NORMAN HALL'S

POSTAL EXAM

PREPARATION BOOK

NORMAN HALL'S
POSTAL EXAM
PREPARATION BOOK

COMPLETELY REVISED
SECOND EDITION

ADAMS MEDIA CORPORATION
Holbrook, Massachusetts

Published by Adams Media Corporation
260 Center Street, Holbrook, MA 02343

ISBN: 1-55850-363-3

Printed in the United States of America.

J I H G

Library of Congress Cataloging-in-Publication Data
Hall, Norman.
    [Postal exam preparation book]
    Norman Hall's postal exam preparation book.
        p.   cm.
    ISBN 1-55850-363-3
    1. Postal service—United States—Examinations, questions, etc. I. Title. II. Title: Postal exam preparation book.
    HE6499.H36   1994
    383'.145'076—dc20

                                                                94-9167
                                                                CIP

This publication is designed to provide accurate and authoritative information with regard to the subject matter covered. It is sold with the understanding that the publisher is not engaged in rendering legal, accounting, or other professional advice. If legal advice or other expert assistance is required, the services of a competent professional person should be sought.
    — From a *Declaration of Principles* jointly adopted by a Committee of the American Bar Association and a Committee of Publishers and Associations

This book is available at quantity discounts for bulk purchases.
For information, call 1-800-872-5627 (in Massachusetts, 781-767-8100).

Visit our home page at http://www.adamsmedia.com

Table of Contents

Preface

Congratulations! You've taken an important step toward getting the job you want at the United States Postal Service. Purchasing this study guide to help you prepare for the Postal exam indicates your determination to be a successful candidate and to give yourself a head start.

Competition for Postal jobs is intense. Considering the current economy, unemployment figures in some areas, and the number of people desiring to work for the Postal Service, it's easy to see how only the best candidates are successful. Too often, applicants fail to adequately prepare for the required exam, and as a consequence, receive only an average test score. A high test score is the key to getting hired. Thorough preparation for this exam offers the means to achieve this goal.

By using this study guide to prepare, you will, without question, gain a competitive edge over others. At the completion of your studies, you will know exactly what to expect on the exam, how to manage your time during the test, how to best handle the difficult memory test section, and how to avoid common mistakes or pitfalls.

You can be certain that you will be able to approach the exam with confidence and a sense of ease. Furthermore, we offer **Guaranteed Test Results**. If, after using this manual, you do not score 90 percent or better on your Postal exam, you can return this study guide to the publisher for a complete refund. (See the back page for details.) No other publication offers such a policy. This should indicate to you how serious we are about helping you in your endeavor to work for the Postal Service, where job satisfaction is high, and the service you provide to the community is invaluable.

— Norman S. Hall

Introduction

The United States Postal Service, which has long been thought of as a tax-supported governmental agency has, in fact, been a private self-supporting organization since 1982. The Postal Service is the eighth largest corporation in this nation, with annual revenues of almost $48 billion. This amounts to approximately 1 percent of the total U.S. economy. With over 680,000 career employees in more than 39,000 post offices, the Postal Service is recognized as this nation's largest civilian employer. According to recent statistics (published in an area update), the type of positions within the Postal Service are as follows:

EMPLOYEES
(Statistics as of June 11, 1993)

Total Career Employees:	**682,390**
Headquarters	1,757
Headquarters Field Support Units	8,263
Area Offices	1,035
**Headquarters & Related Field Units & Regions	471
Inspection Service (Field)	4,286
Postmasters	25,241
Supervisors	32,048
Professional/Administrative/Technician	10,286
Clerks	252,634
Motor Vehicle Operators	6,958
Mail Handlers	49,713
Rural Carriers	43,595
Special Delivery Messengers	1,569
Building and Equipment Maintenance	34,029
Vehicle Maintenance	4,511
Nurses	232
City Delivery Carriers	210,048
Total Noncareer Employees:	**86,297**
Casuals	28,754
Nonbargaining Temporary	1,444
Substitute Rural Carriers	44,069
Postmaster Relief & Leave Replacements	12,030

** Pending reassignments due to restructuring

As shown by this chart, City and Rural Carriers, Clerks, and Mail Handlers comprise the largest percentage of the work force. The annual personnel turnover rate within these crafts can range anywhere from 5-15 percent. This rate can be attributed to retirements, promotions, transfers, disabilities, or employees leaving the service for unspecified personal reasons. Whatever the reason for normal attrition, active registers of qualified applicants must be kept to fill vacancies as they arise.

The frequency of exams to the general public varies. Ordinarily, exams are opened to the public once every one to two years. However, at least up until fall of 1993, some area registers had not been opened for a period of three or more years due to the advent of automation and the desire to downsize the work force in compliance with leaner budgetary mandates. Now that this has been accomplished (100,000 fewer employees since 1989), testing availability to the general public should become more common. (It should be noted here that the Postal Service did not resort to layoffs for a reduction in the work force. Early retirements, in addition to normal attrition, accounted for this downsizing. The Post Office is, in fact, one of only a few corporations that has never laid off workers. Job security is tantamount to this organization.)

When an area register does open, public announcements are made several weeks in advance of the exam in the local media (usually newspapers and/or radio) specifying when and where individuals can apply for the test.

Test application Form 2479-B should be picked up from the Post Office and completed, then returned to the Post Office prior to the announced closure date. This same form will be mailed to you later, and will specify the time and place of the exam. Keep this form: It is your admissions card to the exam. Along with this form you will receive a supplemental packet of information which you must complete prior to the exam. This supplement contains: a brief overview of the written exam; a map showing the place of examination (if necessary); and a list of things that you should bring with you to the exam. For more information about this subject, see Test Taking Strategies.

In addition to the written exam, there are some minimum requirements that job applicants must meet for employment eligibility. You must:

- Be at least eighteen years of age at the time of appointment or be a high school graduate.
- Be a U.S. citizen or have been granted Permanent Resident Alien status in the U.S.
- Be in possession of a valid state driver's license and have a safe driving record.
- Have vision of 20/40 (Snellen) in at least one eye and demonstrate the ability to read typewritten characters without strain. Corrective lenses are permitted. **NOTE:** Exceptions to this requirement are people desiring to work either as a Distribution Clerk Machine Operator or Flat Sorting Machine Operator. See Job Descriptions for further information.
- Pass a urinalysis drug screen prior to appointment.
- Meet minimum medical and health standards as set forth by the Postal Service. This normally is accomplished by sending an applicant to an appointed physician for a thorough physical. Further specifics concerning medical evaluations can be obtained by contacting the personnel department at your local Post Office.
- Have not received a dishonorable discharge from military service.

In addition: Men born after December 12, 1959, must be registered with the Selective Service System in accordance to Section 3 of the Military Selective Service Act. (This requirement is subject to certain exceptions.) Men between the ages of eighteen and twenty-six may pick up a Selective Service Registration form at any Post Office or, if outside the U.S., at any Consular Office.

GENERAL JOB DESCRIPTION OF PROCESSING, DISTRIBUTION AND DELIVERY POSITIONS

Mail processing and delivery is still a labor intensive industry, despite some of the advances made in automation. Consequently, this gives a Postal Service applicant several choices. Listed below are the most common jobs available for entry level personnel and a brief description of what is required, as well as basic salary packages. Most, if not all, of these jobs are available in metropolitan areas. However, smaller cities or towns that lack the necessary facilities to process mail will have fewer positions available. The supplemental packet of information sent to you prior to the exam will stipulate what options are available for your given area.

CLERK: Essentially this is an indoor position that requires sorting and distribution of mails according to Zip Code or area schematics. It may involve prolonged periods of standing, reaching, or lifting (as much as 70 pounds at one time). Clerks may also be required to work with the public by conducting window services. This can involve such transactions as selling postage stamps, weighing parcels, handling Express (overnight) Mail, customer parcel pickup or other accountable mail such as Certified or Registered pieces. It can also entail fielding a wide array of customer questions about other services, or helping to solve customer problems. Window clerks are personally responsible for all stamp stock assigned to them and the money they receive from daily postal transactions.

The basic starting wage for this position is $10.29 per hour and can range as high as $15.29 per hour with cost of living adjustments. Work hours may be irregular.

CITY CARRIER/RURAL CARRIER: Both positions require sorting mail indoors according to the route assigned. Here again, prolonged standing, walking, and being able to lift up to 70 pounds will be required. Additionally, city carriers are required to carry a mail bag on the route that can weigh as much as 35 pounds. Once mail has been organized according to route schematics, it is then the responsibility of the carrier to deliver as well as collect the mail on the route (regardless of prevailing weather conditions). Driving to and from the route requires not only a valid state driver's license, but also a Government Motor Vehicle Operator's Identification Card obtained by passing a standardized driving test. Carriers are also responsible for handling accountable mails such as Express Mail, CODs, and Registered or Certified mailings. The basic starting wage for city carrier positions is $10.29 per hour, and can range as high as $15.29 per hour with cost of living adjustments. Work hours are fairly regular. **NOTE:** Rural Carrier positions differ in the respect that the carrier must use his or her own vehicle to deliver the mail. A valid state driver's license, and a minimum of two years driving experience are required. Compensation for rural carrier associates can vary; however, the average hourly rate paid is $9.29 per hour; Additionally equipment maintenance allowance is provided for use of a personal vehicle. Work hours can be irregular.

MAIL PROCESSOR: This is an indoor position that requires employees to stand for prolonged periods of time while loading and unloading mail from various automated processing equipment. Vision requirements are the same as stipulated earlier, however it is desirable (not mandated) that craft employees be able to distinguish basic colors and shades. The Postal Service has adopted a color code scheme that dictates when certain mails are to be distributed during the course of the week. While color blindness can impair that discernment, it doesn't entirely preclude an employee from filling such a position. Most color-coded material provides sufficient information for correct distribution. The basic starting wage for Mail Processors is $9.58 per hour and can range as high as $14.87 per hour with cost of living adjustments. Work hours for this craft can be irregular and include nights and weekends.

AUTOMATED MARK-UP CLERK: This is an indoor position that requires employees to enter change of address information into a computer data base, process various mails, and perform miscellaneous clerical duties. Employees must have a minimum of six months experience operating clerical or office machinery. Applicants are required to pass a typing test. Minimal accepted proficiency will require the applicant to type 14 correct lines of information within the scope of 4 minutes. That roughly translates into 60 words per minute without error. Vision requirements are the same as described for Mail Processors. The basic starting wage for Automated Mark-up Clerks is $9.58 per hour and can range as high as $14.87 per hour with cost of living adjustments. Work hours for this craft can be irregular and include nights and weekends.

FLAT SORTING MACHINE OPERATOR AND DISTRIBUTION CLERK MACHINE OPERATOR: Both of these crafts involve indoor work, operating machinery that sorts letters and/or flats (oversized envelopes or magazines) according to city schematics or Zip Code. Employees are required to read address Zip Codes and then enter that information into special purpose keyboards (comparable to 10 key). To determine an applicant's proficiency for this kind of exercise, he or she is entered into a dexterity training program. For a total of 16 hours (1 hour per day), applicants learn the keyboard format and how to type in the appropriate information. At the close of this training period, an applicant must be able to successfully type in 250 items within 5 minutes with 98 percent accuracy. Vision requirements for a Flat Sorting Operator are 20/30 (Snellen) in one eye and 20/50 (Snellen) in the other. Here again, corrective lenses are permitted. The ability to distinguish basic colors is also preferred. The basic starting wage for both of these position is $10.29 per hour and can range as high as $15.29 per hour with cost of living adjustments. Work hours for both of these crafts may be irregular and include nights and weekends.

MAIL HANDLER: Employees in this craft mostly work in an industrial environment. The job requires loading and unloading sacks of packages and mail that can weigh up to 70 pounds. Some of this work will be performed inside a Postal facility, while at other times it will involve working outdoors on a loading dock or platform. Applicants desiring this position must pass a short (approximately 10 minute) strength and stamina test. It simply involves being able to lift a 70-pound sack and moving it to a location a few feet away. Examiners want to be certain that you are able to accomplish such tasks without excessive exertion or, worse, hurting yourself in the attempt. Proper lifting techniques will be demonstrated prior to the test. The basic starting wage for this position is $9.58 per hour and can range as high as $14.87 per hour with cost of living adjustments. Work hours for this craft may be irregular and include nights and weekends.

Once an applicant passes the initial screening process (i.e., written exam, interview, physical, etc.) and successfully passes any necessary job simulated performance exercises, he or she is hired on a probationary basis for 90 days. During this period, supervisors closely scrutinize the candidate's performance of tasks that are required of them. The individual's motivation, ability to follow directions, and safety are taken into consideration as well. If, at any point during probation, an immediate supervisor has reason to believe an applicant does not meet expectations, the person in question is released from employment. If, on the other hand, supervisors appreciate the person's job performance and willingness to "go the extra mile," that person becomes entitled to the full complement of career employment benefits. These include:

- Job security
- Paid vacations
- Paid holidays
- Sick leave
- Subsidized health insurance
- Life insurance
- Promotional opportunities
- Retirement

Further information about wages or benefits can be acquired by contacting the Post Office to which you are applying.

TEST TAKING STRATEGIES

When you receive Form 2479-B in the mail saying when and where the written exam will be given, pay particular attention to the supplemental information sent. This supplement spells out exactly what your responsibilities are prior to actually taking the exam. A sample answer sheet will also be sent with step-by-step instructions on how to properly fill in the answer sheet grid with your personal information. Such things as your name, home address, Social Security Number, birth date, race, sex, any disabilities, or veteran status, if applicable, need to be filled out. Information pertinent to the exam itself, such as job choice, and preferred work location need to be identified as well. You are expected to bring this completed answer sheet to the place of examination. If it is not correctly or completely filled out as instructed, you will not be allowed to take the exam. Also required are your Form 2479-B notice, a photo ID or driver's license, and two No. 2 pencils. The lack of any of these will bar you from taking the exam. DO NOT under any circumstances arrive late for the exam. Latecomers are not permitted to take the exam and it is very likely you will not be able to reschedule. Plan to arrive at the exam room at least 30 minutes early.

Once inside the exam room, you will be given a short period of time to transfer what information you have on your sample answer sheet to another answer sheet provided by the examiner. Listen carefully to any and all instructions given by the examiner. Do not deviate in any manner from established test procedures or you will disqualify yourself from further employment consideration.

Prior to fall 1993, the Postal Service had a separate and altogether different exam for each of the job choices described earlier. In what has been viewed as a significant cost cutting measure, the Postal Service consolidated these exams into one basic test (referred to now as the 460 and 470 series). Some portions of the old tests were combined to make up the new test, while other formats were discontinued altogether (e.g., Rural Carrier Associate Exam). Points of emphasis no longer involve reading comprehension, vocabulary, or mathematics relating to postage rates. Instead, the new exam focuses on address comparison, memory, number series, and following directions. Each of these areas of study will be discussed at the beginning of this study guide and then followed by sample test questions and answers. Test strategy and hints will also be discussed as they apply to each subject area.

The format of the exam questions is multiple choice. This makes your job a little easier because you know that one of the choices offered has to be correct. Even if the answer is not immediately apparent, you have a 20 percent chance of guessing answer correctly. Also, if you find that you are running out of time in an exercise, randomly answering the remaining items will more than likely give you a higher test score than leaving answers blank. The one exception to this is the section called, Address Cross Comparison. Even though you have a higher chance of guessing the correct answer because there are fewer choices in this section, all incorrect answers will be counted against those that are correct. Consequently, exam scores for this section can suffer if one guesses with reckless abandon.

While multiple choice exams are fairly easy to complete, you may be surprised at how many people do poorly or don't pass at all because of improper marking. An example of an answer blank is provided below to demonstrate how to mark an answer properly.

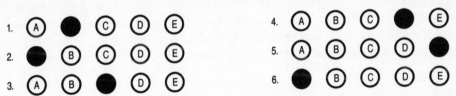

The following examples are answer blanks that have been improperly marked, leading to a poor test score.

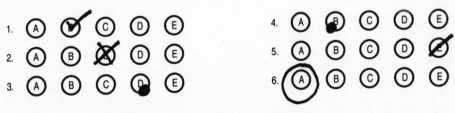

Answer sheets are not hand scored. Rather, they are scanned by machine and the machine is indifferent to whatever the reason may be for sloppiness. It will score the answer wrong (even though it may, in fact, be the correct selection) if not enough effort is made to completely fill in the circle. On this same point, however, do not waste too much time filling in answers. As you work through the sample exercises in this book, you will establish an effective balance between speed and accuracy. Practice is the key.

Another costly mistake is accidentally marking answers that do not correspond to the question you are presently working. A simple way to prevent this problem is to check every ten questions or so to verify what was marked corresponds with the question at hand. Nothing can be more frustrating than completing all of the questions given and then learn that you are one answer short on the answer sheet. There will not be enough time to backtrack to discover where the error was made. Also, if you decide to skip a question that you are unsure of, be certain to skip the corresponding answer blank for the same reason. One last point about marking a multiple choice answer sheet: If you change your mind about any answer, be certain to erase the original answer COMPLETELY. If two answers are apparently marked, the scanner will consider the answer incorrect. Be aware too, that, statistically, the first answer arrived at is generally the correct choice.

STUDY SUGGESTIONS

The Postal Service examination is not the kind of exam on which you can hope for a high test score after "cramming" the night before. Good study habits have a profound impact on how well you do on the exam. If you follow these few simple guidelines, you can approach the exam more relaxed and confident, two essential ingredients for top performance on any exam.

Regular study times should be established and tailored to your comfort. Each person's schedule is different. Some people prefer to study for one or two hours at a time and then take a break, while others prefer several hours of straight study. Regardless of how you study, it is important that you do it regularly; do not rely on a marathon. You will remember the subject matter more easily and comprehend it better if you establish regular study habits.

Where you study is important, too. Eliminate any distractions that can disrupt your studies. The television, the telephone, and children can hinder quality study time. It is suggested that you set aside one room in your home as a study place and use it to isolate yourself from distractions. If you elect to use a bedroom as a study area, avoid lying in bed while you read. Otherwise, you may find yourself more inclined to sleep than to learn. It is important to have a good desk, a comfortable chair, and adequate lighting; anything less can hamper studying. If studying in your home is not feasible, go to your local library or some other place that offers an environment conducive to study.

Again, be sure to get plenty of rest. It is counterproductive to try to study when you are overly tired. It is also important not to skip meals. Your level of concentration during the exam can suffer if you lack proper nutrition. Coffee and other stimulants are not recommended because you will not be allowed to leave the exam room for any reason until the exam is finished. Too much coffee and a little test anxiety can add up to be a very embarrassing situation or worse, disqualification.

Address Cross Comparison

Every stage of the mail sorting process must be done accurately and efficiently. If either a Postal Clerk or Carrier misreads an address, mail is misdirected or delayed. Therefore, Postal personnel must be able to tell whether two addresses are the same or if they represent two entirely different destinations. Sometimes, differences between addresses are subtle—small differences in spelling, for example, or transposed numerals. An applicant must be able to quickly scan the address lists in this section and make an accurate determination to this effect.

At first glance, most people view this exercise as perhaps the easiest section in the exam. However, there is only a limited amount of time allowed (6 minutes) to complete the ninety-five questions given. Therefore, it is important to spend as little time as possible on each question, and yet, be thorough enough to select the correct answer without guessing. In fact, because of the time constraints, examiners will point out at the beginning of this test that you are not expected to finish.

This section of the test provides ninety-five pairs of addresses. You need to determine if each pair of addresses is different or exactly alike. The answer sheet to this test will have two choices from which you may select. Darken answer (A) if the pair of addresses shown are exactly alike. Darken answer (D) if the addresses are different. The ten pairs of sample addresses that follow will lend a general understanding of how this test is constructed. Take no more than 30 seconds to complete the samples.

1.	40407 Hayworth Ave.	44007 Hayworth Ave.	(A) (D)
2.	Chatowaga Blvd. S	Chatowega Blvd S	(A) (D)
3.	Phoenix, Arizona 80553	Phoenix, Arizona 80553	(A) (D)
4.	New York, NY 05130	New Haven, CT 05130	(A) (D)
5.	Newport, KY	Newport, KY	(A) (D)
6.	498 W. 12th Ave.	498 12th Ave. W.	(A) (D)
7.	1156 Beaumont Cr.	1156 Beaumont Cr.	(A) (D)
8.	Roanoke, VA 32075	Roanoke, VA 32075	(A) (D)
9.	4200 3rd St. Apt 2400	2400 3rd ST. Apt 4200	(A) (D)
10.	Reno, NV	Reno, NV	(A) (D)

Only pairs number 3, 5, 7, 8, and 10 are exactly alike and should have the answer Ⓐ darkened. Answer Ⓓ would be darkened for the remaining pairs (1, 2, 4, 6, and 9). If you missed any of these samples, review the pairs and determine what was overlooked.

As you can see, subtle differences in either the numbers or the spelling can be unrecognizable at first glance. Most people, for one reason or another, can spot transposed numbers in either the Zip Code or the street address. However, applicants frequently overlook differences in addresses that sound the same. Pay particularly close attention to addresses of this nature before marking your answer sheet. Caution exercised here will pay off in terms of a higher test score.

You may have noticed too, that while working on the sample exercises a straightedge or ruler could have helped reduce confusion. Unfortunately, such aids are not allowed in the examination room. However, you are allowed two pencils, one of which can serve as a crude straightedge, if necessary.

One other helpful trick to reduce confusion while comparing a set of addresses is to place your index finger on one column of addresses and your little finger on the other column. As you proceed with each pair, move your fingers in unison down the page. This does essentially the same thing as a straight edge. Using this method makes it substantially easier to focus your attention on just the two addresses you are comparing. You also save precious time by not having to search for where you left off in order to mark your answer sheet.

Three practice exercises are provided in this chapter. Tear the answer sheets out of the book for your convenience in marking answers. To help you get an idea of how the actual exam is conducted, you should use a kitchen timer or have someone time you for the allotted six minutes as you work each exercise. This will protect you from the unnecessary distraction of timing yourself. When time is called, do not work any further on the exercise. If you continue, you will lose the true sense of what will be required of you on the actual exam.

A scale is provided at the end of each exercise to allow you to determine your standings. Simply count the number of correct answers you have made and then subtract those that were missed. As mentioned earlier, this is the one exercise in which applicants are penalized for wrong answers. Guessing answers for this part of the exam is not recommended.

1.	Burien Ave.	Burein Avenue
2.	12137 Hartford Dr.	12317 Hartford Dr.
3.	Marguriete Pl.	Margurete Pl.
4.	4731 E. 19th St.	4731 E. 19th St.
5.	Truman W.	Trueman W.
6.	45-D Levenworth Ave.	45-D Levenworth Ave.
7.	Cottage Blvd.	Hut Blvd.
8.	753 Pinecone	753 Pinecone
9.	Ft. Worth, TX	Ft. Apache, AR
10.	Oakland, CA 94371	Oakland, CA 94371
11.	Deception Pass	Deseption Pass
12.	20-L Hogan Ln.	20-L Hogan Ln.
13.	4536 SW 103rd St.	4536 NW 103rd St.
14.	Hutchinson Blvd.	Hutchenson Blvd.
15.	30785 Elliot Bay Rd.	30785 Elliot Bay Rd.
16.	Sparks, NV	Sparks, NY
17.	Springfield, MO 97132	Springfield, MO 97132
18.	Coos Lane	Coos Ln.
19.	Evergreen, ND	Evergrein, MD
20.	Butt, MT 05317	Butte, MT 03517
21.	41-RT 3 Colo, IA	41-RT 3 Colo, IA
22.	Highland Pl.	Highland Place
23.	478 Beach Dr.	478 Beach Dr.

24.	22 Falcon W.	33 Falcon W.
25.	Anderson Heights	Andersin Heights
26.	Falcon Hills Rd.	Eagle Hills Rd.
27.	3249 Brice Pl.	3249 Brice Pl.
28.	42-A Savon DR.	42-D Savon Dr.
29.	Jamestown, NJ	Jameston, NJ
30.	Victoria, BC 090	Victoria, BC 090
31.	359119 Galloway Ln.	359119 Galloway Ln.
32.	Rome, Georgia 31152	Rome, Georgia 31152
33.	Phinney Place	Phiney Place
34.	Constantine Rd.	Constantine Rd.
35.	44-AB Wilkes Dr.	44-AB Wilikes Dr.
36.	Ft. Collins, Colo.	Ft. Collins, CO
37.	2780 ST. John Rd.	2780 ST. Johns Rd.
38.	Livingston Blvd.	Livingston Blvd.
39.	Bloomington, Ill 61653	Bloomington, Ill 61563
40.	4802-E Blaine	4802-W Blaine
41.	Dallas, TX 25109	Dallas, TX 25108
42.	3103 Porter Way	3103 Porter Way
43.	Snohomish, WA	Snohamish, VA
44.	2516 Johnson Pl.	2516 Johnston Pl.
45.	32-D Jensen Way	354 Jensen Way
46.	4012 Rolling Oaks Rd.	4012 Rolling Oaks Rd.
47.	3710 Harsten Blvd.	3710 Harsten Blvd.
48.	Ankorage, AL	Anchorage, AK

49.	Petersville, KY 45108	Petersville, KY 45108
50.	3845 Reid Dr.	3844 Reid Dr.
51.	401-A Westin Pl.	401-A Westin Pl.
52.	20121 Dakota Point	20211 Dakota Point
53.	Faunterloy Center	Founterloy Center
54.	4013 Brussels Dr.	4013 Brussels Dr.
55.	Stovington, Conn.	Stovers, CO 43212
56.	12 Ash Place	12 Ash Pl.
57.	9040 Country Ln.	9040 Country Ln.
58.	Marguriette Ave.	Marguriete Ave.
59.	7140 Constitution Dr.	140 Constitution Pl.
60.	30-R Bloomfield Apts.	30-R Bloomfield Apts.
61.	4099 Harbel Rd.	4099 Harbel Rd.
62.	W. Palm Beach, CA	Palm Beach, CA
63.	Phoenix, Ariz	Phoenix, AR 85021
64.	4037 Nipsic Pl.	4037 Nipsic Pl.
65.	1109 Tangerine Dr.	1109 Tangerine Dr.
66.	20A Abernathy Ct.	20A Abernathy Ct.
67.	Newberry, W. VA	Newberry, W. VA
68.	3401 E. 19th St.	3401 E. 20th St.
69.	1280 12th Ave.	1280 13th Ave.
70.	7800 Forest Ridge	7800 Forest Ridge
71.	Montgomery Pl.	Montgomery Pl.
72.	10 Pierce Grahm Cr.	10 Pierce Grahm Cr.
73.	New York, NY 11940	New York, NY 19140

74.	7780 Proxmire Rd.	8077 Proxmire Rd.
75.	1341 Ivy Terrace	1341 Ivy Terrace
76.	257 Rampert Dr.	275 Ramport Dr.
77.	Newport, WA 99510	Newport, PA 99510
78.	1144 60th St. SW	4411 60th St. NW
79.	117 Chespeke Ct.	117 Chesepeak Ct.
80.	Willow Way E.	Willow Way E.
81.	3030 Prairie Pl.	3030 Prairie Pl.
82.	1212 Seneca Point	2121 Seneca Court
83.	7999 Mercury Blvd.	7999 Mercury Blvd.
84.	Waterloo, IA 50578	Waterloo, IA 50758
85.	14818 1st Ave.	14818 2nd Ave.
86.	S. 120th Pl.	S. 120th Pl.
87.	South Port, KY 98451	South Port, WY 98950
88.	Twelve Oaks, MI	Twelve Oaks, MI
89.	4045 S. Duff St.	4045 N. Duff St.
90.	1391 Fremont Pkwy	1931 Preemont Pksy
91.	Terrington Park	Terrington Park
92.	Essex, MD	Essex, MD
93.	Covings, NM 53845	Sante Fe, NM
94.	Bessert Dr.	Bessert Dr.
95.	30921 W. Hamilton	93021 W. Hamilton

-END OF TEST-

ANSWER SHEET TO ADDRESS CROSS COMPARISON/EXERCISE 1

1. (A) (D)	33. (A) (D)	65. (A) (D)
2. (A) (D)	34. (A) (D)	66. (A) (D)
3. (A) (D)	35. (A) (D)	67. (A) (D)
4. (A) (D)	36. (A) (D)	68. (A) (D)
5. (A) (D)	37. (A) (D)	69. (A) (D)
6. (A) (D)	38. (A) (D)	70. (A) (D)
7. (A) (D)	39. (A) (D)	71. (A) (D)
8. (A) (D)	40. (A) (D)	72. (A) (D)
9. (A) (D)	41. (A) (D)	73. (A) (D)
10. (A) (D)	42. (A) (D)	74. (A) (D)
11. (A) (D)	43. (A) (D)	75. (A) (D)
12. (A) (D)	44. (A) (D)	76. (A) (D)
13. (A) (D)	45. (A) (D)	77. (A) (D)
14. (A) (D)	46. (A) (D)	78. (A) (D)
15. (A) (D)	47. (A) (D)	79. (A) (D)
16. (A) (D)	48. (A) (D)	80. (A) (D)
17. (A) (D)	49. (A) (D)	81. (A) (D)
18. (A) (D)	50. (A) (D)	82. (A) (D)
19. (A) (D)	51. (A) (D)	83. (A) (D)
20. (A) (D)	52. (A) (D)	84. (A) (D)
21. (A) (D)	53. (A) (D)	85. (A) (D)
22. (A) (D)	54. (A) (D)	86. (A) (D)
23. (A) (D)	55. (A) (D)	87. (A) (D)
24. (A) (D)	56. (A) (D)	88. (A) (D)
25. (A) (D)	57. (A) (D)	89. (A) (D)
26. (A) (D)	58. (A) (D)	90. (A) (D)
27. (A) (D)	59. (A) (D)	91. (A) (D)
28. (A) (D)	60. (A) (D)	92. (A) (D)
29. (A) (D)	61. (A) (D)	93. (A) (D)
30. (A) (D)	62. (A) (D)	94. (A) (D)
31. (A) (D)	63. (A) (D)	95. (A) (D)
32. (A) (D)	64. (A) (D)	

(This page may be removed to mark answers.)

ADDRESS CROSS COMPARISON/EXERCISE 1 ANSWERS

1.	D	33.	D	65.	A
2.	D	34.	A	66.	A
3.	D	35.	D	67.	A
4.	A	36.	D	68.	D
5.	D	37.	D	69.	D
6.	A	38.	A	70.	A
7.	D	39.	D	71.	A
8.	A	40.	D	72.	A
9.	D	41.	D	73.	D
10.	A	42.	A	74.	D
11.	D	43.	D	75.	A
12.	A	44.	D	76.	D
13.	D	45.	D	77.	D
14.	D	46.	A	78.	D
15.	A	47.	A	79.	D
16.	D	48.	D	80.	A
17.	A	49.	A	81.	A
18.	D	50.	D	82.	D
19.	D	51.	A	83.	A
20.	D	52.	D	84.	D
21.	A	53.	D	85.	D
22.	D	54.	A	86.	A
23.	A	55.	D	87.	D
24.	D	56.	D	88.	A
25.	D	57.	A	89.	D
26.	D	58.	D	90.	D
27.	A	59.	D	91.	A
28.	D	60.	A	92.	A
29.	D	61.	A	93.	D
30.	A	62.	D	94.	A
31.	A	63.	D	95.	D
32.	A	64.	A		

If you scored:
90 or more correct, you have an excellent score.
85-89 correct, you have a good score.
84 or fewer correct, you should practice more.

1.	2103 Highland Ave.	3102 Highland Ave.
2.	4609 Simpson Pkwy	4609 Simson Parkway
3.	404-C Trenton Park	404-C Trentan Park
4.	Bowling Green, KY	Bowling Green, KY
5.	New Haven, CT 07510	New Haven, CT 07510
6.	Covington Cove SW	SW Covington Cove
7.	St. Louis, MO 44881	St. Louis, MO 88441
8.	Yuma, AZ	Yuma, AZ
9.	Santa Cruz, CA 99580	Santa Clara, NM 99580
10.	Erwin Point Dr.	Erwin Point Dr.
11.	Petersberg Ave. NE	21 Petersberg Ave. NE
12.	47109 Nome St.	47109 Nome St.
13.	558 E. 16th St.	558 W. 16th St.
14.	89D Turner Blvd	89D Turner Blvd
15.	Harrisburg, PA 01184	Harrington, PA 01184
16.	Reno, Nevada 42851	Reno, Nevada 42851
17.	77 E. Fleming Rd.	77 E. Fleming Rd.
18.	Farmington Hills, CT	303 Farmington, Hills, CT
19.	1685 Jensen Way	1685 Jensen Way
20.	SW Tiffany Ct.	SW Tiffany Ct.
21.	3287 Front St.	3287 Front St.
22.	31-D McAllen Rd.	31-D McAllen Rd.
23.	791 Penny Square	719 Penny Square

24.	NE Pinchont View	NE Pinchant View
25.	2413 Wheaton Way	2413 Wheaton Way
26.	443 E. 102nd Ave.	443 E. 107th St.
27.	Elsinore Blvd	Elsinore Blvd
28.	Montgomery Place S.	Montgomery Place S.
29.	742 Callahan Pl.	742 Calahan Pl.
30.	66 Tremont St.	99 Tremont St.
31.	Pershing Blvd. Apt. 37	Pershing Blvd. Apt. 37
32.	11 Finland Ave.	11 Finland Ave.
33.	Atlanta, GA 01789	Atlanta, GA 01789
34.	Gainesville, Fla 22190	Gainesville, Fla 22190
35.	2140 E. Carlson	2140 E. Carlson
36.	40301 SW Seneca	40301 NE Seneca
37.	Fremont, NE 57510	Freemont, NE 57510
38.	2020 N. Parkington	2020 N. Parkington
39.	47-D Spruce	47-D Spruce
40.	Suite N Columbia Square	Suite N Columbia Sq.
41.	Waco, TX	Waco, TX
42.	278 Fontain Dr.	278 Fountain Dr.
43.	521 Essex Blvd.	521 Crown Blvd.
44.	1449 Bloomington St.	1449 Bloomington St.
45.	332 Edgingston Way	322 Edgingston Way
46.	Hazelwood Pkwy.	Hazelwood Pkwy.
47.	Island Lake Dr.	Island Lake Dr.
48.	29471 Chicago St.	29417 Chicago St.

49.	774 NE 42nd Ave.	774 NE 42nd Ave.
50.	Little Rock, Ark.	Little Stone, Ark.
51.	Norfolk, VA 11191	Norfolk, VA 11197
52.	3050 Lebaron Way	412 NE 19th ST.
53.	4640 NW 11th ST.	46 N Cable St.
54.	7793 Halverson Dr.	7793 Halverson Dr.
55.	12-A Nordstrom Way	12-A Nordstrom Way
56.	Presley Ct.	Presley Ct.
57.	Z44 E. 22nd	Z44 E. 22nd
58.	2020 Ramport St.	202 Ramport St.
59.	Forsythe Ln.	Forsithe Ln.
60.	12178 Knoll Dr.	12178 Knoll Rd.
61.	E. 40th Place	S. 40th Place
62.	3047 Evansdale W.	3047 Evansdale W.
63.	SW Hampshire Ln.	SW Hampshire Ln.
64.	23 Flamingo Dr.	23 Flamingo St.
65.	Boise, ID 47814	Boise, ID 47814
66.	4700 Kitsap Way	7400 Kitsap Way
67.	Chepowacket Blvd.	Chepowackat Blvd.
68.	1010 Tanner St.	42 Sloan Ct.
69.	Greensboro, NC 21478	Greensbor, NC 21478
70.	Palo Alto, CA	Palo Alto, CA
71.	38841 Padock S.	33814 Padock St.
72.	2511 Cascade Trail	2511 Cascade Trail
73.	2324 Parker Place	2423 Parker Place

74.	South Shore, WA 99944	South Shore, WA 99944
75.	1710 Symington Ct.	1710 Symington Ct.
76.	Fairbanks, Alaska	Fairbanks, Alaska
77.	SE Karrington Blvd.	SE Karry Blvd
78.	11111 Tisdale Ln.	1111 Tisdale Ln.
79.	3781 Livingston Sq.	3781 Livingston Sq.
80.	Brockton, Mass. 01171	Brockton, Mas. 01171
81.	734 A Twin Bay	734 B Twin Bay
82.	4000 Elsinora Beach	4000 Elsinore Beach
83.	308 Frampton Ave.	308 Frampton Ave.
84.	7901 Havelin Blvd.	7091 Havelin Blvd.
85.	Portland, ME 00521	Portland, ME 05021
86.	Sweitzer Way	Sweitzer Way
87.	44331 Bellingham	43431 Bellingham
88.	807 Terryington Ave.	807 Terryington Ave.
89.	Paradise Valley, AZ	Paridise Valley, AZ
90.	1201 Westin Lake Dr.	1201 Westin Lake Dr.
91.	4100 Hildalgo Park	4100 Hildalgo Park
92.	17181 Austin Center	17181 Astin Center
93.	2510 Stephenson Ave.	2510 Stehensen Ave.
94.	Reno, NV	Reno, NV
95.	2222 Hoffman Dr.	2222 Hoffman Dr.

-END OF TEST-

ANSWER SHEET TO ADDRESS CROSS COMPARISON/ EXERCISE 2

1. (A) (D)	33. (A) (D)	65. (A) (D)
2. (A) (D)	34. (A) (D)	66. (A) (D)
3. (A) (D)	35. (A) (D)	67. (A) (D)
4. (A) (D)	36. (A) (D)	68. (A) (D)
5. (A) (D)	37. (A) (D)	69. (A) (D)
6. (A) (D)	38. (A) (D)	70. (A) (D)
7. (A) (D)	39. (A) (D)	71. (A) (D)
8. (A) (D)	40. (A) (D)	72. (A) (D)
9. (A) (D)	41. (A) (D)	73. (A) (D)
10. (A) (D)	42. (A) (D)	74. (A) (D)
11. (A) (D)	43. (A) (D)	75. (A) (D)
12. (A) (D)	44. (A) (D)	76. (A) (D)
13. (A) (D)	45. (A) (D)	77. (A) (D)
14. (A) (D)	46. (A) (D)	78. (A) (D)
15. (A) (D)	47. (A) (D)	79. (A) (D)
16. (A) (D)	48. (A) (D)	80. (A) (D)
17. (A) (D)	49. (A) (D)	81. (A) (D)
18. (A) (D)	50. (A) (D)	82. (A) (D)
19. (A) (D)	51. (A) (D)	83. (A) (D)
20. (A) (D)	52. (A) (D)	84. (A) (D)
21. (A) (D)	53. (A) (D)	85. (A) (D)
22. (A) (D)	54. (A) (D)	86. (A) (D)
23. (A) (D)	55. (A) (D)	87. (A) (D)
24. (A) (D)	56. (A) (D)	88. (A) (D)
25. (A) (D)	57. (A) (D)	89. (A) (D)
26. (A) (D)	58. (A) (D)	90. (A) (D)
27. (A) (D)	59. (A) (D)	91. (A) (D)
28. (A) (D)	60. (A) (D)	92. (A) (D)
29. (A) (D)	61. (A) (D)	93. (A) (D)
30. (A) (D)	62. (A) (D)	94. (A) (D)
31. (A) (D)	63. (A) (D)	95. (A) (D)
32. (A) (D)	64. (A) (D)	

(This page may be removed to mark answers.)

1.	D	33.	A	65.	A
2.	D	34.	A	66.	D
3.	D	35.	A	67.	D
4.	A	36.	D	68.	D
5.	A	37.	D	69.	D
6.	D	38.	A	70.	A
7.	D	39.	A	71.	D
8.	A	40.	D	72.	A
9.	D	41.	A	73.	D
10.	A	42.	D	74.	A
11.	D	43.	D	75.	A
12.	A	44.	A	76.	A
13.	D	45.	D	77.	D
14.	A	46.	A	78.	D
15.	D	47.	A	79.	A
16.	A	48.	D	80.	D
17.	A	49.	A	81.	D
18.	D	50.	D	82.	D
19.	A	51.	D	83.	A
20.	A	52.	D	84.	D
21.	A	53.	D	85.	D
22.	A	54.	A	86.	A
23.	D	55.	A	87.	D
24.	D	56.	A	88.	A
25.	A	57.	A	89.	D
26.	D	58.	D	90.	A
27.	A	59.	D	91.	A
28.	A	60.	D	92.	D
29.	D	61.	D	93.	D
30.	D	62.	A	94.	A
31.	A	63.	A	95.	A
32.	A	64.	D		

If you scored:

90 or more correct, you have an excellent score.
85-89 correct, you have a good score.
84 or fewer correct, you should practice more.

1.	1216 W. 6th Ave.	1216 S. 6th Ave.
2.	2020 Poplar Bluff Dr.	2020 Popular Bluff Dr.
3.	1402 Wasau Terrace	1402 Wasau Terrace
4.	Eau Claire, Wis. 76944	Eau Clare, Wis 76944
5.	7088 Benton Ave.	7088 Benton Ave.
6.	Pocatello, ID 86713	Pocatello, ID 87613
7.	113-D Rochestor Blvd.	113-D Rochestor Blvd.
8.	8755 Ironwood Dr.	8755 NE Ironwood Dr.
9.	6467 Ramsey Lane S.	6467 Ramsey Lane S.
10.	Salida, Colo. 78435	Salada, Colo. 78435
11.	5000 Natchez	5000 Natchez
12.	Chillicothe, MO 54311	Chilliclothe, MO 54311
13.	4039 Vicksburg St.	4039 Vicksburg St.
14.	50571 Coleman Dr.	50751 Coleman Dr.
15.	Tucumcari, NM 60681	Tucumcary, NM 60681
16.	7135 Roswell Way	7135 Rosewell Way
17.	970 Odessa Ave.	970 Odessa Ave.
18.	Amarillo, Texas 49873	Amabrillo, Texas 49873
19.	1023 Buffalo Pass	1023 Buffalo Pass
20.	Hannibal, MO 45555	Hanninbol, MO 45555
21.	60741 Ottumwa Dr.	67041 Ottumwa Dr.
22.	1010 Remington Cr.	1010 Remington Cr.
23.	W. Palm Beach, Fla.	E. Palm Beach, Fla.

24.	80473 McComb Ave.	80473 MacComb Ave.
25.	1519 67th St. NW	1519 67th St. W.
26.	2040 Albert Lane	2040 Albert Lane
27.	Prescott, Ariz 84988	Prescott, Ariz 84998
28.	1795 Casper Place	1795 Casper Place
29.	603 Craig	603 Craig
30.	4111 Montrose Ave.	4111 Montrose Dr.
31.	15990 Humboldt NE	15909 Humboldt NE
32.	Pierre, SD 77135	Pierre SD 77185
33.	4030 Cookie Pk.	4030 Cooke Pk.
34.	Missoula, MT 88803	Missoula, MD 88803
35.	33810 Mitchell Dr.	33810 Mitchell Dr.
36.	44-C Shenandoah Apts.	44-C Senandoah Apts.
37.	4848 Roanoke Dr.	4848 Roanoke Dr.
38.	Alpena, Mich. 38911	Alpena, Mich. 38911
39.	47811 Sherbrook	47881 Sherbrook
40.	32323 Roman Circle	32323 Romon Circle
41.	Charlotte, NC 12443	Charlette, NC 12443
42.	412 Peterbouroghs	412 Peterboroughs
43.	7651 Corbin St.	7651 Corbin St.
44.	3044 Violet Dr. NW	3404 Violet Dr. NW
45.	450-B Deer Park	450-B Deer Pk
46.	31571 Barrington Ave.	31571 Barrington Ave.
47.	3215 Dundee Dr.	3215 Dundee Dr.
48.	747 Kane St.	747 Kane St.

49.	3011 Foxhill Ave.	3011 Foxhill Ave.
50.	1205 Helm	1502 Helm
51.	1414 Millbern Rd.	1414 Millburn Rd.
52.	7350 Holdridge Dr.	7350 Holdridge Dr.
53.	351 Belvidere Pt.	315 Belvidere Pt.
54.	80913 Sullivan Pl.	80913 N Sullivan Pl.
55.	10009 Callahan Ln.	10009 Callahan Ln.
56.	2023 Gardner Blvd.	2023 Gardner Blvd.
57.	440-442 Greenwood Apts.	440-442 Greenwood Apts.
58.	1199 Hawley Ave.	1999 Hawley Ave.
59.	3000 Scribner Dr.	3000 Scribner Dr.
60.	4458 Countryside Ct.	4458 Countryside Court
61.	Chicago, Ill 60691	Chicago, ID 60691
62.	3008 Ivanhoe Ave.	3080 Ivanhoe Ave.
63.	7777 Kirchoff	9999 Kirchoff
64.	13133 Schaumburgh Dr.	13133 Schaumburgh Dr.
65.	1705 E. Addison Blvd.	1705 S. Addison Blvd.
66.	104 Glen Ellyn	104 Glenn Ellyn
67.	12-E Barber Corners	12-E Barbara Corners
68.	99661 Westmont Ave.	99661 Westmont Ave.
69.	7001 Liberty View	7001 Liberty View
70.	125 88th St. NE	125 88th Dr. NE
71.	Wytheville, VA 15891	Wytheville, VA 15891
72.	8903 Wheaton Way	8309 Wheaton Way
73.	79900 Indian Hts. SW	79900 Indian Hts. SW

74.	345 Lambert Lane	345 Lamburt Lane
75.	4646 Camalot Dr.	6464 Camalot Dr.
76.	8873 Stickney Blvd.	8873 Stickney Blvd.
77.	31371 Hammond Dr.	33171 Hammond Dr.
78.	304 Wilmette Ridge	304 Wilmette Ridge
79.	Bend, Ore. 80077	Bend, Oregon 80077
80.	Springfield, OH 39411	Springfield, OH 39441
81.	7979 Baldwin Pt.	7979 Baldwin Pt.
82.	14001 Prospect Dr.	1401 Prospect Dr.
83.	307 Elm St.	307 Elm St.
84.	409 Kittyhawk Pl	409 Kityhawk Pl.
85.	16073 Algoquin Ave.	16073 Algoquin Dr.
86.	2000 Euclid Blvd.	4000 Euclid Blvd.
87.	7581 Lincolnshire Dr.	7581 Lincolnshire Dr.
88.	180-D Turnball Woods	180-D Turnball Woods
89.	3042 Hintz St.	3042 Hienz St.
90.	393 Twin Orchard Ln.	393 Twin Orchid Ln.
91.	150 Central Ave.	150 Central Ave.
92.	6167 Hoffman Estates	6716 Hoffman Estates
93.	4311 Devon Dr.	4311 Devon Dr. S
94.	2222 Nickols Ave.	2222 Nickols Ave.
95.	111 82nd St.	111 82nd St.

-END OF TEST-

ANSWER SHEET TO ADDRESS CROSS COMPARISON/EXERCISE 3

1. (A) (D)	33. (A) (D)	65. (A) (D)
2. (A) (D)	34. (A) (D)	66. (A) (D)
3. (A) (D)	35. (A) (D)	67. (A) (D)
4. (A) (D)	36. (A) (D)	68. (A) (D)
5. (A) (D)	37. (A) (D)	69. (A) (D)
6. (A) (D)	38. (A) (D)	70. (A) (D)
7. (A) (D)	39. (A) (D)	71. (A) (D)
8. (A) (D)	40. (A) (D)	72. (A) (D)
9. (A) (D)	41. (A) (D)	73. (A) (D)
10. (A) (D)	42. (A) (D)	74. (A) (D)
11. (A) (D)	43. (A) (D)	75. (A) (D)
12. (A) (D)	44. (A) (D)	76. (A) (D)
13. (A) (D)	45. (A) (D)	77. (A) (D)
14. (A) (D)	46. (A) (D)	78. (A) (D)
15. (A) (D)	47. (A) (D)	79. (A) (D)
16. (A) (D)	48. (A) (D)	80. (A) (D)
17. (A) (D)	49. (A) (D)	81. (A) (D)
18. (A) (D)	50. (A) (D)	82. (A) (D)
19. (A) (D)	51. (A) (D)	83. (A) (D)
20. (A) (D)	52. (A) (D)	84. (A) (D)
21. (A) (D)	53. (A) (D)	85. (A) (D)
22. (A) (D)	54. (A) (D)	86. (A) (D)
23. (A) (D)	55. (A) (D)	87. (A) (D)
24. (A) (D)	56. (A) (D)	88. (A) (D)
25. (A) (D)	57. (A) (D)	89. (A) (D)
26. (A) (D)	58. (A) (D)	90. (A) (D)
27. (A) (D)	59. (A) (D)	91. (A) (D)
28. (A) (D)	60. (A) (D)	92. (A) (D)
29. (A) (D)	61. (A) (D)	93. (A) (D)
30. (A) (D)	62. (A) (D)	94. (A) (D)
31. (A) (D)	63. (A) (D)	95. (A) (D)
32. (A) (D)	64. (A) (D)	

(This page may be removed to mark answers.)

ADDRESS CROSS COMPARISON/EXERCISE 3 ANSWERS

1.	D	33.	D	65.	D
2.	D	34.	D	66.	D
3.	A	35.	A	67.	D
4.	D	36.	D	68.	A
5.	A	37.	A	69.	A
6.	D	38.	A	70.	D
7.	A	39.	D	71.	A
8.	D	40.	D	72.	D
9.	A	41.	D	73.	A
10.	D	42.	D	74.	D
11.	A	43.	A	75.	D
12.	D	44.	D	76.	A
13.	A	45.	D	77.	D
14.	D	46.	A	78.	A
15.	D	47.	A	79.	D
16.	D	48.	A	80.	D
17.	A	49.	A	81.	A
18.	D	50.	D	82.	D
19.	A	51.	D	83.	A
20.	D	52.	A	84.	D
21.	D	53.	D	85.	D
22.	A	54.	D	86.	D
23.	D	55.	A	87.	A
24.	D	56.	A	88.	A
25.	D	57.	A	89.	D
26.	A	58.	D	90.	D
27.	D	59.	A	91.	A
28.	A	60.	D	92.	D
29.	A	61.	D	93.	D
30.	D	62.	D	94.	A
31.	D	63.	D	95.	A
32.	D	64.	A		

If you scored:

90 or more correct, you have an excellent score.
85-89 correct, you have a good score.
84 or fewer correct, you should practice more.

Memory

The second portion of this test involves memorization. Most postal employees are required to memorize city-wide route schematics in order to become proficient at sorting mail. Depending on the size of city in question, those schemes can become quite involved. If an employee cannot memorize what is required, he or she will have little chance of retaining a job beyond probation. This is no doubt a test section that many people struggle with. Doing well on this section should make the difference between excelling and settling for average. This is not meant to minimize the importance of doing well on the rest of the test. However, the other three sections of this test are fairly straight forward and most people will do fairly well on them, even if their preparation for this exam is minimal. Assuming that you do not possess a photographic memory, the memory system described in this book is designed to help you. This system of memory is easy to learn. Over 100,000 people who have purchased this study guide have successfully employed this technique on their exams.

On the exam you will be given a key such as the one provided below that will contain twenty-five addresses in five categories (A through E). Ten addresses are plain street names while the remainder are numerical street addresses.

A	B	C	D	E
1200-1299 Brewster	6700-6799 Brewster	6900-6999 Brewster	2100-2199 Brewster	1300-1399 Brewster
Hoover Ct.	Highland St.	Beaver Ave.	Lamplight Ct.	Bellvue St.
1400-1499 Lakemont	2700-2799 Lakemont	3100-3199 Lakemont	4200-4299 Lakemont	0900-0999 Lakemont
Sycamore St.	Aspen Dr.	Johnson Ave.	Time Square	Harbor View
9200-9299 Terrace	5800-5899 Terrace	1800-1899 Terrace	8700-8799 Terrace	4300-4399 Terrace

You will be given 11 minutes to study this key at which point further reference is not permitted. You then have five minutes to answer as many of the eighty-eight questions pertaining to the key as possible.

Even if you have marginal memory skills, the techniques discussed here (imagery and association) will help you improve in this area. The technique requires you to form images in your mind related to the items to be memorized. Each of these images is then linked together in a specific order by means of association. It may sound complicated, but learning to stretch the boundaries of your imagination can be enjoyable.

A. NAMES
Street names will be among the items that need to be committed to memory for the exam. Use the following street names as examples:

> Jorganson Street
> Phillips Avenue
> Tremont
> Tricia
> Edgewater Boulevard
> Bloomington

Many people approach this exercise by rote memorization, or in other words, drilling the street names into their head by sheer repetition. Not only is this a boring way to memorize, but this method of recall lasts only a short time. On the other hand, imagery and association techniques can be fun and your ability to recall can be substantially extended.

Now, look at those same street names again and see what key word derivatives have been used and what images we can associate with them.

For example:

Jorganson Street—Jogger
Phillips Avenue—Phillips screwdriver
Tremont—Tree
Tricia—Tricycle
Edgewater—Edge
Bloomington—Blossoms

Carry the process one step further and place those key word derivatives in a bizarre context, story or situation. Using this process, we have developed the following story:

A JOGGER with his pockets completely stuffed with PHILLIPS SCREWDRIVERS wasn't paying attention and ran into a giant TREE. After dusting himself off, he jumped on a child's TRICYCLE and pedaled it to the EDGE of a pool filled with flower BLOSSOMS.

Sounds ridiculous, doesn't it? However, because of its strong images, you will not easily forget this kind of story.

Another advantage of the imagery technique is that you can remember items in their respective order by simply reviewing where they fit in relation to the other items in the story.

Look at each of the street names below and develop a story using imagery. There are no right or wrong key word derivatives. What is important is that the images conjure up a clear picture in your mind and then interlink.

Work on each of these columns separately:

Bedford Ave.	Apple Dr.	Anderson Blvd.	Bayberry Rd.
Wellington	Constantine Way	Cannon Ave.	Hickory Ridge
Walker St.	Bristol	Foxtail Run	Ebony Ln.
Penny Ln.	Echo Ave.	Arsenal Way	Ester Ct.
Ridgemont Dr	Darrington	Jacobson St.	Steinbald Ln.
Bowmont	Smalley St.	Prince Williams	Georgia St.

Once you have finished this exercise, cover the street names and see if you can remember all 24 items. If your four stories are bizarre enough, you can have this entire list committed to long-term memory in a short time.

B. NUMBERS

Numbers are another problem in memory recall. For most people, numbers are difficult to memorize because they are intangible. To rectify this problem, numbers can be transposed into letters so that words can be formed and associated accordingly. Below is the format for transposition. Remember this format as if it were your Social Security number because on the exam you will draw from it regularly.

0	1	2	3	4	5	6	7	8	9
/ \	/ \	/ \	/ \	|	|	|	|	|	|
G or V	B or D	C or K	F or P	M	N	R	S	T	L

(All other letters can be incorporated into words without any significance.)

For instance, let's say you are given the number 10603328157. Memorizing this number so well that you can recall it after any length of time could be very difficult. However, by using this memory system, you could use the number to spell out a variety of memorable things. Here is your chance to use your creativity!

After you have had the chance to figure out what words can code such a number, one problem becomes apparent: The more numbers you try to cram into one word, the harder it is to find a compatible word in the English vocabulary. To simplify matters, there are two alternative ways to form words. The first method is to take two numbers at a time, form a word and associate it with the next word. Dealing with the same number (10603328157) DOG could be derived from the number 10, RUG from 60, PIPE from 33, CAT from 28, BONE from 15, and S from 7. There are many ways you could imagine and link these words. One possibility would be a DOG lying on a RUG and smoking a PIPE while a CAT prances by carrying a BONE shaped like an S. This is just one way to memorize this long number. Other words and stories could work just as well.

The second alternative, which offers greater flexibility, is using words of any length but making only the first two significant letters of the word applicable to your story. For example, the word DIG/GING could represent 10 in the number 10603328157.

RAV/EN = RUG/BY = REV/OLVER = 60
POP/ULATION = PUP/PY = PEP/PER = 33
CAT/ERPILLAR = CAT/TLE = COT/TON = 28
BIN/OCULAR = BEAN/S = DIN/NER = 15

By doing this, you have a larger number of words at your disposal to put into stories. With a little originality, it can be fun to see what you can imagine for any number given.

Below are exercises to help you apply this system. The first group of numbers is meant to be used as a transposition exercise. See how many different words you can use to represent each number. The second series is for practice with transposition and story fabrication. This technique may seem difficult at first, but with practice, you will enhance your memory capabilities.

I.

44	63	86	40
53	97	93	32
61	10	48	26
13	3	60	91
12	57	35	99
8	52	27	16
41	11	21	68

II.

17547321158 10	63211347890
69804215 69497	145322175328
14729944710	917403218977
83213555572119	638146119900
488770509453	433351896487
15301978 65321	765321046991

Now that you have a basic grasp of how to remember street names and numbers more easily, let's take a typical test sample and break it down into the order in which the material should be memorized.

A	B	C	D	E
1200-1299 Brewster	6700-6799 Brewster	6900-6999 Brewster	2100-2199 Brewster	1300-1399 Brewster
Hoover Ct.	Highland St.	Beaver Ave.	Lamplight Ct.	Bellvue St.
1400-1499 Lakemont	2700-2799 Lakemont	3100-3199 Lakemont	4200-4299 Lakemont	0900-0999 Lakemont
Sycamore St.	Aspen Dr.	Johnson Ave.	Time Square	Harbor View
9200-9299 Terrace	5800-5899 Terrace	1800-1899 Terrace	8700-8799 Terrace	4300-4399 Terrace

What should become immediately apparent by looking at the key is the fact that all numerical addresses are redundant with respect to street name and all but the first two numbers in each address shown are redundant as well. A lot of time and effort can be saved by looking at the key in the manner shown below.

A	B	C	D	E
BREWSTER - 12	67	69	21	13
Hoover Ct.	Highland St.	Beaver Ave.	Lamplight Ct.	Bellvue St.
LAKEMONT - 14	27	31	42	09
Sycamore St.	Aspen Dr.	Johnson Ave.	Time Square	Harbor View
TERRACE - 92	58	18	87	43

Now, each line of information needs to be set up in story format so that recall references can be easily made. As an example, let's use the sequence of numbers that represents Brewster on the exam.

A	B	C	D	E
12	67	69	21	13

There are virtually thousands of different words that can be transposed from these numbers, but for this particular illustration, we'll use the words BUCKET, ROSES, ROLLING, KID and DIP. Imagine, if you will, a BUC/KET (fashioned from a huge beer can) full of ROS/ES ROL/LING down a hillside knocks over a KID trying to balance a 30-DIP ice cream cone. This is a strange story, but the underlying principle is quite effective. Not only can you reference the street name (i.e., beer represents BREW or BREWSTER) but, as long as the story's chronological order remains intact, you can easily determine the category (i.e., A through E) that each number belongs under.

For example, let's say on the test you were asked what category 1300-1399 Brewster belongs to? (Look at it as the number 13.) Referring back to the BREW-BUCKET story, the number 13 represents the word DIP. Since DIP was the last image in the story, we would know that it belongs in category E and the answer E should be marked accordingly on our answer sheet.

As another example, let's say you were asked in what category 6700-6799 Brewster belongs. Since 67 was transposed into the word ROS/ES in the BEER-BUCKET story, and it was the second image in our story, answer B would be the correct choice.

Now let's examine the next line of street names and see what kind of bizarre story can be concocted.

A	B	C	D	E
Hoover Ct.	Highland St.	Beaver Ave.	Lamplight Ct.	Bellvue St.

How about a HOOVER vacuum cleaner that has arms, both of which are waving to say HI to a BEAVER standing beneath a street LAMP with a huge BELL for a tail? Quiz yourself. At what point in the story did the beaver stand beneath the street lamp (i.e., Lamplight Ct.)? It was the fourth image in the story. Had this been an actual exam question, category D would have been marked as the answer.

As a final example to this system of memory, let's look at the third line of information in the key and work up another story format.

A	B	C	D	E
14	27	31	42	09

How about the Lakemont DAM which instead of retaining water, retains Hershey KIS/SES. At the base of the DAM was a PUD/DLE of melted chocolate that had oozed forth from a crack in the DAM. Standing in the middle of the PUDDLE was a MEC/HANIC frantically attempting to stop the leak by stuffing his GL/OVES into the crack.

At this point, you should be getting a pretty good idea of how this concept works. Transposition of numbers to letters and then back again may seem a little difficult at first. However, the more you practice at using this system, the easier it will become.

During the actual exam, you will be given a 3 minute pretest with a *sample* key and a short sample answer sheet. Examiners almost always fail to tell you that the sample key is the same key used on the rest of the exam. In other words, you will actually be provided an extra 3 minutes to study the key.

Don't bother marking the sample answer sheets in the pretest: Focus all of your attention on making up your five story lines. If you have a solid feel for your stories, you will be able to answer questions accurately and without hesitation. At the close of the first 3 minutes, the examiner will instruct you to turn the page, where the answer key is provided by itself. You are then given 3 minutes to work on your stories. After this time period is up, you will again be instructed to flip another page where the same key and a full length practice question and answer sheet will be provided. You are allotted three more minutes to either study the key or work practice exercises. Again, it is suggested that you completely ignore the practice exercises and continue working on your stories. If you feel compelled to check yourself, limit answering questions to only a few.

After the 3 minutes are up, you will be instructed to turn to the next page in your booklet, which has practice questions and an answer sheet minus the key. You have 3 minutes to work as many practice questions as you feel comfortable doing. Here again, it is strongly recommended that you simply ignore this section and continue working the stories in your mind. Close your eyes if you want to alleviate any visual distractions. If you still feel it necessary to work the practice questions, keep it to an absolute minimum. When time is up, you will be instructed to turn to the next page in the booklet which has only the key. You will be given 5 more minutes to study. At this point, you should know your five stories forward and backward. By the time the actual exam has begun, you should be able to answer all eighty-eight questions in well under 5 minutes.

A couple of words of caution are needed here. If, by chance, you somehow have a mental block to an occasional question, waste no time and skip over it. Be absolutely certain that you also skip over the corresponding answer blank. You can come back to the question later and make an educated guess, if necessary.

The second point is that the new postal exams will intentionally try to confuse you by utilizing duplicate numbers. In other words, there may be three or four 2400-2499 street addresses. Rest assured that if you keep all of your various stories in their respective orders, duplicate numbers on an exam will matter very little. The practice exams toward the back of this study guide are all comparable to what will be seen on the actual test. The practice exams in this chapter are somewhat easier due to a minimum of duplicate numbers. This will allow you to work up to proficiency before attempting the more challenging exercises.

Before you begin any of these exercises, get yourself a timer with an alarm. Set it for the allotted time for each part of the exercise. This will spare you from losing time watching the clock. If you finish before the exam is finished, you can always check your answers once over for accuracy as well as neatness. Erase any miscellaneous marks on the answer sheet because as mentioned earlier, it can impact your test score at the time of grading. A scale is provided at the end of each exercise to allow you to determine your standings.

MEMORIZATION/EXERCISE 1   **STEP 1 TIME: 3 MINUTES**
                                                               STEP 4 TIME: 5 MINUTES

A	B	C	D	E
3300-3399 Burns	3900-3999 Burns	4500-4599 Burns	3600-3699 Burns	4000-4099 Burns
Harrison Dr.	Beaver Ave.	Liberty Rd.	Gregory Blvd.	Sunset Ln.
0800-0899 Pine	1100-1199 Pine	1000-1099 Pine	1500-1599 Pine	0700-0799 Pine
Olympic Ave.	Beatrice St.	Charlette Ct.	Salem	Monteray Pl.
9500-9599 Dibb	7300-7399 Dibb	8400-8499 Dibb	7600-7699 Dibb	8500-8599 Dibb

(STEP 1) Study the address key above for 3 minutes.

(STEP 2) Then turn to the practice exercise on the next page and either study the key or work the practice questions provided for 3 minutes.

(STEP 3) Cover the address key (no reference permitted) and work as many of the practice exercises as possible for 3 minutes.

(STEP 4) Then turn back to this page and study the address key above for another 5 minutes.

(STEP 5) When your time is up, turn two pages over to the actual test and answer as many of the eighty-eight questions as possible within a 5 minute time frame. DO NOT exceed any of the time limits specified or look at the key while doing the actual test. If you do, you forfeit the true sense of how the real exam will be conducted.

NOTE: Remember Step 3 is purely optional. Failure to complete some or all of the practice questions given will NOT affect your test score. Time may well be better spent mentally reviewing your story fabrications.

PRACTICE MEMORIZATION/EXERCISE 1

A	B	C	D	E
3300-3399 Burns Harrison Dr. 0800-0899 Pine Olympic Ave. 9500-9599 Dibb	3900-3999 Burns Beaver Ave. 1100-1199 Pine Beatrice St. 7300-7399 Dibb	4500-4599 Burns Liberty Rd. 1000-1099 Pine Charlette Ct. 8400-8499 Dibb	3600-3699 Burns Gregory Blvd. 1500-1599 Pine Salem 7600-7699 Dibb	4000-4099 Burns Sunset Ln. 0700-0799 Pine Monteray Pl. 8500-8599 Dibb

1. Beatrice St.
2. 3300-3399 Burns
3. 3900-3999 Burns
4. Salem
5. Olympic Ave.
6. 0800-0899 Pine
7. 8400-8499 Dibb
8. Harrison Dr.
9. 4000-4099 Burns
10. 1000-1099 Pine
11. 7600-7699 Dibb
12. Harrison Dr.
13. Liberty Rd.
14. Beaver Ave.
15. 1500-1599 Pine
16. Monteray Pl.
17. 4500-4599 Burns
18. 9500-9599 Dibb
19. 8500-8599 Dibb
20. Gregory Blvd.
21. 1100-1199 Pine
22. Sunset Ln.
23. Charlette Ct.
24. 4500-4599 Burns
25. 3300-3399 Burns
26. Beatrice St.
27. Sunset Ln.
28. 1000-1099 Pine
29. 7300-7399 Dibb
30. Olympic Ave.
31. 3900-3999 Burns
32. Liberty Rd.
33. 8500-8599 Dibb
34. 1500-1599 Pine
35. Salem
36. Gregory Blvd.
37. 4000-4099 Burns
38. 8500-8599 Dibb
39. 1500-1599 Pine
40. Monteray Pl.
41. Gregory Blvd.
42. Charlette Ct.
43. 8500-8599 Dibb
44. 3600-3699 Burns
45. 0800-0899 Pine
46. 7300-7399 Dibb
47. Salem
48. Harrison Dr.
49. 3300-3399 Burns
50. 1100-1199 Pine
51. Beatrice St.
52. Beaver Ave.
53. 3600-3699 Burns
54. Monteray Pl.
55. 0700-0799 Pine
56. 9500-9599 Dibb
57. Olympic Ave.
58. 8400-8499 Dibb
59. 1100-1199 Pine
60. 4000-4099 Burns
61. Charlette Ct.
62. 1000-1099 Pine
63. 9500-9599 Dibb
64. 4500-4599 Burns
65. Beatrice St.
66. Harrison Dr.
67. 7300-7399 Dibb
68. 1500-1599 Pine
69. Monteray Pl.
70. 7600-7699 Dibb
71. 4500-4599 Burns
72. Sunset Ln.
73. Liberty Rd.
74. 8400-8499 Dibb
75. Beaver Ave.
76. 0700-0799 Pine
77. 7600-7699 Dibb
78. Salem
79. Gregory Blvd.
80. 0700-0799 Pine
81. 0800-0899 Pine
82. Olympic Ave.
83. Charlette Ct.
84. 3600-3699 Burns
85. Liberty Rd.
86. 1100-1199 Pine
87. 3900-3999 Burns
88. Salem

PRACTICE ANSWER SHEET TO MEMORIZATION/EXERCISE 1

1. (A) (B) (C) (D) (E)
2. (A) (B) (C) (D) (E)
3. (A) (B) (C) (D) (E)
4. (A) (B) (C) (D) (E)
5. (A) (B) (C) (D) (E)
6. (A) (B) (C) (D) (E)
7. (A) (B) (C) (D) (E)
8. (A) (B) (C) (D) (E)
9. (A) (B) (C) (D) (E)
10. (A) (B) (C) (D) (E)
11. (A) (B) (C) (D) (E)
12. (A) (B) (C) (D) (E)
13. (A) (B) (C) (D) (E)
14. (A) (B) (C) (D) (E)
15. (A) (B) (C) (D) (E)
16. (A) (B) (C) (D) (E)
17. (A) (B) (C) (D) (E)
18. (A) (B) (C) (D) (E)
19. (A) (B) (C) (D) (E)
20. (A) (B) (C) (D) (E)
21. (A) (B) (C) (D) (E)
22. (A) (B) (C) (D) (E)
23. (A) (B) (C) (D) (E)
24. (A) (B) (C) (D) (E)
25. (A) (B) (C) (D) (E)
26. (A) (B) (C) (D) (E)
27. (A) (B) (C) (D) (E)
28. (A) (B) (C) (D) (E)
29. (A) (B) (C) (D) (E)
30. (A) (B) (C) (D) (E)

31. (A) (B) (C) (D) (E)
32. (A) (B) (C) (D) (E)
33. (A) (B) (C) (D) (E)
34. (A) (B) (C) (D) (E)
35. (A) (B) (C) (D) (E)
36. (A) (B) (C) (D) (E)
37. (A) (B) (C) (D) (E)
38. (A) (B) (C) (D) (E)
39. (A) (B) (C) (D) (E)
40. (A) (B) (C) (D) (E)
41. (A) (B) (C) (D) (E)
42. (A) (B) (C) (D) (E)
43. (A) (B) (C) (D) (E)
44. (A) (B) (C) (D) (E)
45. (A) (B) (C) (D) (E)
46. (A) (B) (C) (D) (E)
47. (A) (B) (C) (D) (E)
48. (A) (B) (C) (D) (E)
49. (A) (B) (C) (D) (E)
50. (A) (B) (C) (D) (E)
51. (A) (B) (C) (D) (E)
52. (A) (B) (C) (D) (E)
53. (A) (B) (C) (D) (E)
54. (A) (B) (C) (D) (E)
55. (A) (B) (C) (D) (E)
56. (A) (B) (C) (D) (E)
57. (A) (B) (C) (D) (E)
58. (A) (B) (C) (D) (E)
59. (A) (B) (C) (D) (E)
60. (A) (B) (C) (D) (E)

61. (A) (B) (C) (D) (E)
62. (A) (B) (C) (D) (E)
63. (A) (B) (C) (D) (E)
64. (A) (B) (C) (D) (E)
65. (A) (B) (C) (D) (E)
66. (A) (B) (C) (D) (E)
67. (A) (B) (C) (D) (E)
68. (A) (B) (C) (D) (E)
69. (A) (B) (C) (D) (E)
70. (A) (B) (C) (D) (E)
71. (A) (B) (C) (D) (E)
72. (A) (B) (C) (D) (E)
73. (A) (B) (C) (D) (E)
74. (A) (B) (C) (D) (E)
75. (A) (B) (C) (D) (E)
76. (A) (B) (C) (D) (E)
77. (A) (B) (C) (D) (E)
78. (A) (B) (C) (D) (E)
79. (A) (B) (C) (D) (E)
80. (A) (B) (C) (D) (E)
81. (A) (B) (C) (D) (E)
82. (A) (B) (C) (D) (E)
83. (A) (B) (C) (D) (E)
84. (A) (B) (C) (D) (E)
85. (A) (B) (C) (D) (E)
86. (A) (B) (C) (D) (E)
87. (A) (B) (C) (D) (E)
88. (A) (B) (C) (D) (E)

MEMORIZATON/EXERCISE 1   **STEP 5 TIME: 5 MINUTES**

1. 9500-9599 Dibb	31. Beatrice St.	61. 0700-0799 Pine
2. 0800-0899 Pine	32. Harrison Dr.	62. 3900-3999 Burns
3. Harrison Dr.	33. 8400-8499 Dibb	63. Harrison Dr.
4. Beaver Ave.	34. Salem	64. Monteray Pl.
5. 8400-8499 Dibb	35. 7300-7399 Dibb	65. 9500-9599 Dibb
6. 3900-3999 Burns	36. Liberty Rd.	66. 4000-4099 Burns
7. Gregory Blvd.	37. 0800-0899 Pine	67. Beaver Ave.
8. 7300-7399 Dibb	38. 3900-3999 Burns	68. Gregory Blvd.
9. 1100-1199 Pine	39. 9500-9599 Dibb	69. 7300-7399 Dibb
10. Beatrice St.	40. Beaver Ave.	70. 1100-1199 Pine
11. 3300-3399 Burns	41. Sunset Ln.	71. 3600-3699 Burns
12. 0700-0799 Pine	42. 1000-1099 Pine	72. Beatrice St.
13. Liberty Rd.	43. 3300-3399 Burns	73. 0800-0899 Pine
14. 7600-7699 Dibb	44. Beatrice St.	74. 4500-4599 Burns
15. 4000-4099 Burns	45. 1100-1199 Pine	75. 8400-8499 Dibb
16. Sunset Ln.	46. 3600-3699 Burns	76. Charlette Ct.
17. Salem	47. Olympic Ave.	77. Monteray Pl.
18. 1000-1099 Pine	48. Monteray Pl.	78. 7600-7699 Dibb
19. 3600-3699 Burns	49. 9500-9599 Dibb	79. Beaver Ave.
20. 0700-0799 Pine	50. 4500-4599 Burns	80. 4500-4599 Burns
21. Charlette Ct.	51. Gregory Blvd.	81. Olympic Ave.
22. 8400-8499 Dibb	52. 8500-8599 Dibb	82. Sunset Ln.
23. 3300-3399 Burns	53. Charlette Ct.	83. 8500-8599 Dibb
24. Monteray Pl.	54. 1000-1099 Pine	84. Salem
25. Gregory Blvd.	55. 4000-4099 Burns	85. 0800-0899 Pine
26. Olympic Ave.	56. Liberty Rd.	86. 3300-3399 Burns
27. 8500-8599 Dibb	57. 7600-7699 Dibb	87. Liberty Rd.
28. 3900-3999 Burns	58. Sunset Ln.	88. Harrison Dr.
29. Charlette Ct.	59. Olympic Ave.	
30. 1100-1199 Pine	60. Salem	

ANSWER SHEET TO MEMORIZATION/EXERCISE 1

1. (A) (B) (C) (D) (E)
2. (A) (B) (C) (D) (E)
3. (A) (B) (C) (D) (E)
4. (A) (B) (C) (D) (E)
5. (A) (B) (C) (D) (E)
6. (A) (B) (C) (D) (E)
7. (A) (B) (C) (D) (E)
8. (A) (B) (C) (D) (E)
9. (A) (B) (C) (D) (E)
10. (A) (B) (C) (D) (E)
11. (A) (B) (C) (D) (E)
12. (A) (B) (C) (D) (E)
13. (A) (B) (C) (D) (E)
14. (A) (B) (C) (D) (E)
15. (A) (B) (C) (D) (E)
16. (A) (B) (C) (D) (E)
17. (A) (B) (C) (D) (E)
18. (A) (B) (C) (D) (E)
19. (A) (B) (C) (D) (E)
20. (A) (B) (C) (D) (E)
21. (A) (B) (C) (D) (E)
22. (A) (B) (C) (D) (E)
23. (A) (B) (C) (D) (E)
24. (A) (B) (C) (D) (E)
25. (A) (B) (C) (D) (E)
26. (A) (B) (C) (D) (E)
27. (A) (B) (C) (D) (E)
28. (A) (B) (C) (D) (E)
29. (A) (B) (C) (D) (E)
30. (A) (B) (C) (D) (E)

31. (A) (B) (C) (D) (E)
32. (A) (B) (C) (D) (E)
33. (A) (B) (C) (D) (E)
34. (A) (B) (C) (D) (E)
35. (A) (B) (C) (D) (E)
36. (A) (B) (C) (D) (E)
37. (A) (B) (C) (D) (E)
38. (A) (B) (C) (D) (E)
39. (A) (B) (C) (D) (E)
40. (A) (B) (C) (D) (E)
41. (A) (B) (C) (D) (E)
42. (A) (B) (C) (D) (E)
43. (A) (B) (C) (D) (E)
44. (A) (B) (C) (D) (E)
45. (A) (B) (C) (D) (E)
46. (A) (B) (C) (D) (E)
47. (A) (B) (C) (D) (E)
48. (A) (B) (C) (D) (E)
49. (A) (B) (C) (D) (E)
50. (A) (B) (C) (D) (E)
51. (A) (B) (C) (D) (E)
52. (A) (B) (C) (D) (E)
53. (A) (B) (C) (D) (E)
54. (A) (B) (C) (D) (E)
55. (A) (B) (C) (D) (E)
56. (A) (B) (C) (D) (E)
57. (A) (B) (C) (D) (E)
58. (A) (B) (C) (D) (E)
59. (A) (B) (C) (D) (E)
60. (A) (B) (C) (D) (E)

61. (A) (B) (C) (D) (E)
62. (A) (B) (C) (D) (E)
63. (A) (B) (C) (D) (E)
64. (A) (B) (C) (D) (E)
65. (A) (B) (C) (D) (E)
66. (A) (B) (C) (D) (E)
67. (A) (B) (C) (D) (E)
68. (A) (B) (C) (D) (E)
69. (A) (B) (C) (D) (E)
70. (A) (B) (C) (D) (E)
71. (A) (B) (C) (D) (E)
72. (A) (B) (C) (D) (E)
73. (A) (B) (C) (D) (E)
74. (A) (B) (C) (D) (E)
75. (A) (B) (C) (D) (E)
76. (A) (B) (C) (D) (E)
77. (A) (B) (C) (D) (E)
78. (A) (B) (C) (D) (E)
79. (A) (B) (C) (D) (E)
80. (A) (B) (C) (D) (E)
81. (A) (B) (C) (D) (E)
82. (A) (B) (C) (D) (E)
83. (A) (B) (C) (D) (E)
84. (A) (B) (C) (D) (E)
85. (A) (B) (C) (D) (E)
86. (A) (B) (C) (D) (E)
87. (A) (B) (C) (D) (E)
88. (A) (B) (C) (D) (E)

ANSWERS TO MEMORIZATION/EXERCISE 1

1.	A	31.	B	61.	E
2.	A	32.	A	62.	B
3.	A	33.	C	63.	A
4.	B	34.	D	64.	E
5.	C	35.	B	65.	A
6.	B	36.	C	66.	E
7.	D	37.	A	67.	B
8.	B	38.	B	68.	D
9.	B	39.	A	69.	B
10.	B	40.	B	70.	B
11.	A	41.	E	71.	D
12.	E	42.	C	72.	B
13.	C	43.	A	73.	A
14.	D	44.	B	74.	C
15.	E	45.	B	75.	C
16.	E	46.	D	76.	C
17.	D	47.	A	77.	E
18.	C	48.	E	78.	D
19.	D	49.	A	79.	B
20.	E	50.	C	80.	C
21.	C	51.	D	81.	A
22.	C	52.	E	82.	E
23.	A	53.	C	83.	E
24.	E	54.	C	84.	D
25.	D	55.	E	85.	A
26.	A	56.	C	86.	A
27.	E	57.	D	87.	C
28.	B	58.	E	88.	A
29.	C	59.	A		
30.	B	60.	D		

If you scored:
84 or more correct, you have an excellent score.
78-83 correct, you have a good score.
77 or fewer, you should practice more.

MEMORIZATION/EXERCISE 2

A	B	C	D	E
7700-7799 Rose	6200-6299 Rose	7100-7199 Rose	5400-5499 Rose	6600-6699 Rose
Cactus Ln.	Maleroy Rd.	Phillips Dr.	Falcon Ridge	Franklin
6100-6199 Clem	4900-4999 Clem	8500-8599 Clem	6000-6099 Clem	5900-5999 Clem
Beechnut Dr.	Carver Blvd.	Washington Ave.	Scotts Bluff	Keyport St.
2300-2399 King	2700-2799 King	1900-1999 King	3000-3099 King	2000-2099 King

PRACTICE MEMORIZATION/EXERCISE 2

STEP 2 TIME: 3 MINUTES
STEP 3 TIME: 3 MINUTES (cover key)

A	B	C	D	E
7700-7799 Rose Cactus Ln. 6100-6199 Clem Beechnut Dr. 2300-2399 King	6200-6299 Rose Maleroy Rd. 4900-4999 Clem Carver Blvd. 2700-2799 King	7100-7199 Rose Phillips Dr. 8500-8599 Clem Washington Ave. 1900-1999 King	5400-5499 Rose Falcon Ridge 6000-6099 Clem Scotts Bluff 3000-3099 King	6600-6699 Rose Franklin 5900-5999 Clem Keyport St. 2000-2099 King

1. Maleroy Rd.
2. Phillips Dr.
3. 7700-7799 Rose
4. 4900-4999 Clem
5. Falcon Ridge
6. 1900-1999 King
7. Cactus Ln.
8. 6200-6299 Rose
9. Washington Ave.
10. 2300-2399 King
11. Beechnut Dr.
12. 8500-8599 Clem
13. 5400-5499 Rose
14. Franklin
15. 2000-2099 King
16. 6000-6099 Clem
17. Carver Blvd.
18. Keyport St.
19. 6600-6699 Rose
20. Scotts Bluff
21. 5400-5499 Rose
22. 6100-6199 Clem
23. Cactus Ln.
24. Washington Ave.
25. Franklin
26. 7700-7799 Rose
27. Maleroy Rd.
28. 5900-5999 Clem
29. Falcon Ridge
30. 1900-1999 King

31. Beechnut Dr.
32. 6000-6099 Clem
33. 2000-2099 King
34. 7100-7199 Rose
35. Phillips Dr.
36. 7700-7799 Rose
37. Scotts Bluff
38. 8500-8599 Clem
39. 2000-2099 King
40. Carver Blvd.
41. Falcon Ridge
42. Keyport St.
43. 1900-1999 King
44. Beechnut Dr.
45. 6000-6099 Clem
46. 2000-2099 King
47. Franklin
48. 6100-6199 Clem
49. 2700-2799 King
50. Cactus Ln.
51. Maleroy Rd.
52. 7100-7199 Rose
53. 3000-3099 King
54. Carver Blvd.
55. 6200-6299 Rose
56. 5900-5999 Clem
57. Scotts Bluff
58. 2300-2399 King
59. 6600-6699 Rose
60. Washington Ave.

61. 4900-4999 Clem
62. Keyport St.
63. 3000-3099 King
64. 7700-7799 Rose
65. Cactus Ln.
66. Phillips Dr.
67. 2700-2799 King
68. 6100-6199 Clem
69. 7100-7199 Rose
70. 6000-6099 Clem
71. Maleroy Rd.
72. 3000-3099 King
73. 8500-8599 Clem
74. Scotts Bluff
75. 5400-5499 Rose
76. 5900-5999 Clem
77. Keyport St.
78. Franklin
79. 6600-6699 Rose
80. Scotts Bluff
81. Phillips Dr.
82. 2300-2399 King
83. Falcon Ridge
84. 4900-4999 Clem
85. 6200-6299 Rose
86. Beechnut Dr.
87. Washington Ave.
88. Carver Blvd.

PRACTICE ANSWER SHEET TO MEMORIZATION/EXERCISE 2

1. (A) (B) (C) (D) (E)
2. (A) (B) (C) (D) (E)
3. (A) (B) (C) (D) (E)
4. (A) (B) (C) (D) (E)
5. (A) (B) (C) (D) (E)
6. (A) (B) (C) (D) (E)
7. (A) (B) (C) (D) (E)
8. (A) (B) (C) (D) (E)
9. (A) (B) (C) (D) (E)
10. (A) (B) (C) (D) (E)
11. (A) (B) (C) (D) (E)
12. (A) (B) (C) (D) (E)
13. (A) (B) (C) (D) (E)
14. (A) (B) (C) (D) (E)
15. (A) (B) (C) (D) (E)
16. (A) (B) (C) (D) (E)
17. (A) (B) (C) (D) (E)
18. (A) (B) (C) (D) (E)
19. (A) (B) (C) (D) (E)
20. (A) (B) (C) (D) (E)
21. (A) (B) (C) (D) (E)
22. (A) (B) (C) (D) (E)
23. (A) (B) (C) (D) (E)
24. (A) (B) (C) (D) (E)
25. (A) (B) (C) (D) (E)
26. (A) (B) (C) (D) (E)
27. (A) (B) (C) (D) (E)
28. (A) (B) (C) (D) (E)
29. (A) (B) (C) (D) (E)
30. (A) (B) (C) (D) (E)

31. (A) (B) (C) (D) (E)
32. (A) (B) (C) (D) (E)
33. (A) (B) (C) (D) (E)
34. (A) (B) (C) (D) (E)
35. (A) (B) (C) (D) (E)
36. (A) (B) (C) (D) (E)
37. (A) (B) (C) (D) (E)
38. (A) (B) (C) (D) (E)
39. (A) (B) (C) (D) (E)
40. (A) (B) (C) (D) (E)
41. (A) (B) (C) (D) (E)
42. (A) (B) (C) (D) (E)
43. (A) (B) (C) (D) (E)
44. (A) (B) (C) (D) (E)
45. (A) (B) (C) (D) (E)
46. (A) (B) (C) (D) (E)
47. (A) (B) (C) (D) (E)
48. (A) (B) (C) (D) (E)
49. (A) (B) (C) (D) (E)
50. (A) (B) (C) (D) (E)
51. (A) (B) (C) (D) (E)
52. (A) (B) (C) (D) (E)
53. (A) (B) (C) (D) (E)
54. (A) (B) (C) (D) (E)
55. (A) (B) (C) (D) (E)
56. (A) (B) (C) (D) (E)
57. (A) (B) (C) (D) (E)
58. (A) (B) (C) (D) (E)
59. (A) (B) (C) (D) (E)
60. (A) (B) (C) (D) (E)

61. (A) (B) (C) (D) (E)
62. (A) (B) (C) (D) (E)
63. (A) (B) (C) (D) (E)
64. (A) (B) (C) (D) (E)
65. (A) (B) (C) (D) (E)
66. (A) (B) (C) (D) (E)
67. (A) (B) (C) (D) (E)
68. (A) (B) (C) (D) (E)
69. (A) (B) (C) (D) (E)
70. (A) (B) (C) (D) (E)
71. (A) (B) (C) (D) (E)
72. (A) (B) (C) (D) (E)
73. (A) (B) (C) (D) (E)
74. (A) (B) (C) (D) (E)
75. (A) (B) (C) (D) (E)
76. (A) (B) (C) (D) (E)
77. (A) (B) (C) (D) (E)
78. (A) (B) (C) (D) (E)
79. (A) (B) (C) (D) (E)
80. (A) (B) (C) (D) (E)
81. (A) (B) (C) (D) (E)
82. (A) (B) (C) (D) (E)
83. (A) (B) (C) (D) (E)
84. (A) (B) (C) (D) (E)
85. (A) (B) (C) (D) (E)
86. (A) (B) (C) (D) (E)
87. (A) (B) (C) (D) (E)
88. (A) (B) (C) (D) (E)

MEMORIZATION/EXERCISE 2   **STEP 5: 5 MINUTES**

1. Franklin	31. Carver Blvd.	61. 3000-3099 King
2. Carver Blvd.	32. 2300-2399 King	62. Falcon Ridge
3. 1900-1999 King	33. 6200-6299 Rose	63. 6000-6099 Clem
4. 6000-6099 Clem	34. 5900-5999 Clem	64. 7100-7100 Rose
5. 2700-2799 King	35. Cactus Ln.	65. Maleroy Rd.
6. Cactus Ln.	36. Maleroy Rd.	66. Keyport St.
7. 6200-6299 Rose	37. 8500-8599 Clem	67. 2000-2099 King
8. 8500-8599 Clem	38. 2700-2799 King	68. Beechnut Dr.
9. 2000-2099 King	39. 6600-6699 Rose	69. 6200-6299 Rose
10. Beechnut Dr.	40. Phillips Dr.	70. Washington Ave.
11. Maleroy Rd.	41. Keyport St.	71. 2700-2799 King
12. 6100-6199 Clem	42. Washington Ave.	72. 7100-7199 Rose
13. 5400-5499 Rose	43. Falcon Ridge	73. 6000-6099 Clem
14. Falcon Ridge	44. Franklin	74. Keyport St.
15. Scotts Bluff	45. 6100-6199 Clem	75. Franklin
16. 2300-2399 King	46. Scotts Bluff	76. Washington Ave.
17. 7700-7799 Rose	47. 7700-7799 Rose	77. 5900-5999 Clem
18. Phillips Dr.	48. 4900-4999 Clem	78. Scotts Bluff
19. Keyport St.	49. 3000-3099 King	79. Maleroy Rd.
20. 6200-6299 Rose	50. Beechnut Dr.	80. 2000-2099 King
21. 4900-4999 Clem	51. 8500-8599 Clem	81. 7700-7799 Rose
22. 1900-1999 King	52. 6600-6699 Rose	82. 6100-6199 Clem
23. 3000-3099 King	53. Cactus Ln.	83. Phillips Dr.
24. 6600-6699 Rose	54. Scotts Bluff	84. Falcon Ridge
25. Washington Ave.	55. 3000-3099 King	85. 1900-1999 King
26. Franklin	56. 5900-5999 Clem	86. 2300-2399 King
27. 5400-5499 Rose	57. Carver Blvd.	87. Carver Blvd.
28. 8500-8599 Clem	58. Phillips Dr.	88. Cactus Ln.
29. Beechnut Dr.	59. 5400-5499 Rose	
30. 7100-7199 Rose	60. 4900-4999 Clem	

ANSWER SHEET TO MEMORIZATION/EXERCISE 2

1. Ⓐ Ⓑ Ⓒ Ⓓ Ⓔ
2. Ⓐ Ⓑ Ⓒ Ⓓ Ⓔ
3. Ⓐ Ⓑ Ⓒ Ⓓ Ⓔ
4. Ⓐ Ⓑ Ⓒ Ⓓ Ⓔ
5. Ⓐ Ⓑ Ⓒ Ⓓ Ⓔ
6. Ⓐ Ⓑ Ⓒ Ⓓ Ⓔ
7. Ⓐ Ⓑ Ⓒ Ⓓ Ⓔ
8. Ⓐ Ⓑ Ⓒ Ⓓ Ⓔ
9. Ⓐ Ⓑ Ⓒ Ⓓ Ⓔ
10. Ⓐ Ⓑ Ⓒ Ⓓ Ⓔ
11. Ⓐ Ⓑ Ⓒ Ⓓ Ⓔ
12. Ⓐ Ⓑ Ⓒ Ⓓ Ⓔ
13. Ⓐ Ⓑ Ⓒ Ⓓ Ⓔ
14. Ⓐ Ⓑ Ⓒ Ⓓ Ⓔ
15. Ⓐ Ⓑ Ⓒ Ⓓ Ⓔ
16. Ⓐ Ⓑ Ⓒ Ⓓ Ⓔ
17. Ⓐ Ⓑ Ⓒ Ⓓ Ⓔ
18. Ⓐ Ⓑ Ⓒ Ⓓ Ⓔ
19. Ⓐ Ⓑ Ⓒ Ⓓ Ⓔ
20. Ⓐ Ⓑ Ⓒ Ⓓ Ⓔ
21. Ⓐ Ⓑ Ⓒ Ⓓ Ⓔ
22. Ⓐ Ⓑ Ⓒ Ⓓ Ⓔ
23. Ⓐ Ⓑ Ⓒ Ⓓ Ⓔ
24. Ⓐ Ⓑ Ⓒ Ⓓ Ⓔ
25. Ⓐ Ⓑ Ⓒ Ⓓ Ⓔ
26. Ⓐ Ⓑ Ⓒ Ⓓ Ⓔ
27. Ⓐ Ⓑ Ⓒ Ⓓ Ⓔ
28. Ⓐ Ⓑ Ⓒ Ⓓ Ⓔ
29. Ⓐ Ⓑ Ⓒ Ⓓ Ⓔ
30. Ⓐ Ⓑ Ⓒ Ⓓ Ⓔ
31. Ⓐ Ⓑ Ⓒ Ⓓ Ⓔ
32. Ⓐ Ⓑ Ⓒ Ⓓ Ⓔ
33. Ⓐ Ⓑ Ⓒ Ⓓ Ⓔ
34. Ⓐ Ⓑ Ⓒ Ⓓ Ⓔ
35. Ⓐ Ⓑ Ⓒ Ⓓ Ⓔ
36. Ⓐ Ⓑ Ⓒ Ⓓ Ⓔ
37. Ⓐ Ⓑ Ⓒ Ⓓ Ⓔ
38. Ⓐ Ⓑ Ⓒ Ⓓ Ⓔ
39. Ⓐ Ⓑ Ⓒ Ⓓ Ⓔ
40. Ⓐ Ⓑ Ⓒ Ⓓ Ⓔ
41. Ⓐ Ⓑ Ⓒ Ⓓ Ⓔ
42. Ⓐ Ⓑ Ⓒ Ⓓ Ⓔ
43. Ⓐ Ⓑ Ⓒ Ⓓ Ⓔ
44. Ⓐ Ⓑ Ⓒ Ⓓ Ⓔ
45. Ⓐ Ⓑ Ⓒ Ⓓ Ⓔ
46. Ⓐ Ⓑ Ⓒ Ⓓ Ⓔ
47. Ⓐ Ⓑ Ⓒ Ⓓ Ⓔ
48. Ⓐ Ⓑ Ⓒ Ⓓ Ⓔ
49. Ⓐ Ⓑ Ⓒ Ⓓ Ⓔ
50. Ⓐ Ⓑ Ⓒ Ⓓ Ⓔ
51. Ⓐ Ⓑ Ⓒ Ⓓ Ⓔ
52. Ⓐ Ⓑ Ⓒ Ⓓ Ⓔ
53. Ⓐ Ⓑ Ⓒ Ⓓ Ⓔ
54. Ⓐ Ⓑ Ⓒ Ⓓ Ⓔ
55. Ⓐ Ⓑ Ⓒ Ⓓ Ⓔ
56. Ⓐ Ⓑ Ⓒ Ⓓ Ⓔ
57. Ⓐ Ⓑ Ⓒ Ⓓ Ⓔ
58. Ⓐ Ⓑ Ⓒ Ⓓ Ⓔ
59. Ⓐ Ⓑ Ⓒ Ⓓ Ⓔ
60. Ⓐ Ⓑ Ⓒ Ⓓ Ⓔ
61. Ⓐ Ⓑ Ⓒ Ⓓ Ⓔ
62. Ⓐ Ⓑ Ⓒ Ⓓ Ⓔ
63. Ⓐ Ⓑ Ⓒ Ⓓ Ⓔ
64. Ⓐ Ⓑ Ⓒ Ⓓ Ⓔ
65. Ⓐ Ⓑ Ⓒ Ⓓ Ⓔ
66. Ⓐ Ⓑ Ⓒ Ⓓ Ⓔ
67. Ⓐ Ⓑ Ⓒ Ⓓ Ⓔ
68. Ⓐ Ⓑ Ⓒ Ⓓ Ⓔ
69. Ⓐ Ⓑ Ⓒ Ⓓ Ⓔ
70. Ⓐ Ⓑ Ⓒ Ⓓ Ⓔ
71. Ⓐ Ⓑ Ⓒ Ⓓ Ⓔ
72. Ⓐ Ⓑ Ⓒ Ⓓ Ⓔ
73. Ⓐ Ⓑ Ⓒ Ⓓ Ⓔ
74. Ⓐ Ⓑ Ⓒ Ⓓ Ⓔ
75. Ⓐ Ⓑ Ⓒ Ⓓ Ⓔ
76. Ⓐ Ⓑ Ⓒ Ⓓ Ⓔ
77. Ⓐ Ⓑ Ⓒ Ⓓ Ⓔ
78. Ⓐ Ⓑ Ⓒ Ⓓ Ⓔ
79. Ⓐ Ⓑ Ⓒ Ⓓ Ⓔ
80. Ⓐ Ⓑ Ⓒ Ⓓ Ⓔ
81. Ⓐ Ⓑ Ⓒ Ⓓ Ⓔ
82. Ⓐ Ⓑ Ⓒ Ⓓ Ⓔ
83. Ⓐ Ⓑ Ⓒ Ⓓ Ⓔ
84. Ⓐ Ⓑ Ⓒ Ⓓ Ⓔ
85. Ⓐ Ⓑ Ⓒ Ⓓ Ⓔ
86. Ⓐ Ⓑ Ⓒ Ⓓ Ⓔ
87. Ⓐ Ⓑ Ⓒ Ⓓ Ⓔ
88. Ⓐ Ⓑ Ⓒ Ⓓ Ⓔ

ANSWERS TO MEMORIZATION/EXERCISE 2

1.	E	31.	B	61.	D
2.	B	32.	A	62.	D
3.	C	33.	B	63.	D
4.	D	34.	E	64.	C
5.	B	35.	A	65.	B
6.	A	36.	B	66.	E
7.	B	37.	C	67.	E
8.	C	38.	B	68.	A
9.	E	39.	E	69.	B
10.	A	40.	C	70.	C
11.	B	41.	E	71.	B
12.	A	42.	C	72.	C
13.	D	43.	D	73.	D
14.	D	44.	E	74.	E
15.	D	45.	A	75.	E
16.	A	46.	D	76.	C
17.	A	47.	A	77.	E
18.	C	48.	B	78.	D
19.	E	49.	D	79.	B
20.	B	50.	A	80.	E
21.	B	51.	C	81.	A
22.	C	52.	E	82.	A
23.	D	53.	A	83.	C
24.	E	54.	D	84.	D
25.	C	55.	D	85.	C
26.	E	56.	E	86.	A
27.	D	57.	B	87.	B
28.	C	58.	C	88.	A
29.	A	59.	D		
30.	C	60.	B		

If you scored:
84 or more correct, you have an excellent score.
78-83 correct, you have a good score.
77 or fewer correct, you should practice more.

MEMORIZATION/EXERCISE 3

A	B	C	D	E
3700-3799 Boston Eagle Ct.	4300-4399 Boston Michigan Ave.	3500-3599 Boston Alderwood	4000-4099 Boston Falkner Dr.	5000-5099 Boston Stevens Ln.
8200-8299 Sievers Apache Jct.	8700-8799 Sievers Mt. Springs	9400-9499 Sievers Caldwell	9000-9099 Sievers Swanson Ave.	8000-8099 Sievers Benchard Dr.
0400-0499 St. John	1000-1099 St. John	2500-2599 St. John	0900-0999 St. John	2200-2299 St. John

PRACTICE MEMORIZATION/EXERCISE 3

STEP 2 TIME: 3 MINUTES
STEP 3 TIME: 3 MINUTES (cover key)

A	B	C	D	E
3700-3799 Boston	4300-4399 Boston	3500-3599 Boston	4000-4099 Boston	5000-5099 Boston
Eagle Ct.	Michigan Ave.	Alderwood	Falkner Dr.	Stevens Ln.
8200-8299 Sievers	8700-8799 Sievers	9400-9499 Sievers	9000-9099 Sievers	8000-8099 Sievers
Apache Jct.	Mt. Springs	Caldwell	Swanson Ave.	Benchard Dr.
0400-0499 St. John	1000-1099 St. John	2500-2599 St. John	0900-0999 St. John	2200-2299 St. John

1. 8700-8799 Sievers
2. 4300-4399 Boston
3. Michigan Ave.
4. 0400-0499 St. John
5. Eagle Ct.
6. Mt. Springs
7. 9000-9099 Sievers
8. 2200-2299 St. John
9. 5000-5099 Boston
10. Stevens Ln.
11. Alderwood
12. 1000-1099 St. John
13. 9400-9499 Sievers
14. Apache Jct.
15. Swanson Ave.
16. 3500-3599 Boston
17. Benchard Dr.
18. 8000-8099 Sievers
19. 2500-2599 St. John
20. Caldwell
21. Mt. Springs
22. 8000-8099 Sievers
23. 3700-3799 Boston
24. Falkner Dr.
25. 0900-0999 St. John
26. 8700-8799 Sievers
27. Eagle Ct.
28. 4000-4099 Boston
29. Michigan Ave.
30. Stevens Ln.
31. 4300-4399 Boston
32. 8200-8299 Sievers
33. 2500-2599 St. John
34. Alderwood
35. Apache Jct.
36. Michigan Ave.
37. Benchard Dr.
38. 9000-9099 Sievers
39. 2200-2299 St. John
40. Falkner Dr.
41. 5000-5099 Boston
42. Caldwell
43. Swanson Ave.
44. 1000-1099 St. John
45. 4300-4399 Boston
46. Apache Jct.
47. Mt. Springs
48. Stevens Ln.
49. 0400-0499 St. John
50. 8200-8299 Sievers
51. Caldwell
52. Eagle Ct.
53. 1000-1099 St. John
54. 4000-4099 Boston
55. 8700-8799 Sievers
56. Falkner Dr.
57. 3500-3599 Boston
58. 3700-3799 Boston
59. Swanson Ave.
60. Alderwood
61. 2200-2299 St. John
62. 3500-3599 Boston
63. 8200-8299 Sievers
64. Eagle Ct.
65. Benchard Dr.
66. 3700-3799 Boston
67. 8000-8099 Sievers
68. 2500-2599 St. John
69. Caldwell
70. 5000-5099 Boston
71. 9400-9499 Sievers
72. 0900-0999 St. John
73. Mt. Springs
74. 4000-4099 Boston
75. Swanson Ave.
76. Stevens Ln.
77. Benchard Dr.
78. 3700-3799 Boston
79. 9000-9099 Sievers
80. Caldwell
81. 9400-9499 Sievers
82. Michigan Ave.
83. 0400-0499 St. John
84. Alderwood
85. 0900-0999 St. John
86. 1000-1099 St. John
87. Falkner Dr.
88. Apache Jct.

PRACTICE ANSWER SHEET TO MEMORIZATION/EXERCISE 3

1. Ⓐ Ⓑ Ⓒ Ⓓ Ⓔ
2. Ⓐ Ⓑ Ⓒ Ⓓ Ⓔ
3. Ⓐ Ⓑ Ⓒ Ⓓ Ⓔ
4. Ⓐ Ⓑ Ⓒ Ⓓ Ⓔ
5. Ⓐ Ⓑ Ⓒ Ⓓ Ⓔ
6. Ⓐ Ⓑ Ⓒ Ⓓ Ⓔ
7. Ⓐ Ⓑ Ⓒ Ⓓ Ⓔ
8. Ⓐ Ⓑ Ⓒ Ⓓ Ⓔ
9. Ⓐ Ⓑ Ⓒ Ⓓ Ⓔ
10. Ⓐ Ⓑ Ⓒ Ⓓ Ⓔ
11. Ⓐ Ⓑ Ⓒ Ⓓ Ⓔ
12. Ⓐ Ⓑ Ⓒ Ⓓ Ⓔ
13. Ⓐ Ⓑ Ⓒ Ⓓ Ⓔ
14. Ⓐ Ⓑ Ⓒ Ⓓ Ⓔ
15. Ⓐ Ⓑ Ⓒ Ⓓ Ⓔ
16. Ⓐ Ⓑ Ⓒ Ⓓ Ⓔ
17. Ⓐ Ⓑ Ⓒ Ⓓ Ⓔ
18. Ⓐ Ⓑ Ⓒ Ⓓ Ⓔ
19. Ⓐ Ⓑ Ⓒ Ⓓ Ⓔ
20. Ⓐ Ⓑ Ⓒ Ⓓ Ⓔ
21. Ⓐ Ⓑ Ⓒ Ⓓ Ⓔ
22. Ⓐ Ⓑ Ⓒ Ⓓ Ⓔ
23. Ⓐ Ⓑ Ⓒ Ⓓ Ⓔ
24. Ⓐ Ⓑ Ⓒ Ⓓ Ⓔ
25. Ⓐ Ⓑ Ⓒ Ⓓ Ⓔ
26. Ⓐ Ⓑ Ⓒ Ⓓ Ⓔ
27. Ⓐ Ⓑ Ⓒ Ⓓ Ⓔ
28. Ⓐ Ⓑ Ⓒ Ⓓ Ⓔ
29. Ⓐ Ⓑ Ⓒ Ⓓ Ⓔ
30. Ⓐ Ⓑ Ⓒ Ⓓ Ⓔ

31. Ⓐ Ⓑ Ⓒ Ⓓ Ⓔ
32. Ⓐ Ⓑ Ⓒ Ⓓ Ⓔ
33. Ⓐ Ⓑ Ⓒ Ⓓ Ⓔ
34. Ⓐ Ⓑ Ⓒ Ⓓ Ⓔ
35. Ⓐ Ⓑ Ⓒ Ⓓ Ⓔ
36. Ⓐ Ⓑ Ⓒ Ⓓ Ⓔ
37. Ⓐ Ⓑ Ⓒ Ⓓ Ⓔ
38. Ⓐ Ⓑ Ⓒ Ⓓ Ⓔ
39. Ⓐ Ⓑ Ⓒ Ⓓ Ⓔ
40. Ⓐ Ⓑ Ⓒ Ⓓ Ⓔ
41. Ⓐ Ⓑ Ⓒ Ⓓ Ⓔ
42. Ⓐ Ⓑ Ⓒ Ⓓ Ⓔ
43. Ⓐ Ⓑ Ⓒ Ⓓ Ⓔ
44. Ⓐ Ⓑ Ⓒ Ⓓ Ⓔ
45. Ⓐ Ⓑ Ⓒ Ⓓ Ⓔ
46. Ⓐ Ⓑ Ⓒ Ⓓ Ⓔ
47. Ⓐ Ⓑ Ⓒ Ⓓ Ⓔ
48. Ⓐ Ⓑ Ⓒ Ⓓ Ⓔ
49. Ⓐ Ⓑ Ⓒ Ⓓ Ⓔ
50. Ⓐ Ⓑ Ⓒ Ⓓ Ⓔ
51. Ⓐ Ⓑ Ⓒ Ⓓ Ⓔ
52. Ⓐ Ⓑ Ⓒ Ⓓ Ⓔ
53. Ⓐ Ⓑ Ⓒ Ⓓ Ⓔ
54. Ⓐ Ⓑ Ⓒ Ⓓ Ⓔ
55. Ⓐ Ⓑ Ⓒ Ⓓ Ⓔ
56. Ⓐ Ⓑ Ⓒ Ⓓ Ⓔ
57. Ⓐ Ⓑ Ⓒ Ⓓ Ⓔ
58. Ⓐ Ⓑ Ⓒ Ⓓ Ⓔ
59. Ⓐ Ⓑ Ⓒ Ⓓ Ⓔ
60. Ⓐ Ⓑ Ⓒ Ⓓ Ⓔ

61. Ⓐ Ⓑ Ⓒ Ⓓ Ⓔ
62. Ⓐ Ⓑ Ⓒ Ⓓ Ⓔ
63. Ⓐ Ⓑ Ⓒ Ⓓ Ⓔ
64. Ⓐ Ⓑ Ⓒ Ⓓ Ⓔ
65. Ⓐ Ⓑ Ⓒ Ⓓ Ⓔ
66. Ⓐ Ⓑ Ⓒ Ⓓ Ⓔ
67. Ⓐ Ⓑ Ⓒ Ⓓ Ⓔ
68. Ⓐ Ⓑ Ⓒ Ⓓ Ⓔ
69. Ⓐ Ⓑ Ⓒ Ⓓ Ⓔ
70. Ⓐ Ⓑ Ⓒ Ⓓ Ⓔ
71. Ⓐ Ⓑ Ⓒ Ⓓ Ⓔ
72. Ⓐ Ⓑ Ⓒ Ⓓ Ⓔ
73. Ⓐ Ⓑ Ⓒ Ⓓ Ⓔ
74. Ⓐ Ⓑ Ⓒ Ⓓ Ⓔ
75. Ⓐ Ⓑ Ⓒ Ⓓ Ⓔ
76. Ⓐ Ⓑ Ⓒ Ⓓ Ⓔ
77. Ⓐ Ⓑ Ⓒ Ⓓ Ⓔ
78. Ⓐ Ⓑ Ⓒ Ⓓ Ⓔ
79. Ⓐ Ⓑ Ⓒ Ⓓ Ⓔ
80. Ⓐ Ⓑ Ⓒ Ⓓ Ⓔ
81. Ⓐ Ⓑ Ⓒ Ⓓ Ⓔ
82. Ⓐ Ⓑ Ⓒ Ⓓ Ⓔ
83. Ⓐ Ⓑ Ⓒ Ⓓ Ⓔ
84. Ⓐ Ⓑ Ⓒ Ⓓ Ⓔ
85. Ⓐ Ⓑ Ⓒ Ⓓ Ⓔ
86. Ⓐ Ⓑ Ⓒ Ⓓ Ⓔ
87. Ⓐ Ⓑ Ⓒ Ⓓ Ⓔ
88. Ⓐ Ⓑ Ⓒ Ⓓ Ⓔ

MEMORIZATION/EXERCISE 3   **STEP 5 TIME: 5 MINUTES**

1. 2500-2599 St. John
2. Benchard Dr.
3. Alderwood
4. 8700-8799 Sievers
5. Mt. Springs
6. Eagle Ct.
7. 0400-0499 St. John
8. 9000-9099 Sievers
9. 5000-5099 Boston
10. Michigan Ave.
11. 0900-0999 St. John
12. 8200-8299 Sievers
13. Apache Jct.
14. Stevens Ln.
15. 2200-2299 St. John
16. 1000-1099 St. John
17. Swanson Ave.
18. 9400-9499 Sievers
19. 3700-3799 Boston
20. Falkner Dr.
21. 4000-4099 Boston
22. 3500-3599 Boston
23. 8000-8099 Sievers
24. Alderwood
25. Caldwell
26. Michigan Ave.
27. 8000-8099 Sievers
28. 5000-5099 Boston
29. Apache Jct.
30. 2500-2599 St. John
31. 8700-8799 Sievers
32. Benchard Dr.
33. 4000-4099 Boston
34. Mt. Springs
35. 4300-4399 Boston
36. 8000-8099 Sievers
37. Falkner Dr.
38. 0400-0499 St. John
39. Swanson Ave.
40. Caldwell
41. Eagle Ct.
42. Stevens Ln.
43. 8700-8799 Sievers
44. Alderwood
45. 1000-1099 St. John
46. 3500-3599 Boston
47. Mt. Springs
48. 9400-9499 Sievers
49. Benchard Dr.
50. Falkner Dr.
51. Caldwell
52. Stevens Ln.
53. 2200-2299 St. John
54. 9000-9099 Sievers
55. 4300-4399 Boston
56. Michigan Ave.
57. Benchard Dr.
58. 4000-4099 Boston
59. 0900-0999 St. John
60. Alderwood
61. 8200-8299 Sievers
62. 5000-5099 Boston
63. Apache Jct.
64. Alderwood
65. 2500-2599 St. John
66. Eagle Ct.
67. 8700-8799 Sievers
68. Michigan Ave.
69. Stevens Ln.
70. 3700-3799 Boston
71. 3500-3599 Boston
72. 9400-9499 Sievers
73. Benchard Dr.
74. 2200-2299 St. John
75. Swanson Ave.
76. Eagle Ct.
77. Falkner Dr.
78. 0900-0999 St. John
79. 4300-4399 Boston
80. Apache Jct.
81. 1000-1099 St. John
82. Mt. Springs
83. Caldwell
84. 3700-3799 Boston
85. 9000-9099 Sievers
86. Swanson Ave.
87. 8200-8299 Sievers
88. 0400-0499 St. John

ANSWER SHEET TO MEMORIZATION/EXERCISE 3

1. Ⓐ Ⓑ Ⓒ Ⓓ Ⓔ
2. Ⓐ Ⓑ Ⓒ Ⓓ Ⓔ
3. Ⓐ Ⓑ Ⓒ Ⓓ Ⓔ
4. Ⓐ Ⓑ Ⓒ Ⓓ Ⓔ
5. Ⓐ Ⓑ Ⓒ Ⓓ Ⓔ
6. Ⓐ Ⓑ Ⓒ Ⓓ Ⓔ
7. Ⓐ Ⓑ Ⓒ Ⓓ Ⓔ
8. Ⓐ Ⓑ Ⓒ Ⓓ Ⓔ
9. Ⓐ Ⓑ Ⓒ Ⓓ Ⓔ
10. Ⓐ Ⓑ Ⓒ Ⓓ Ⓔ
11. Ⓐ Ⓑ Ⓒ Ⓓ Ⓔ
12. Ⓐ Ⓑ Ⓒ Ⓓ Ⓔ
13. Ⓐ Ⓑ Ⓒ Ⓓ Ⓔ
14. Ⓐ Ⓑ Ⓒ Ⓓ Ⓔ
15. Ⓐ Ⓑ Ⓒ Ⓓ Ⓔ
16. Ⓐ Ⓑ Ⓒ Ⓓ Ⓔ
17. Ⓐ Ⓑ Ⓒ Ⓓ Ⓔ
18. Ⓐ Ⓑ Ⓒ Ⓓ Ⓔ
19. Ⓐ Ⓑ Ⓒ Ⓓ Ⓔ
20. Ⓐ Ⓑ Ⓒ Ⓓ Ⓔ
21. Ⓐ Ⓑ Ⓒ Ⓓ Ⓔ
22. Ⓐ Ⓑ Ⓒ Ⓓ Ⓔ
23. Ⓐ Ⓑ Ⓒ Ⓓ Ⓔ
24. Ⓐ Ⓑ Ⓒ Ⓓ Ⓔ
25. Ⓐ Ⓑ Ⓒ Ⓓ Ⓔ
26. Ⓐ Ⓑ Ⓒ Ⓓ Ⓔ
27. Ⓐ Ⓑ Ⓒ Ⓓ Ⓔ
28. Ⓐ Ⓑ Ⓒ Ⓓ Ⓔ
29. Ⓐ Ⓑ Ⓒ Ⓓ Ⓔ
30. Ⓐ Ⓑ Ⓒ Ⓓ Ⓔ
31. Ⓐ Ⓑ Ⓒ Ⓓ Ⓔ
32. Ⓐ Ⓑ Ⓒ Ⓓ Ⓔ
33. Ⓐ Ⓑ Ⓒ Ⓓ Ⓔ
34. Ⓐ Ⓑ Ⓒ Ⓓ Ⓔ
35. Ⓐ Ⓑ Ⓒ Ⓓ Ⓔ
36. Ⓐ Ⓑ Ⓒ Ⓓ Ⓔ
37. Ⓐ Ⓑ Ⓒ Ⓓ Ⓔ
38. Ⓐ Ⓑ Ⓒ Ⓓ Ⓔ
39. Ⓐ Ⓑ Ⓒ Ⓓ Ⓔ
40. Ⓐ Ⓑ Ⓒ Ⓓ Ⓔ
41. Ⓐ Ⓑ Ⓒ Ⓓ Ⓔ
42. Ⓐ Ⓑ Ⓒ Ⓓ Ⓔ
43. Ⓐ Ⓑ Ⓒ Ⓓ Ⓔ
44. Ⓐ Ⓑ Ⓒ Ⓓ Ⓔ
45. Ⓐ Ⓑ Ⓒ Ⓓ Ⓔ
46. Ⓐ Ⓑ Ⓒ Ⓓ Ⓔ
47. Ⓐ Ⓑ Ⓒ Ⓓ Ⓔ
48. Ⓐ Ⓑ Ⓒ Ⓓ Ⓔ
49. Ⓐ Ⓑ Ⓒ Ⓓ Ⓔ
50. Ⓐ Ⓑ Ⓒ Ⓓ Ⓔ
51. Ⓐ Ⓑ Ⓒ Ⓓ Ⓔ
52. Ⓐ Ⓑ Ⓒ Ⓓ Ⓔ
53. Ⓐ Ⓑ Ⓒ Ⓓ Ⓔ
54. Ⓐ Ⓑ Ⓒ Ⓓ Ⓔ
55. Ⓐ Ⓑ Ⓒ Ⓓ Ⓔ
56. Ⓐ Ⓑ Ⓒ Ⓓ Ⓔ
57. Ⓐ Ⓑ Ⓒ Ⓓ Ⓔ
58. Ⓐ Ⓑ Ⓒ Ⓓ Ⓔ
59. Ⓐ Ⓑ Ⓒ Ⓓ Ⓔ
60. Ⓐ Ⓑ Ⓒ Ⓓ Ⓔ
61. Ⓐ Ⓑ Ⓒ Ⓓ Ⓔ
62. Ⓐ Ⓑ Ⓒ Ⓓ Ⓔ
63. Ⓐ Ⓑ Ⓒ Ⓓ Ⓔ
64. Ⓐ Ⓑ Ⓒ Ⓓ Ⓔ
65. Ⓐ Ⓑ Ⓒ Ⓓ Ⓔ
66. Ⓐ Ⓑ Ⓒ Ⓓ Ⓔ
67. Ⓐ Ⓑ Ⓒ Ⓓ Ⓔ
68. Ⓐ Ⓑ Ⓒ Ⓓ Ⓔ
69. Ⓐ Ⓑ Ⓒ Ⓓ Ⓔ
70. Ⓐ Ⓑ Ⓒ Ⓓ Ⓔ
71. Ⓐ Ⓑ Ⓒ Ⓓ Ⓔ
72. Ⓐ Ⓑ Ⓒ Ⓓ Ⓔ
73. Ⓐ Ⓑ Ⓒ Ⓓ Ⓔ
74. Ⓐ Ⓑ Ⓒ Ⓓ Ⓔ
75. Ⓐ Ⓑ Ⓒ Ⓓ Ⓔ
76. Ⓐ Ⓑ Ⓒ Ⓓ Ⓔ
77. Ⓐ Ⓑ Ⓒ Ⓓ Ⓔ
78. Ⓐ Ⓑ Ⓒ Ⓓ Ⓔ
79. Ⓐ Ⓑ Ⓒ Ⓓ Ⓔ
80. Ⓐ Ⓑ Ⓒ Ⓓ Ⓔ
81. Ⓐ Ⓑ Ⓒ Ⓓ Ⓔ
82. Ⓐ Ⓑ Ⓒ Ⓓ Ⓔ
83. Ⓐ Ⓑ Ⓒ Ⓓ Ⓔ
84. Ⓐ Ⓑ Ⓒ Ⓓ Ⓔ
85. Ⓐ Ⓑ Ⓒ Ⓓ Ⓔ
86. Ⓐ Ⓑ Ⓒ Ⓓ Ⓔ
87. Ⓐ Ⓑ Ⓒ Ⓓ Ⓔ
88. Ⓐ Ⓑ Ⓒ Ⓓ Ⓔ

ANSWERS TO MEMORIZATION/EXERCISE 3

1.	C	31.	B	61.	A
2.	E	32.	E	62.	E
3.	C	33.	D	63.	A
4.	B	34.	B	64.	C
5.	B	35.	B	65.	C
6.	A	36.	E	66.	A
7.	A	37.	D	67.	B
8.	D	38.	A	68.	B
9.	E	39.	D	69.	E
10.	B	40.	C	70.	A
11.	D	41.	A	71.	C
12.	A	42.	E	72.	C
13.	A	43.	B	73.	E
14.	E	44.	C	74.	E
15.	E	45.	B	75.	D
16.	B	46.	C	76.	A
17.	D	47.	B	77.	D
18.	C	48.	C	78.	D
19.	A	49.	E	79.	B
20.	D	50.	D	80.	A
21.	D	51.	C	81.	B
22.	C	52.	E	82.	B
23.	E	53.	E	83.	C
24.	C	54.	D	84.	A
25.	C	55.	B	85.	D
26.	B	56.	B	86.	D
27.	E	57.	E	87.	A
28.	E	58.	D	88.	A
29.	A	59.	D		
30.	C	60.	C		

If you scored:
84 or more correct, you have an excellent score.
78-83 correct, you have a good score.
77 or fewer correct, you should practice more.

Number Series

Number series tests are used to determine your skill at discerning number patterns. For clerks, this has direct relevance to code recognition as information is typed into a special purpose keyboard to sort either letters or flats.

Number series tests are not difficult if you can quickly establish the pattern in the numbers listed. For example, look at the question below:

| 2 | 4 | 6 | 8 | 10 | 12 | ? | ? |

As you can see, there is an addition constant of +2 between each number. Therefore, the next two numbers in the sequence should be 14 and 16.

2	4	6	8	10	12	14	16
+2	+2	+2	+2	+2	+2	+2	

Subtraction and multiplication number series are much the same as the prior example. An example of each is given below. Try to determine what the last two numbers are in each of the number sequences.

| 23 | 20 | 17 | 14 | 11 | 8 | ? | ? |

| 1 | 3 | 9 | 27 | 81 | ? | ? |

The first example shown is a subtraction number series. If you determined that there was a subtraction constant of -3 between numbers, you were correct. So the last two numbers in the first sequence should be 5 and 2.

23	20	17	14	11	8	5	2
-3	-3	-3	-3	-3	-3	-3	

The second example represents a multiplication number series. If you determined that there was a multiplication constant of 3 between the numbers in the sequence, you were right again. Therefore, the last two numbers in this series are 243 and 729.

1	3	9	27	81	243	729
x3	x3	x3	x3	x3	x3	

The last kind of number series that will appear on the exam is an alternating number series. This kind of number sequence is a little more involved and consequently takes extra time to solve. The series involves alternating uses of addition and/or subtraction to create a pattern. A pattern may not be immediately evident but with a little diligence, it should become apparent. Two examples are given below. Try to determine what the last two numbers are in each sequence.

| 0 | 12 | 10 | 3 | 6 | 8 | 6 | 9 | ? | ? |

| 0 | 16 | 17 | 4 | 18 | 19 | 8 | 20 | ? | ? |

If you guessed 12 and 4, and 21 and 12, respectively, you are right. You can see how these patterns can become a bit more complicated.

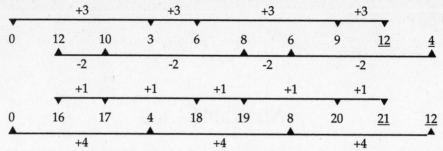

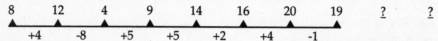

If a pattern in an alternating number series is not discernable, there is a method you can use to help. The first step involves determining the differences between each successive number in sequence. For example:

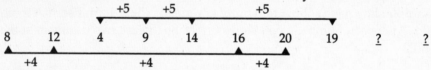

Note that there are two +4 and two +5 constants. The next step is to check these differences to see if, indeed, some kind of pattern can be established. Let's start with the +4 constant. The numbers involved are 8, 12, 16, and 20. What should become evident is that this series of four numbers represents an addition number series pattern. To better clarify the pattern, if you diagram it as shown below, it should alleviate some confusion

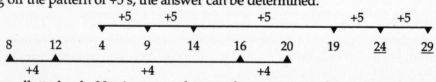

If there were one more answer blank, the number 24 would be the right answer. However, the addition number series pattern already established does not encompass the two answer blanks. Now, look at the remaining numbers: 4, 9, 14, and 19. Do you see a pattern emerge there? If you determined the series is another addition number series with +5 as a constant, you are correct.

By blocking off the pattern of +5's, the answer can be determined.

Since you are allotted only 20 minutes on the actual exam to complete twenty-four number series questions, time is of the essence. If an answer to an alternating number series question is not apparent within the scope of 30 seconds, skip the question and go on to the next one. If you have any time remaining after you have completed the test questions that you know, return to those questions you skipped, and try to solve them. If you still have trouble determining the answer, systematically plug in each of the options provided and by the process of elimination you can determine the correct answer. This is somewhat time consuming, but it is better than just guessing. Whatever the case, don't leave any answers blank. Guess only as a last resort.

For your convenience, the first number series exercise questions have been segregated into the four number series groups (i.e., addition, subtraction, multiplication, and alternating). This should clue you in as to what kind of pattern to be searching for. However, you will not be given the same convenience on number series exercises 2 and 3. On those exams, the series will be relatively well mixed for variety. The answers will provide the correct number combinations and establish the set pattern involved. Thus, you can see how the answer to the question was determined. A scale has been provided for determination of your performance on each exam.

NUMBER SERIES/EXERCISE 1

Addition Number Series

1.   7   10   13   16   19   22   ___   ___

     A.   25, 28   C.   23, 27   E.   27, 30
     B.   23, 24   D.   25, 26

2.   24   30   36   42   48   54   ___   ___

     A.   56, 66   C.   60, 56   E.   60, 66
     B.   58, 64   D.   58, 66

3.   18   27   36   45   54   63   ___   ___

     A.   70, 81   C.   72, 81   E.   72, 83
     B.   71, 81   D.   71, 82

4.   4   20   36   52   68   84   ___   ___

     A.   96, 114   C.   100, 110   E.   110, 116
     B.   98, 110   D.   100, 116

5.   13   15   17   19   21   23   ___   ___

     A.   24, 25   C.   25, 28   E.   26, 28
     B.   27, 28   D.   25, 27

6.   1   18   35   52   69   86   ___   ___

     A.   105, 122   C.   101, 119   E.   105, 120
     B.   103, 120   D.   103, 102

Subtraction Number Series

7.   14   12   10   8   6   4   ___   ___

     A.   2, 0   C.   2, 2   E.   0, 0
     B.   4, 2   D.   0, 2

8.   174   150   126   102   78   54   ___   ___

     A.   40, 6   C.   30, 6   E.   28, 2
     B.   30, 4   D.   28, 4

9.   45   40   35   30   25   20   ___   ___

     A.   10, 5   C.   10, 15   E.   15, 10
     B.   15, 5   D.   5, 10

10.   81   72   63   54   45   36   ___   ___

     A.   18, 27   C.   17, 28   E.   27, 18
     B.   28, 17   D.   26, 18

11.   163   149   135   121   107   93   ___   ___

     A.   65, 79   C.   81, 67   E.   67, 81
     B.   79, 65   D.   79, 59

12.   1205   1088   971   854   737   620   ___   ___

     A.   386, 503   C.   503, 286   E.   500, 286
     B.   403, 386   D.   503, 386

Multiplication Number Series

13. 2   4   8   16   32   ___   ___

    A. 32, 64   C. 64, 128   E. 60, 128
    B. 64, 32   D. 60, 120

14. 4   20   100   500   2500   ___   ___

    A. 5000, 12,500   C. 62,500, 12,500   E. 12,000, 60,000
    B. 12,500, 62,500   D. 18,500, 25,500

15. 3   9   27   81   243   ___   ___

    A. 729, 2187   C. 739, 2187   E. 723, 2187
    B. 715, 2180   D. 715, 2387

16. 1   7   49   343   ___   ___

    A. 2401, 16,807   C. 2401, 16,907   E. 4085, 17,250
    B. 2400, 16,000   D. 2400, 16,807

17. 6   12   24   48   96   ___   ___

    A. 182, 384   C. 192, 375   E. 192, 384
    B. 190, 380   D. 195, 380

18. 2   8   32   128   512   ___   ___

    A. 2408, 8192   C. 2348, 8792   E. 2040, 8029
    B. 2580, 8092   D. 2048, 8192

Alternating Number Series

19. 12   10   16   17   8   6   18   ___   ___

    A. 19, 2   C. 2, 20   E. 20, 3
    B. 4, 19   D. 19, 4

20. 7   11   3   8   13   15   19   18   ___   ___

    A. 25, 28   C. 23, 24   E. 22, 28
    B. 23, 28   D. 21, 23

21. 20   3   6   9   17   14   12   15   18   ___   ___

    A. 5, 8   C. 11, 8   E. 8, 11
    B. 7, 11   D. 12, 8

22. 30   20   25   28   30   35   26   40   ___   ___

    A. 45, 24   C. 47, 24   E. 41, 22
    B. 46, 25   D. 43, 25

23. 18   14   13   16   12   11   14   10   ___   ___

    A. 8, 10   C. 10, 9   E. 10, 8
    B. 9, 12   D. 12, 9

24. 36   42   35   28   45   21   14   7   ___   ___

    A. 54, 0   C. 43, 14   E. 48, 7
    B. 36, 7   D. 48, 0

ANSWER SHEET TO NUMBER SERIES/EXERCISE 1

1. Ⓐ Ⓑ Ⓒ Ⓓ Ⓔ
2. Ⓐ Ⓑ Ⓒ Ⓓ Ⓔ
3. Ⓐ Ⓑ Ⓒ Ⓓ Ⓔ
4. Ⓐ Ⓑ Ⓒ Ⓓ Ⓔ
5. Ⓐ Ⓑ Ⓒ Ⓓ Ⓔ
6. Ⓐ Ⓑ Ⓒ Ⓓ Ⓔ
7. Ⓐ Ⓑ Ⓒ Ⓓ Ⓔ
8. Ⓐ Ⓑ Ⓒ Ⓓ Ⓔ

9. Ⓐ Ⓑ Ⓒ Ⓓ Ⓔ
10. Ⓐ Ⓑ Ⓒ Ⓓ Ⓔ
11. Ⓐ Ⓑ Ⓒ Ⓓ Ⓔ
12. Ⓐ Ⓑ Ⓒ Ⓓ Ⓔ
13. Ⓐ Ⓑ Ⓒ Ⓓ Ⓔ
14. Ⓐ Ⓑ Ⓒ Ⓓ Ⓔ
15. Ⓐ Ⓑ Ⓒ Ⓓ Ⓔ
16. Ⓐ Ⓑ Ⓒ Ⓓ Ⓔ

17. Ⓐ Ⓑ Ⓒ Ⓓ Ⓔ
18. Ⓐ Ⓑ Ⓒ Ⓓ Ⓔ
19. Ⓐ Ⓑ Ⓒ Ⓓ Ⓔ
20. Ⓐ Ⓑ Ⓒ Ⓓ Ⓔ
21. Ⓐ Ⓑ Ⓒ Ⓓ Ⓔ
22. Ⓐ Ⓑ Ⓒ Ⓓ Ⓔ
23. Ⓐ Ⓑ Ⓒ Ⓓ Ⓔ
24. Ⓐ Ⓑ Ⓒ Ⓓ Ⓔ

(This page may be removed to mark answers.)

[This page intentionally blank.]

ANSWERS TO NUMBER SERIES/EXERCISE 1

1. A. 7   10   13   16   19   22   25   28
       +3   +3   +3   +3   +3   +3   +3

2. E. 24   30   36   42   48   54   60   66
       +6   +6   +6   +6   +6   +6   +6

3. C. 18   27   36   45   54   63   72   81
       +9   +9   +9   +9   +9   +9   +9

4. D. 4   20   36   52   68   84   100   116
      +16   +16   +16   +16   +16   +16   +16

5. D. 13   15   17   19   21   23   25   27
       +2   +2   +2   +2   +2   +2   +2

6. B. 1   18   35   52   69   86   103   120
      +17   +17   +17   +17   +17   +17   +17

7. A. 14   12   10   8   6   4   2   0
       -2   -2   -2   -2   -2   -2   -2

8. C. 174   150   126   102   78   54   30   6
       -24   -24   -24   -24   -24   -24   -24

9. E. 45   40   35   30   25   20   15   10
       -5   -5   -5   -5   -5   -5   -5

10. E. 81   72   63   54   45   36   27   18
        -9   -9   -9   -9   -9   -9   -9

11. B. 163   149   135   121   107   93   79   65
        -14   -14   -14   -14   -14   -14   -14

12. D. 1205   1088   971   854   737   620   503   386
        -117   -117   -117   -117   -117   -117   -117

13. C. 2   4   6   8   16   32   64   128
       x2   x2   x2   x2   x2   x2   x2

14. B. 4   20   100   500   2500   12,500   62,500
       x5   x5   x5   x5   x5   x5

15. A. 3   9   27   81   243   729   2187
       x3   x3   x3   x3   x3   x3

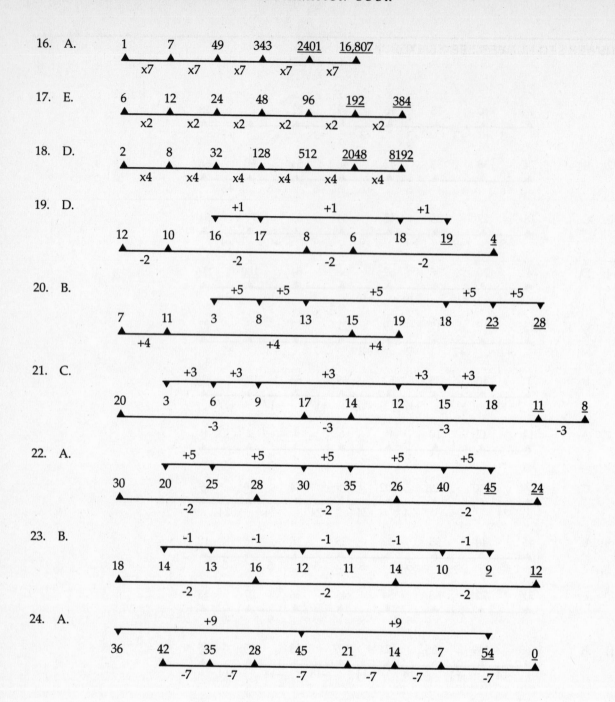

16. A.
1   7   49   343   2401   16,807
    x7   x7   x7   x7   x7

17. E.
6   12   24   48   96   192   384
    x2   x2   x2   x2   x2   x2

18. D.
2   8   32   128   512   2048   8192
    x4   x4   x4   x4   x4   x4

19. D.
                +1   +1   +1
12   10   16   17   8   6   18   19   4
    -2   -2   -2   -2

20. B.
            +5   +5   +5   +5   +5
7   11   3   8   13   15   19   18   23   28
    +4   +4   +4

21. C.
        +3   +3   +3   +3   +3
20   3   6   9   17   14   12   15   18   11   8
    -3   -3   -3   -3

22. A.
        +5   +5   +5   +5   +5
30   20   25   28   30   35   26   40   45   24
    -2   -2   -2

23. B.
        -1   -1   -1   -1   -1
18   14   13   16   12   11   14   10   9   12
    -2   -2   -2

24. A.
        +9   +9
36   42   35   28   45   21   14   7   54   0
    -7   -7   -7   -7   -7   -7

If you scored:
22 or more correct, you have an excellent score.
20 or 21 correct, you have a good score.
19 or fewer correct, you need more practice.

NUMBER SERIES/EXERCISE 2   **TIME: 20 MINUTES**

1. 12   16   20   24   28   ___   ___
    A. 29, 32   C. 32, 24   E. 32, 36
    B. 30, 36   D. 30, 32

2. 1   4   16   64   256   ___   ___
    A. 1042, 4096   C. 1024, 4096   E. 1042, 5000
    B. 1096, 4024   D. 1034, 5000

3. 21   20   18   24   15   28   ___   ___
    A. 13, 23   C. 14, 32   E. 12, 23
    B. 12, 32   D. 10, 30

4. 17 27 37 32 47 57 67 30 ___ ___
    A. 77, 87   C. 87, 28   E. 67, 28
    B. 77, 28   D. 87, 34

5. 3   6   12   24   48   ___   ___
    A. 90, 196   C. 92, 196   E. 100, 196
    B. 96, 129   D. 96, 192

6. 29 7 23 13 17 19 11 25 ___ ___
    A. 4, 31   C. 5, 31   E. 31, 4
    B. 4, 30   D. 31, 5

7. 18 12 20 28 21 36 44 ___ ___
    A. 50, 24   C. 52, 24   E. 52, 42
    B. 52, 34   D. 50, 34

8. 19   17   15   13   11   ___   ___
    A. 10, 6   C. 9, 6   E. 9, 7
    B. 9, 8   D. 8, 7

9. 14   15   23   19   32   23   ___   ___
    A. 40, 26   C. 27, 40   E. 41, 30
    B. 41, 27   D. 26, 14

10. 23   40   57   74   91   ___   ___
    A. 98, 115   C. 103, 115   E. 118, 125
    B. 108, 125   D. 98, 108

11. 4   3   5   3   7   9   ___   ___
    A. 10, 2   C. 11, 15   E. 1, 10
    B. 2, 11   D. 3, 10

12. 27   25   23   20   19   15   ___   ___
    A. 10, 15   C. 17, 15   E. 19, 20
    B. 12, 10   D. 15, 10

13. 9   18   27   36   45   ___   ___

     A.   54, 63   C.   53, 64   E.   50, 63
     B.   53, 63   D.   55, 64

14. 4   7   15   9   26   11   ___   ___

     A.   37, 13   C.   28, 37   E.   13, 27
     B.   27, 12   D.   39, 13

15. 37   40   41   39   43   46   37   ___   ___

     A.   33, 48   C.   35, 49   E.   37, 50
     B.   35, 48   D.   30, 49

16. 1   7   6   14   36   28   ___   ___

     A.   224, 56   C.   216, 56   E.   202, 60
     B.   220, 50   D.   230, 52

17. 15   20   25   30   35   40   ___   ___

     A.   40, 45   C.   45, 55   E.   50, 45
     B.   50, 60   D.   45, 50

18. 1   21   9   19   17   17   25   ___   ___

     A.   33, 17   C.   20, 37   E.   15, 33
     B.   15, 30   D.   12, 35

19. 12   40   39   24   38   37   36   36   ___   ___

     A.   36, 42   C.   35, 40   E.   35, 48
     B.   37, 46   D.   39, 44

20. 68   60   52   44   36   ___   ___

     A.   28, 20   C.   24, 18   E.   16, 28
     B.   20, 28   D.   22, 20

21. 7   12   10   14   13   16   ___   ___

     A.   18, 20   C.   16, 18   E.   14, 23
     B.   18, 16   D.   14, 20

22. 15   12   18   19   9   6   20   ___   ___

     A.   22, 0   C.   24, 0   E.   27, 4
     B.   21, 3   D.   25, 2

23. 4   12   36   108   ___   ___

     A.   304, 912   C.   324, 902   E.   312, 936
     B.   314, 942   D.   324, 972

24. 6   8   7   6   7   8   5   4   ___   ___

     A.   2, 8   C.   2, 9   E.   0, 8
     B.   1, 10   D.   3, 9

ANSWER SHEET TO NUMBER SERIES/EXERCISE 2

1. (A) (B) (C) (D) (E)
2. (A) (B) (C) (D) (E)
3. (A) (B) (C) (D) (E)
4. (A) (B) (C) (D) (E)
5. (A) (B) (C) (D) (E)
6. (A) (B) (C) (D) (E)
7. (A) (B) (C) (D) (E)
8. (A) (B) (C) (D) (E)

9. (A) (B) (C) (D) (E)
10. (A) (B) (C) (D) (E)
11. (A) (B) (C) (D) (E)
12. (A) (B) (C) (D) (E)
13. (A) (B) (C) (D) (E)
14. (A) (B) (C) (D) (E)
15. (A) (B) (C) (D) (E)
16. (A) (B) (C) (D) (E)

17. (A) (B) (C) (D) (E)
18. (A) (B) (C) (D) (E)
19. (A) (B) (C) (D) (E)
20. (A) (B) (C) (D) (E)
21. (A) (B) (C) (D) (E)
22. (A) (B) (C) (D) (E)
23. (A) (B) (C) (D) (E)
24. (A) (B) (C) (D) (E)

(This page may be removed to mark answers.)

[This page intentionally blank.]

ANSWERS TO NUMBER SERIES/EXERCISE 2

1. E.
12 16 20 24 28 <u>32</u> <u>36</u>
+4 +4 +4 +4 +4 +4

2. C.
1 4 16 64 256 <u>1024</u> <u>4096</u>
x4 x4 x4 x4 x4 x4

3. B.
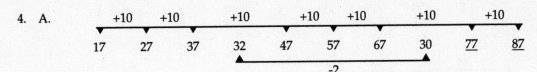
+4   +4   +4
21 20 18 24 15 28 <u>12</u> <u>32</u>
-3   -3   -3

4. A.
+10 +10   +10   +10 +10   +10   +10
17 27 37 32 47 57 67 30 <u>77</u> <u>87</u>
-2

5. D.
3 6 12 24 48 <u>96</u> <u>192</u>
x2 x2 x2 x2 x2 x2

6. C.
+6   +6   +6   +6
29 7 23 13 17 19 11 25 <u>5</u> <u>31</u>
-6   -6   -6   -6

7. C.
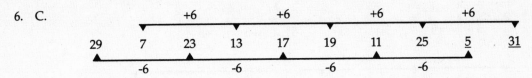
+8 +8   +8   +8 +8
18 12 20 28 21 36 44 <u>52</u> <u>24</u>
+3   +3

8. E.
19 17 15 13 11 <u>9</u> <u>7</u>
-2 -2 -2 -2 -2 -2

9. B.
+9   +9   +9
14 15 23 19 32 23 <u>41</u> <u>27</u>
+4   +4   +4

10. B.
23 40 57 74 91 <u>108</u> <u>125</u>
+17 +17 +17 +17 +17 +17

11. B.
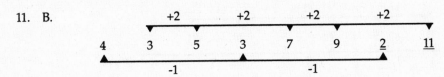
+2   +2   +2   +2
4 3 5 3 7 9 <u>2</u> <u>11</u>
-1   -1

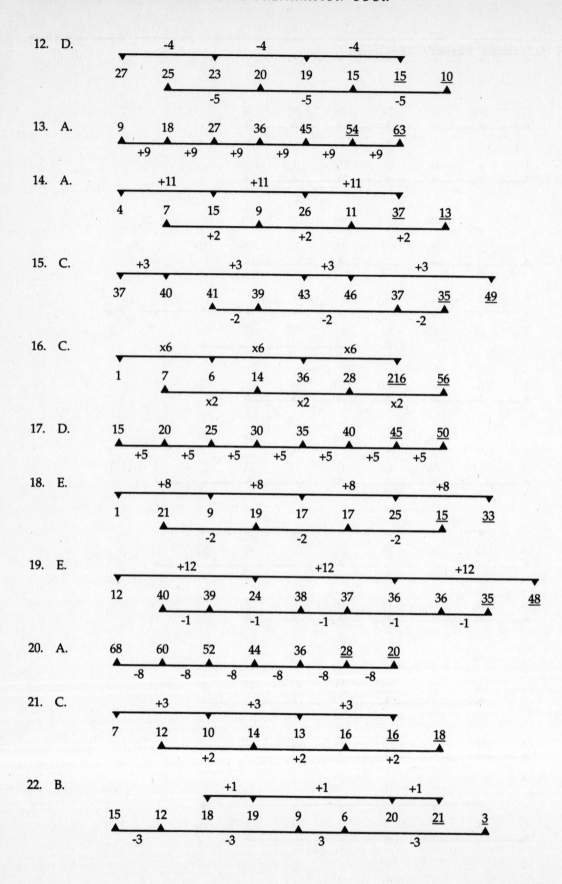

12. D.

-4   -4   -4

27   25   23   20   19   15   15   10

-5   -5   -5

13. A.

9   18   27   36   45   54   63

+9   +9   +9   +9   +9   +9

14. A.

+11   +11   +11

4   7   15   9   26   11   37   13

+2   +2   +2

15. C.

+3   +3   +3   +3

37   40   41   39   43   46   37   35   49

-2   -2   -2

16. C.

x6   x6   x6

1   7   6   14   36   28   216   56

x2   x2   x2

17. D.

15   20   25   30   35   40   45   50

+5   +5   +5   +5   +5   +5   +5

18. E.

+8   +8   +8   +8

1   21   9   19   17   17   25   15   33

-2   -2   -2

19. E.

+12   +12   +12

12   40   39   24   38   37   36   36   35   48

-1   -1   -1   -1   -1

20. A.

68   60   52   44   36   28   20

-8   -8   -8   -8   -8   -8

21. C.

+3   +3   +3

7   12   10   14   13   16   16   18

+2   +2   +2

22. B.

+1   +1   +1

15   12   18   19   9   6   20   21   3

-3   -3   3   -3

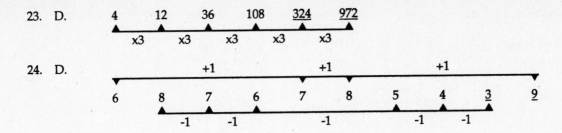

23. D.   4   12   36   108   <u>324</u>   <u>972</u>
     x3   x3   x3   x3   x3

24. D.   +1   +1   +1
  6   8   7   6   7   8   5   4   <u>3</u>   <u>2</u>
    -1   -1   -1   -1   -1

If you scored:
22 or more correct, you have an excellent score.
20 or 21 correct, you have a good score.
19 or fewer correct, you need more practice.

[This page intentionally blank.]

NUMBER SERIES/EXERCISE 3   **TIME: 20 MINUTES**

1.   6   13   20   27   34   ___   ___
     A.   40, 46   C.   42, 48   E.   43, 50
     B.   41, 48   D.   40, 47

2.   19   16   13   10   7   ___   ___
     A.   4, 0   C.   5, 2   E.   4, 1
     B.   3, 0   D.   5, 3

3.   1   8   64   512   ___   ___
     A.   4069, 32,768   C.   4096, 32,768   E.   4075, 32,300
     B.   5000, 40,000   D.   4080, 32,320

4.   17   19   16   19   13   10   ___   ___
     A.   15, 6   C.   20, 8   E.   21, 6
     B.   17, 6   D.   21, 7

5.   24   27   23   25   26   27   19   ___   ___
     A.   14, 26   C.   16, 26   E.   20, 28
     B.   13, 28   D.   15, 28

6.   16   12   15   14   18   21   ___   ___
     A.   12, 24   C.   20, 19   E.   15, 19
     B.   24, 12   D.   19, 20

7.   3   21   147   ___   ___
     A.   1029, 7203   C.   1029, 7302   E.   1025, 7150
     B.   1000, 3000   D.   7203, 1028

8.   1   8   17   26   7   35   44   ___   ___
     A.   50, 13   C.   53, 12   E.   10, 56
     B.   53, 13   D.   56, 10

9.   64   80   77   75   90   70   ___   ___
     A.   105, 65   C.   103, 56   E.   103, 65
     B.   130, 70   D.   100, 65

10. 11   8   7   13   6   ___   ___
     A.   5, 14   C.   3, 10   E.   7, 20
     B.   5, 15   D.   10, 3

11. 27   34   41   48   55   62   ___   ___
     A.   69, 75   C.   69, 76   E.   75, 70
     B.   68, 76   D.   70, 75

12. 96   81   66   51   36   ___   ___
     A.   20, 6   C.   21, 6   E.   20, 3
     B.   21, 5   D.   18, 0

13. 20   17   15   19   13   11   ___   ___

    A. 18, 9   C. 6, 9   E. 17, 9
    B. 12, 9   D. 10, 2

14. 37   29   30   31   32   32   33   ___   ___

    A. 30, 27   C. 30, 28
    B. 34, 27   D. 34, 34   E. 33, 27

15. 48   58   60   63   72   68   ___   ___

    A. 80, 70   C. 84, 72
    B. 85, 73   D. 84, 73   E. 90, 70

16. 6   10   27   22   48   34   69   ___   ___

    A. 50, 70   C. 42, 88
    B. 64, 80   D. 43, 89   E. 46, 90

17. 25   22   19   16   13   ___   ___

    A. 10, 7   C. 13, 6
    B. 12, 8   D. 6, 4   E. 8, 6

18. 2   5   7   6   5   8   11   4   3   ___   ___

    A. 1, 10   C. 1, 10
    B. 2, 14   D. 10, 12   E. 12, 14

19. 20   16   12   8   ___   ___

    A. 4, 1   C. 4, 0
    B. 3, 2   D. 3, 3   E. 2, 4

20. 1   2   4   8   16   ___   ___

    A. 20, 24   C. 36, 42
    B. 32, 46   D. 30, 62   E. 32, 64

21. 14   21   3   28   35   13   ___   ___

    A. 41, 47   C. 44, 50
    B. 42, 47   D. 43, 49   E. 42, 49

22. 12   11   9   14   10   9   19   24   ___   ___

    A. 6, 5   C. 5, 6
    B. 7, 8   D. 8, 7   E. 7, 5

23. 36   42   48   54   60   66   ___   ___

    A. 70, 74   C. 73, 79
    B. 76, 86   D. 72, 78   E. 75, 89

24. 48   16   28   36   40   52   24   64   ___   ___

    A. 70, 14   C. 76, 0
    B. 76, 12   D. 64, 0   E. 72, 12

ANSWER SHEET TO NUMBER SERIES/EXERCISE 3

1. (A) (B) (C) (D) (E)
2. (A) (B) (C) (D) (E)
3. (A) (B) (C) (D) (E)
4. (A) (B) (C) (D) (E)
5. (A) (B) (C) (D) (E)
6. (A) (B) (C) (D) (E)
7. (A) (B) (C) (D) (E)
8. (A) (B) (C) (D) (E)

9. (A) (B) (C) (D) (E)
10. (A) (B) (C) (D) (E)
11. (A) (B) (C) (D) (E)
12. (A) (B) (C) (D) (E)
13. (A) (B) (C) (D) (E)
14. (A) (B) (C) (D) (E)
15. (A) (B) (C) (D) (E)
16. (A) (B) (C) (D) (E)

17. (A) (B) (C) (D) (E)
18. (A) (B) (C) (D) (E)
19. (A) (B) (C) (D) (E)
20. (A) (B) (C) (D) (E)
21. (A) (B) (C) (D) (E)
22. (A) (B) (C) (D) (E)
23. (A) (B) (C) (D) (E)
24. (A) (B) (C) (D) (E)

(This page may be removed to mark answers.)

[This page intentionally blank.]

ANSWERS TO NUMBER SERIES/EXERCISE 3

1. B.
6   13   20   27   34   <u>41</u>   <u>48</u>
+7 +7 +7 +7 +7 +7

2. E.
19 16 13 10 7 <u>4</u> <u>1</u>
-3 -3 -3 -3 -3 -3

3. C.
1 8 64 512 <u>4096</u> <u>32,768</u>
x8 x8 x8 x8 x8

4. D.
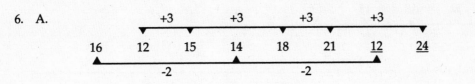
+2 ... +2
17 19 16 19 13 10 <u>21</u> <u>7</u>
-3 -3 -3 -3

5. D.
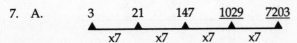
+1 +1 +1 +1
24 27 23 25 26 27 19 <u>15</u> <u>28</u>
-4 -4 -4

6. A.
+3 +3 +3 +3
16 12 15 14 18 21 <u>12</u> <u>24</u>
-2 -2

7. A.
3 21 147 <u>1029</u> <u>7203</u>
x7 x7 x7 x7

8. B.
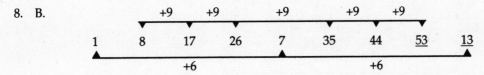
+9 +9 +9 +9 +9
1 8 17 26 7 35 44 <u>53</u> <u>13</u>
+6 +6

9. E.
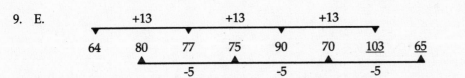
+13 +13 +13
64 80 77 75 90 70 <u>103</u> <u>65</u>
-5 -5 -5

10. B.
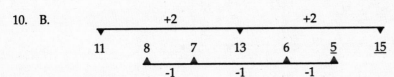
+2 +2
11 8 7 13 6 <u>5</u> <u>15</u>
-1 -1 -1

11. C.
27 34 41 48 55 62 <u>69</u> <u>76</u>
+7 +7 +7 +7 +7 +7 +7

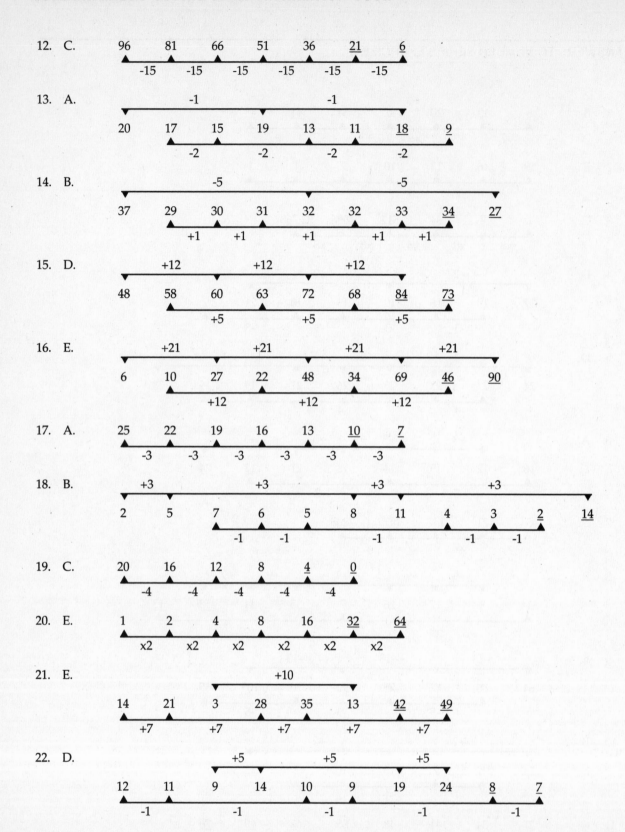

12. C.
13. A.
14. B.
15. D.
16. E.
17. A.
18. B.
19. C.
20. E.
21. E.
22. D.

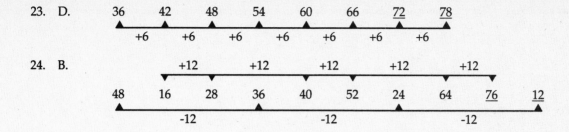

23. D.

36	42	48	54	60	66	<u>72</u>	<u>78</u>
+6	+6	+6	+6	+6	+6	+6	

24. B.

	+12		+12		+12		+12		+12	
48	16	28	36	40	52	24	64	<u>76</u>	<u>12</u>
	-12		-12		-12	

If you scored:
22 or more correct, you have an excellent score.
20 or 21 correct, you have a good score.
19 or fewer correct, you need more practice.

Following Directions

This part of the exam is derived from the old Mail Handler test and is designed to determine how well you follow directions. How you perform here has bearing on the amount of time and effort required by Postal supervisory staff to train you for a specific job. Obviously, a person who needs to be told only once how to do something stands a better chance of being hired than someone who needs directions repeated. This is not a difficult test, particularly if you pay full attention to the examiner's every direction. You will be given ample time between directions to respond on your answer sheet. This is not a time-oriented section. One note of caution here: Be alert for words such as IF, OR, BUT, AND, ONLY, EXCEPT, OTHERWISE, or any other conditional terms, because they alter the instructions. Ignoring such terms will cause you to mark incorrect choices.

In the practice session that follows, a friend or relative will be needed to play the part of the test examiner. He or she will be responsible for reading the directions orally to you at a rate of 75–80 words per minute, pausing where indicated in the test. As a suggestion, have whoever you choose to help you read with a timer until they can judge what the rate of 75–80 words per minute is like. Pauses between directions should be timed also.

When you are ready to do one of the three exercises provided in this chapter, tear out those pages with the directions and give them to the person assisting you. You should be left with only the samples and answer sheets on which to mark your responses. Once a direction has been read by the examiner, it cannot be repeated. If you happen to miss part of a direction or do not understand the direction completely, you can attempt a guess at the correct answer. Place a greater emphasis on listening more closely to the next set of directions given. Most importantly, do not panic if a question has to be skipped. Overlooking one or two questions will not substantially affect your test score.

There are more answer blanks provided than there are directions on the exam, so a great deal of your answer sheet will remain blank after you have completed the test. **NOTE:** Unlike any other test section, the answer sheet in this exercise may not be filled out in numerical order. In other sections, question number 1 corresponds with answer blank number 1, question number 2 with answer blank number 2, etc. On this particular test, however, question number 1 may direct you to darken a particular letter in answer blank number 82; question number 2 many concern answer blank number 25, etc.

The correct answers to practice exams are posted at the end of each exercise. A scale has also been provided to rank your proficiency at following directions.

[This page intentionally blank.]

FOLLOWING DIRECTIONS/EXERCISE 1

Note To Person Assisting In This Exercise:

Remove from this test guide the pages of this exercise that comprise the directions (this page and the reverse). The test applicant should be left with only the samples and the answer sheet.

Read the following directions out loud at the suggested rate of 75-80 words per minute, pausing only where indicated in parentheses. Speak as clearly as possible: Once a statement has been read, it cannot be repeated.

Examine Sample 1. (Pause 2-3 seconds.) If any of the months listed in Sample 1 can be categorized as winter months, find number 12 on your answer sheet and darken the letter E, as in "elephant." Otherwise, find number 14 on your answer sheet and darken the letter A, as in "apple." (Pause 7 seconds.)

Examine Sample 1 again. (Pause 2-3 seconds.) If more than two months begin with the letter J, as in "jack," go to number 15 on your answer sheet and darken the letter B, as in "boy." (Pause 7 seconds.) Otherwise, darken the letter C, as in "cat" on number 5 on your answer sheet. (Pause 7 seconds.)

Examine Sample 2. (Pause 2-3 seconds.) Write the number 17 in the smallest circle shown. Darken the resulting number-letter combination on your answer sheet only if there are two larger circles shown in the sample. (Pause 10 seconds.) Otherwise, write the number 16 in square D, as in "dog," and darken that number-letter combination on your answer sheet. (Pause 10 seconds.)

Examine Sample 3. (Pause 2-3 seconds.) This sample illustrates the respective number of routes originating from each of three Postal substations in a metropolitan area. Select the largest substation, designated by the highest number of routes, and write the letter C, as in "cat," beside it. (Pause 7 seconds.) Darken the resulting number-letter combination on your answer sheet. (Pause 7 seconds.)

Examine Sample 3 again. (Pause 2-3 seconds.) If the Chaney Street station has more routes than the Myers Boulevard station, write the letter B, as in "boy," beside the Clifford Avenue station. (Pause 5 seconds.) If not, write the letter A, as in "apple," beside the Myers Boulevard station (Pause 5 seconds.) Darken the number-letter combination you have selected on your answer sheet. (Pause 7 seconds.)

Examine Sample 4. (Pause 2-3 seconds.) If the third number is greater than the second number, but less than the fifth number, write the letter A, as in "apple," beside 42. (Pause 5 seconds.) Otherwise, write the letter D, as in "dog," beside the fourth number. (Pause 5 seconds.) Darken the number-letter combination that you have selected on your answer sheet. (Pause 7 seconds.)

Examine Sample 3 again. (Pause 2-3 seconds.) Darken the letter D, as in "dog," on number 9 of your answer sheet if the Chaney Street substation has the smallest number of routes. (Pause 7 seconds.) Otherwise, go to number 82 on your answer sheet and darken the letter D, as in "dog." (Pause 7 seconds.)

Examine Sample 4 again. (Pause 2-3 seconds.) If there are any numbers greater than 53, but less than 70, write the letter B, as in "boy," beside that number and darken the resulting number-letter combination on your answer sheet. (Pause 7 seconds.) Otherwise, write the letter E, as in "elephant," beside the second number of the sample and darken that number-letter combination on your answer sheet. (Pause 10 seconds.)

Examine Sample 5. (Pause 2-3 seconds.) This sample shows four numbers, each representing a combined Zip Code and route direct number. The first five digits of each number identify the Zip Code and the last two digits represent intercity route numbers. If all of the Zip Codes in Sample 5 are the same and there is not a route number higher than 50, darken the letter A, as in "apple," on number 50 of your answer sheet. (Pause 10 seconds.) Otherwise, darken the letter C, as in "cat," on number 49 of your answer sheet. (Pause 7 seconds.)

Examine Sample 6. (Pause 2-3 seconds.) Write the letter A, as in "apple," beside the lowest number if the first number in the sample is less than the last number in the sample, and if there is a number greater than 91. (Pause 7 seconds.) Otherwise, write the letter E, as in "elephant," beside the number 30. (Pause 5 seconds.) Darken the number-letter combination you have selected on your answer sheet. (Pause 7 seconds.)

Examine Sample 6 again. (Pause 2-3 seconds.) Write the letter B, as in "boy," beside the number 84 if the preceding number is less than 84. (Pause 5 seconds.) Otherwise, write the letter C, as in "cat," beside 84. (Pause 5 seconds.) Darken the number-letter combination you have chosen on your answer sheet. (Pause 7 seconds.)

Examine Sample 6 one more time. (Pause 2-3 seconds.) If there is a number which is greater than 43, yet less than 53, write the letter D, as in "dog," beside it. Darken that number-letter combination on your answer sheet. (Pause 10 seconds.) If not, go to number 14 on your answer sheet and darken the letter B, as in "boy." (Pause 7 seconds.)

Examine Sample 7. (Pause 2-3 seconds.) If Los Angeles is located in Florida, and Washington, D.C. is in California, write the number 16 on the line beside the letter E, as in "elephant." (Pause 5 seconds.) If the preceding statement is false, write the number 16 beside the letter E, as in "elephant," anyway, and darken the resulting number-letter combinations on your answer sheet. (Pause 10 seconds.)

Examine Sample 8. (Pause 2-3 seconds.) Each of the five boxes show the starting and finishing times of five rural routes on a particular day. The time at the top is the rural carriers' starting time and the time listed below shows when they finished for the day. Find the carrier who spends the longest time on his or her route and write the number 10 beside the letter representing that carrier. (Pause 10 seconds.) Darken your answer sheet with this number-letter combination. (Pause 7 seconds.)

Examine Sample 8 again. (Pause 2-3 seconds.) If Carrier A, as in "apple," finished for the day before Carrier B, as in "boy," write the number 2 beside the letter A, as in "apple." (Pause 5 seconds.) Otherwise, find which of the carriers had the latest starting time and write the number 7 beside the letter representing that carrier. (Pause 7 seconds.) Darken the number-letter combination you have chosen on your answer sheet. (Pause 7 seconds.)

Examine Sample 8 one more time. (Pause 2-3 seconds.) Write the number 11 beside the letter representing the carrier with the second latest finishing time. (Pause 7 seconds.) Darken that number-letter combination on your answer sheet. (Pause 7 seconds.)

Examine Sample 9. (Pause 2-3 seconds.) Write the letter E, as in "elephant," beside the number that is in the circle and darken your answer with the resulting number-letter combination. (Pause 5 seconds.) If there is no circle in the sample, write the number 47 beside the letter within the rectangle and darken that number-letter combination on your answer sheet. (Pause 10 seconds.)

Examine Sample 10. (Pause 2-3 seconds.) If any one of the states shown in the sample is not located in the western part of the United States, go to number 36 on your answer sheet and darken the letter E, as in "elephant." (Pause 7 seconds.) Otherwise, go to number 3 on your answer sheet and darken the letter B, as in "boy." (Pause 7 seconds.)

Examine Sample 10 again. (Pause 2-3 seconds.) If any of the states listed begin with the letter C, as in "cat," go to number 49 on your answer sheet, and darken the letter C, as in "cat." (Pause 7 seconds.)

Examine Sample 11. (Pause 2-3 seconds.) If 9 is greater than 7, and 20 is less than 21, write the number 60 on the line provided and darken that number-letter combination on your answer sheet. (Pause 10 seconds.) Otherwise, go to number 23 on your answer sheet and darken the letter B, as in "boy."

Examine Sample 12. (Pause 2-3 seconds.) Find the number that is greater than 13 and less than 64, and go to that number on your answer sheet and darken the letter C, as in "cat." (Pause 10 seconds.)

Examine Sample 13. (Pause 2-3 seconds.) Choose the number that is shown in identically sized shapes and go to that number on your answer sheet and darken in the letter E, as in "elephant." (Pause 10 seconds.)

Examine Sample 14. (Pause 2-3 seconds.) If 40 is less than 69 and greater than 15, go to 40 on your answer sheet and darken the letter A, as in "apple." (Pause 7 seconds.) If not, write the letter C, as in "cat," beside the number 15 in the sample. (Pause 5 seconds.) Darken that number-letter combination on your answer sheet. (Pause 7 seconds.)

-END OF TEST-

FOLLOWING DIRECTIONS/EXERCISE 1 SAMPLES

1. March : December : November : July : January

2. (A)   (C)   [D]   [E]   (B)

3.
Myers Blvd.	Clifford Ave.	Chaney St.
32___routes	45___routes	9___routes

4. 42_____   1_____   50_____   73_____   79_____

5. 9837841   9837810   9837814   9837813

6. 43_____   27_____   84_____   91_____   30_____   52_____

7. _____B   _____E

8.
7:30 AM 2:45 PM __A	7:00 AM 2:15 PM __B	6:00 AM 4:00 PM __C	6:45 AM 3:30 PM __D	7:00 AM 3:00 PM __E

9. [B_____]   [12_____]   A_____   47_____

10. California : Oregon : Alaska : Florida : Washington

11.   _____D

12.   13   51   64   65   80

13.   [20]   (6)   [20]   (6)

14.   _____A   15_____   69_____   40_____   _____C

ANSWER SHEET TO FOLLOWING DIRECTIONS/EXERCISE 1

1. (A) (B) (C) (D) (E)
2. (A) (B) (C) (D) (E)
3. (A) (B) (C) (D) (E)
4. (A) (B) (C) (D) (E)
5. (A) (B) (C) (D) (E)
6. (A) (B) (C) (D) (E)
7. (A) (B) (C) (D) (E)
8. (A) (B) (C) (D) (E)
9. (A) (B) (C) (D) (E)
10. (A) (B) (C) (D) (E)
11. (A) (B) (C) (D) (E)
12. (A) (B) (C) (D) (E)
13. (A) (B) (C) (D) (E)
14. (A) (B) (C) (D) (E)
15. (A) (B) (C) (D) (E)
16. (A) (B) (C) (D) (E)
17. (A) (B) (C) (D) (E)
18. (A) (B) (C) (D) (E)
19. (A) (B) (C) (D) (E)
20. (A) (B) (C) (D) (E)
21. (A) (B) (C) (D) (E)
22. (A) (B) (C) (D) (E)
23. (A) (B) (C) (D) (E)
24. (A) (B) (C) (D) (E)
25. (A) (B) (C) (D) (E)
26. (A) (B) (C) (D) (E)
27. (A) (B) (C) (D) (E)
28. (A) (B) (C) (D) (E)
29. (A) (B) (C) (D) (E)
30. (A) (B) (C) (D) (E)
31. (A) (B) (C) (D) (E)
32. (A) (B) (C) (D) (E)

33. (A) (B) (C) (D) (E)
34. (A) (B) (C) (D) (E)
35. (A) (B) (C) (D) (E)
36. (A) (B) (C) (D) (E)
37. (A) (B) (C) (D) (E)
38. (A) (B) (C) (D) (E)
39. (A) (B) (C) (D) (E)
40. (A) (B) (C) (D) (E)
41. (A) (B) (C) (D) (E)
42. (A) (B) (C) (D) (E)
43. (A) (B) (C) (D) (E)
44. (A) (B) (C) (D) (E)
45. (A) (B) (C) (D) (E)
46. (A) (B) (C) (D) (E)
47. (A) (B) (C) (D) (E)
48. (A) (B) (C) (D) (E)
49. (A) (B) (C) (D) (E)
50. (A) (B) (C) (D) (E)
51. (A) (B) (C) (D) (E)
52. (A) (B) (C) (D) (E)
53. (A) (B) (C) (D) (E)
54. (A) (B) (C) (D) (E)
55. (A) (B) (C) (D) (E)
56. (A) (B) (C) (D) (E)
57. (A) (B) (C) (D) (E)
58. (A) (B) (C) (D) (E)
59. (A) (B) (C) (D) (E)
60. (A) (B) (C) (D) (E)
61. (A) (B) (C) (D) (E)
62. (A) (B) (C) (D) (E)
63. (A) (B) (C) (D) (E)
64. (A) (B) (C) (D) (E)

65. (A) (B) (C) (D) (E)
66. (A) (B) (C) (D) (E)
67. (A) (B) (C) (D) (E)
68. (A) (B) (C) (D) (E)
69. (A) (B) (C) (D) (E)
70. (A) (B) (C) (D) (E)
71. (A) (B) (C) (D) (E)
72. (A) (B) (C) (D) (E)
73. (A) (B) (C) (D) (E)
74. (A) (B) (C) (D) (E)
75. (A) (B) (C) (D) (E)
76. (A) (B) (C) (D) (E)
77. (A) (B) (C) (D) (E)
78. (A) (B) (C) (D) (E)
79. (A) (B) (C) (D) (E)
80. (A) (B) (C) (D) (E)
81. (A) (B) (C) (D) (E)
82. (A) (B) (C) (D) (E)
83. (A) (B) (C) (D) (E)
84. (A) (B) (C) (D) (E)
85. (A) (B) (C) (D) (E)
86. (A) (B) (C) (D) (E)
87. (A) (B) (C) (D) (E)
88. (A) (B) (C) (D) (E)
89. (A) (B) (C) (D) (E)
90. (A) (B) (C) (D) (E)
91. (A) (B) (C) (D) (E)
92. (A) (B) (C) (D) (E)
93. (A) (B) (C) (D) (E)
94. (A) (B) (C) (D) (E)
95. (A) (B) (C) (D) (E)

(This page may be removed to mark answers.)

ANSWERS TO FOLLOWING DIRECTIONS/EXERCISE 1

1.	12 E	9.	50 A	17.	47 B		
2.	5 C	10.	30 E	18.	36 E		
3.	17 B	11.	84 B	19.	49 C		
4.	45 C	12.	52 D	20.	60 D		
5.	32 A	13.	16 E	21.	51 C		
6.	42 A	14.	10 C	22.	20 E		
7.	9 D	15.	7 A	23.	40 A		
8.	1 E	16.	11 D				

If you scored:
22 or more correct, you have an excellent score.
20 or 21 correct, you have a good score.
19 or fewer correct, you need more practice.

If you have missed any of the questions in this exercise, review the narrative and identify what you misinterpreted. Most often, applicants make errors in this section because they answer too quickly, and miss key phrases. Be sure to listen to the entire question.

FOLLOWING DIRECTIONS/EXERCISE 2

Note To Person Assisting In This Exercise:

Remove from this test guide the pages of this exercise that comprise the directions (this page and the reverse). The test applicant should be left with only the samples and the answer sheet.

Read the following directions out loud at the suggested rate of 75-80 words per minute, pausing only where indicated in parentheses. Speak as clearly as possible: Once a statement has been read, it cannot be repeated.

Examine Sample 1. (Pause 2-3 seconds.) The figures shown represent postal drop boxes, each showing respective collection times. Write the letter B, as in "boy," in the box that has the earliest collection time. (Pause 5 seconds.) Find the numbers that represent the minutes of the collection time you have selected. Go to that number on your answer sheet and darken that letter-number combination. (Pause 7 seconds.)

Examine Sample 2. (Pause 2-3 seconds.) If 30 is more than 27, and 40 is less than 41, write the letter C, as in "cat," beside number 5 in the sample. (Pause 5 seconds.) If not, write the letter E, as in "elephant," beside number 16. (Pause 5 seconds.) Darken the selected number-letter combination on your answer sheet. (Pause 7 seconds.)

Examine Sample 2 again. (Pause 2-3 seconds.) Write the letter E, as in "elephant," beside 16 if 16 is greater than 7. (Pause 5 seconds.) Otherwise, write an A, as in "apple," beside number 7. (Pause 5 seconds.) Darken your chosen number-letter combination on the answer sheet. (Pause 7 seconds.)

Examine Sample 3. (Pause 2-3 seconds.) There are three squares and two circles of different proportions. In the second to the largest square write the number 75. (Pause 7 seconds.) Darken that number-letter combination on your answer sheet. (Pause 7 seconds.)

Examine Sample 3 again. (Pause 2-3 seconds.) If 10 divided by 5 equals 3, then write the number 76 in Square C, as in "cat." (Pause 5 seconds.) If not, write the number 81 in the larger circle. (Pause 5 seconds.) Darken the number-letter combination you have selected on your answer sheet. (Pause 7 seconds.)

Examine Sample 4. (Pause 2-3 seconds.) Write the letter A, as in "apple," beside the second largest number and the letter D, as in "dog," beside the largest number. (Pause 10 seconds.) Of the remaining two numbers, write the letter E, as in "elephant," beside the smallest number of the two. (Pause 5 seconds.) Darken that number-letter combination on your answer sheet. (Pause 7 seconds.)

Examine Sample 5. (Pause 2-3 seconds.) The three boxes shown in this sample represent different classes of mail; each is assigned a letter to reference it. If Box D, as in "dog," is a cheaper means of mailing advertisements than Box A, as in "apple," find number 15 on your answer sheet and darken the letter D, as in "dog." (Pause 7 seconds.) If Box D, as in "dog," is a more expensive means of mailing advertisements, then find number 3 on your answer sheet and darken the letter A, as in "apple." (Pause 7 seconds.)

Examine Sample 6. (Pause 2-3 seconds.) This sample illustrates five numbers each representing the length of a different mail route in terms of mileage. Write the letter C, as in "cat," beside the third longest route if it is over 25 miles in length. (Pause 5 seconds.) Otherwise, write the letter A, as in "apple," beside the smallest route. (Pause 5 seconds.) Darken the number-letter combination you have chosen on your answer sheet. (Pause 7 seconds.)

Examine Sample 6 again. (Pause 2-3 seconds.) Pick out the route that is more than 14 miles long, yet less than 40 miles long. (Pause 5 seconds.) Write the letter A, as in "apple," beside it. (Pause 5 seconds.) Darken the resulting number-letter combination on your answer sheet. (Pause 7 seconds.)

Examine Sample 6 one more time. (Pause 2-3 seconds.) If the longest mail route is exactly 37 miles longer than the shortest route, go to number 3 on your answer sheet and darken the letter C, as in "cat." (Pause 10 seconds.) If it is not exactly 37 miles longer, then find number 8 on your answer sheet and darken the letter E, as in "elephant." (Pause 10 seconds.)

Examine Sample 7. (Pause 2-3 seconds.) Write the letter B, as in "boy," in the triangular shape and the letter C, as in "cat," in the circular shape. (Pause 10 seconds.) If the trapezoid shape represented by the number 24 has more sides than a square, darken the number-letter combination that lies in the triangle on your answer sheet. (Pause 10 seconds.) Otherwise, darken the number-letter combination on your answer sheet that lies in the circle. (Pause 10 seconds.)

Examine Sample 8. (Pause 2-3 seconds.) This sample shows five different numbers. Each number represents the number of parcels delivered by each of five carriers on a particular day. Consider 72 the largest number and 9 the smallest number. If the second largest number is more than 50, write the letter C, as in "cat," beside number 12. (Pause 5 seconds.) Darken this number-letter combination on your answer sheet. (Pause 7 seconds.) If the second smallest number of parcels is less than 11, write the letter E, as in "elephant," beside 45 and darken that number-letter combination on your answer sheet. (Pause 10 seconds.) If none of the previous statements are true, then write the letter C, as in "cat," beside the number 9 and darken your answer sheet accordingly. (Pause 10 seconds.)

Examine Sample 9. (Pause 2-3 seconds.) Write the number 20 beside letter B, as in "boy," if Chicago is located in Alaska. (Pause 5 seconds.) If not, write the number 6 beside letter C, as in "cat," and darken that number-letter combination on your answer sheet. (Pause 10 seconds.)

Examine Sample 9 again. (Pause 2-3 seconds.) If the product of 3 times 3 is greater than the sum of 4 plus 4, then write the number 17 beside the letter E, as in "elephant." (Pause 7 seconds.) Otherwise, write the number 82 beside the letter E, as in "elephant." (Pause 5 seconds.) Darken your answer sheet with the number-letter combination that you have chosen. (Pause 7 seconds.)

Examine Sample 10. (Pause 2-3 seconds.) Sample 10 shows five Mail Volume Index figures. Index numbers located in the upper portion of each circle indicate an above-average mail volume. Index numbers located in the lower portion of each circle indicate a below-average Index figure. If Circle C, as in "cat," and E, as in "elephant," each illustrate a below-average Index figure, find number 27 on your answer sheet and darken the letter D, as in "dog." (Pause 10 seconds.) However, if Circle A, as in "apple," and C, as in "cat," show above average figures, find number 14 on your answer sheet and darken the letter A, as in "apple." (Pause 10 seconds.)

Examine Sample 10 again. (Pause 2-3 seconds.) If Circle A, as in "apple," has a higher Index figure than Circle D, as in "dog," find the number 27 on your answer sheet and darken the letter B, as in "boy." (Pause 7 seconds.) If not, find number 10 on your answer sheet and darken the letter D, as in "dog." (Pause 7 seconds.)

Examine Sample 10 one more time. (Pause 2-3 seconds.) On your answer sheet darken the number-letter combination of the highest Mail Volume Index figure. (Pause 10 seconds.)

Examine Sample 11. (Pause 2-3 seconds.) If 30 is greater than 31, write the number 30 on the line beside the letter C, as in "cat." Darken that number-letter combination on your answer sheet. (Pause 10 seconds.) If not, then write the number 30 on the line beside the letter B, as in "boy," and darken your answer sheet accordingly. (Pause 10 seconds.)

Examine Sample 9 again. (Pause 2-3 seconds.) Go to the fourth letter from the right side of the sample and write the number 32 beside it. (Pause 5 seconds.) Darken this number-letter combination on your answer sheet. (Pause 7 seconds.)

Examine Sample 11 again. (Pause 2-3 seconds.) Write the letter C, as in "cat," beside 30. Darken the number-letter combination on your answer sheet only if 30 is the largest number in the sample. (Pause 10 seconds.) Otherwise, write the letter A, as in "apple," beside 48. Darken your answer on the answer sheet. (Pause 7 seconds.)

Examine Sample 12. (Pause 2-3 seconds.) This sample has four pairs of numbers, each measuring the quantity of letters dropped in a test collection box on four consecutive Mondays. The first number in each pair represents the number of out-of-town letters and the second number represents the number of local delivery letters. If there are more out-of-town letters than there are local letters in each of the pairs, and the testing is conducted on Tuesday, go to number 93 on your answer sheet and darken the letter A, as in "apple." (Pause 7 seconds.) Otherwise, go to number 69 on your answer sheet and darken the letter B, as in "boy." (Pause 7 seconds.)

Examine Sample 12 again. (Pause 2-3 seconds.) Write the letter C, as in "cat," beside the second out-of-town mail count and darken that number-letter combination on your answer sheet. (Pause 10 seconds.)

-END OF TEST-

FOLLOWING DIRECTIONS/EXERCISE 2 SAMPLES

1.
| 1:10 PM _____ | 1:45 PM _____ | 10:45 PM _____ |

2. 5_____   7_____   16_____

3. ____A   ____B   ____C   ____D   ____E

4. 47____   52_____   46_____   2_____

5.
| First Class A | Second Class C | Third Class D |

6. 4_____   13_____   41_____   40_____   24_____

7. 21_____   22_____   23_____   24_____

8. 12____   18_____   9_____   72_____   45_____

9. ____B   ____D   ____X   ____E   ____C

10. A^{83} B_{46} C^{15} D_{10} E^{26}

11.　A＿＿＿＿　　30＿＿＿＿　　C＿＿＿＿　　31＿＿＿＿　　B＿＿＿＿　　48＿＿＿＿

12.　70/10　　　　87/14　　　　90/3　　　　88/69

ANSWER SHEET TO FOLLOWING DIRECTIONS/EXERCISE 2

1. Ⓐ Ⓑ Ⓒ Ⓓ Ⓔ
2. Ⓐ Ⓑ Ⓒ Ⓓ Ⓔ
3. Ⓐ Ⓑ Ⓒ Ⓓ Ⓔ
4. Ⓐ Ⓑ Ⓒ Ⓓ Ⓔ
5. Ⓐ Ⓑ Ⓒ Ⓓ Ⓔ
6. Ⓐ Ⓑ Ⓒ Ⓓ Ⓔ
7. Ⓐ Ⓑ Ⓒ Ⓓ Ⓔ
8. Ⓐ Ⓑ Ⓒ Ⓓ Ⓔ
9. Ⓐ Ⓑ Ⓒ Ⓓ Ⓔ
10. Ⓐ Ⓑ Ⓒ Ⓓ Ⓔ
11. Ⓐ Ⓑ Ⓒ Ⓓ Ⓔ
12. Ⓐ Ⓑ Ⓒ Ⓓ Ⓔ
13. Ⓐ Ⓑ Ⓒ Ⓓ Ⓔ
14. Ⓐ Ⓑ Ⓒ Ⓓ Ⓔ
15. Ⓐ Ⓑ Ⓒ Ⓓ Ⓔ
16. Ⓐ Ⓑ Ⓒ Ⓓ Ⓔ
17. Ⓐ Ⓑ Ⓒ Ⓓ Ⓔ
18. Ⓐ Ⓑ Ⓒ Ⓓ Ⓔ
19. Ⓐ Ⓑ Ⓒ Ⓓ Ⓔ
20. Ⓐ Ⓑ Ⓒ Ⓓ Ⓔ
21. Ⓐ Ⓑ Ⓒ Ⓓ Ⓔ
22. Ⓐ Ⓑ Ⓒ Ⓓ Ⓔ
23. Ⓐ Ⓑ Ⓒ Ⓓ Ⓔ
24. Ⓐ Ⓑ Ⓒ Ⓓ Ⓔ
25. Ⓐ Ⓑ Ⓒ Ⓓ Ⓔ
26. Ⓐ Ⓑ Ⓒ Ⓓ Ⓔ
27. Ⓐ Ⓑ Ⓒ Ⓓ Ⓔ
28. Ⓐ Ⓑ Ⓒ Ⓓ Ⓔ
29. Ⓐ Ⓑ Ⓒ Ⓓ Ⓔ
30. Ⓐ Ⓑ Ⓒ Ⓓ Ⓔ
31. Ⓐ Ⓑ Ⓒ Ⓓ Ⓔ
32. Ⓐ Ⓑ Ⓒ Ⓓ Ⓔ

33. Ⓐ Ⓑ Ⓒ Ⓓ Ⓔ
34. Ⓐ Ⓑ Ⓒ Ⓓ Ⓔ
35. Ⓐ Ⓑ Ⓒ Ⓓ Ⓔ
36. Ⓐ Ⓑ Ⓒ Ⓓ Ⓔ
37. Ⓐ Ⓑ Ⓒ Ⓓ Ⓔ
38. Ⓐ Ⓑ Ⓒ Ⓓ Ⓔ
39. Ⓐ Ⓑ Ⓒ Ⓓ Ⓔ
40. Ⓐ Ⓑ Ⓒ Ⓓ Ⓔ
41. Ⓐ Ⓑ Ⓒ Ⓓ Ⓔ
42. Ⓐ Ⓑ Ⓒ Ⓓ Ⓔ
43. Ⓐ Ⓑ Ⓒ Ⓓ Ⓔ
44. Ⓐ Ⓑ Ⓒ Ⓓ Ⓔ
45. Ⓐ Ⓑ Ⓒ Ⓓ Ⓔ
46. Ⓐ Ⓑ Ⓒ Ⓓ Ⓔ
47. Ⓐ Ⓑ Ⓒ Ⓓ Ⓔ
48. Ⓐ Ⓑ Ⓒ Ⓓ Ⓔ
49. Ⓐ Ⓑ Ⓒ Ⓓ Ⓔ
50. Ⓐ Ⓑ Ⓒ Ⓓ Ⓔ
51. Ⓐ Ⓑ Ⓒ Ⓓ Ⓔ
52. Ⓐ Ⓑ Ⓒ Ⓓ Ⓔ
53. Ⓐ Ⓑ Ⓒ Ⓓ Ⓔ
54. Ⓐ Ⓑ Ⓒ Ⓓ Ⓔ
55. Ⓐ Ⓑ Ⓒ Ⓓ Ⓔ
56. Ⓐ Ⓑ Ⓒ Ⓓ Ⓔ
57. Ⓐ Ⓑ Ⓒ Ⓓ Ⓔ
58. Ⓐ Ⓑ Ⓒ Ⓓ Ⓔ
59. Ⓐ Ⓑ Ⓒ Ⓓ Ⓔ
60. Ⓐ Ⓑ Ⓒ Ⓓ Ⓔ
61. Ⓐ Ⓑ Ⓒ Ⓓ Ⓔ
62. Ⓐ Ⓑ Ⓒ Ⓓ Ⓔ
63. Ⓐ Ⓑ Ⓒ Ⓓ Ⓔ
64. Ⓐ Ⓑ Ⓒ Ⓓ Ⓔ

65. Ⓐ Ⓑ Ⓒ Ⓓ Ⓔ
66. Ⓐ Ⓑ Ⓒ Ⓓ Ⓔ
67. Ⓐ Ⓑ Ⓒ Ⓓ Ⓔ
68. Ⓐ Ⓑ Ⓒ Ⓓ Ⓔ
69. Ⓐ Ⓑ Ⓒ Ⓓ Ⓔ
70. Ⓐ Ⓑ Ⓒ Ⓓ Ⓔ
71. Ⓐ Ⓑ Ⓒ Ⓓ Ⓔ
72. Ⓐ Ⓑ Ⓒ Ⓓ Ⓔ
73. Ⓐ Ⓑ Ⓒ Ⓓ Ⓔ
74. Ⓐ Ⓑ Ⓒ Ⓓ Ⓔ
75. Ⓐ Ⓑ Ⓒ Ⓓ Ⓔ
76. Ⓐ Ⓑ Ⓒ Ⓓ Ⓔ
77. Ⓐ Ⓑ Ⓒ Ⓓ Ⓔ
78. Ⓐ Ⓑ Ⓒ Ⓓ Ⓔ
79. Ⓐ Ⓑ Ⓒ Ⓓ Ⓔ
80. Ⓐ Ⓑ Ⓒ Ⓓ Ⓔ
81. Ⓐ Ⓑ Ⓒ Ⓓ Ⓔ
82. Ⓐ Ⓑ Ⓒ Ⓓ Ⓔ
83. Ⓐ Ⓑ Ⓒ Ⓓ Ⓔ
84. Ⓐ Ⓑ Ⓒ Ⓓ Ⓔ
85. Ⓐ Ⓑ Ⓒ Ⓓ Ⓔ
86. Ⓐ Ⓑ Ⓒ Ⓓ Ⓔ
87. Ⓐ Ⓑ Ⓒ Ⓓ Ⓔ
88. Ⓐ Ⓑ Ⓒ Ⓓ Ⓔ
89. Ⓐ Ⓑ Ⓒ Ⓓ Ⓔ
90. Ⓐ Ⓑ Ⓒ Ⓓ Ⓔ
91. Ⓐ Ⓑ Ⓒ Ⓓ Ⓔ
92. Ⓐ Ⓑ Ⓒ Ⓓ Ⓔ
93. Ⓐ Ⓑ Ⓒ Ⓓ Ⓔ
94. Ⓐ Ⓑ Ⓒ Ⓓ Ⓔ
95. Ⓐ Ⓑ Ⓒ Ⓓ Ⓔ

(This page may be removed to mark answers.)

ANSWERS TO FOLLOWING DIRECTIONS/EXERCISE 2

1.	10 B	9.	24 A	17.	83 A
2.	5 C	10.	3 C	18.	30 B
3.	16 E	11.	23 C	19.	32 D
4.	75 B	12.	9 C	20.	48 A
5.	81 D	13.	6 C	21.	69 B
6.	2 E	14.	17 E	22.	87 C
7.	15 D	15.	14 A		
8.	4 A	16.	27 B		

If you scored:
21 or more correct, you have an excellent score.
19 or 20 correct, you have a good score.
18 or fewer correct, you need more practice.

If you have missed any of the questions in this exercise, review the narrative and identify what you misinterpreted. Most often, applicants make errors in this section because they answer too quickly, and miss key phrases. Remember: Be sure to listen to the entire question.

FOLLOWING DIRECTION/EXERCISE 3

Note To Person Assisting In This Exercise:

Remove from this test guide the pages of this exercise that comprise the directions (this page and the reverse.) The test applicant should be left with only the samples and the answer sheet.

Read the following directions out loud at the suggested rate of 75-80 words per minute, pausing only where indicated in parentheses. Speak as clearly as possible: Once a statement has been read, it cannot be repeated.

Examine Sample 1. (Pause 2-3 seconds.) If any of the numbers shown are greater than 122, go to number 22 on your answer sheet and darken the letter D, as in "dog." (Pause 7 seconds.) If not, go to number 23 on your answer sheet and darken the letter A, as in "apple." (Pause 7 seconds.)

Examine Sample 2. (Pause 2-3 seconds.) Write the letter E, as in "elephant," on the line provided only if the number shown is less than 51. (Pause 5 seconds.) If the number shown is greater than or equal to 51, write the letter B, as in "boy," on the line provided. (Pause 5 seconds.) Darken the number-letter combination you have selected on your answer sheet. (Pause 7 seconds.)

Examine Sample 3. (Pause 2-3 seconds.) Write the number 67 on the shortest line shown. (Pause 5 seconds.) Write the number 68 on the longest line shown. (Pause 5 seconds.) Now, darken on your answer sheet both of the number-letter combinations you have made. (Pause 12 seconds.)

Examine Sample 3 again. (Pause 2-3 seconds.) If any part of the statement that I am about to read is false, write the number 2 on line A, as in "apple." (Pause 3 seconds.) There are seven days in a week, four weeks in a month, and 12 months in a year. (Pause 5 seconds.) However, if the statement is true, write the number 1 on line A, as in "apple." (Pause 3 seconds.) Darken the number-letter combination you have selected for line A, as in "apple," on your answer sheet. (Pause 7 seconds.)

Examine Sample 4. (Pause 2-3 seconds.) Write the letter B, as in "boy," beside the highest number shown within a geometric shape. (Pause 5 seconds.) Darken the resulting number-letter combination on your answer sheet. (Pause 7 seconds.)

Examine Sample 4 again. (Pause 2-3 seconds.) Now, write the letter C, as in "cat," beside the highest number shown in the sample. (Pause 5 seconds.) Darken the number-letter combination on your answer sheet. (Pause 7 seconds.)

Examine Sample 4 one more time. (Pause 2-3 seconds.) Write the letter D, as in "dog," in the circular shape and darken the number-letter combination on your answer sheet. (Pause 10 seconds.)

Examine Sample 5. (Pause 2-3 seconds.) This sample is a record of the time each day that Mr. John Smith returned from his mail route during the week. We will assume that Mr. Smith left the office at the same time each morning to begin his route. (Pause 3 seconds.) If Mr. Smith's delivery time is improving as the week progresses, go to number 86 on your answer sheet and darken the letter E, as in "elephant." (Pause 10 seconds.) If, on the other hand, Mr. Smith seems to be taking more time to deliver his mail as the week progresses, go to number 89 on your answer sheet and darken the letter B, as in "boy." (Pause 7 seconds.)

If 40 is less than 40.5, but greater than 39, go to number 11 on your answer sheet and darken the letter D, as in "dog." (Pause 7 seconds). Otherwise, go to number 15 on your answer sheet and darken the letter E, as in "elephant." (Pause 7 seconds).

Examine Sample 6. (Pause 2-3 seconds.) On the line provided, write the number of letters that are needed to spell the word, "Wednesday." (Pause 10 seconds.) Darken the number-letter combination you have made on your answer sheet. (Pause 7 seconds.)

Examine Sample 7. (Pause 2-3 seconds.) Write the number 53 beside the letter A, as in "apple." (Pause 5 seconds.) If there are more than six letters shown in Sample 7, then darken the number-letter combination you have made on your answer sheet. (Pause 10 seconds.) If not, write the number 57 beside the letter C, as in "cat," and darken that number-letter combination on your answer sheet. (Pause 7 seconds.)

If New York, New York is north of Miami, Florida, and Boston, Massachusetts, is east of San Francisco, California, go to number 38 on your answer sheet and darken the letter D, as in "dog." (Pause 10 seconds.) If any part of the previous statement is incorrect, go to number 36 on your answer sheet and darken the letter B, as in "boy." (Pause 7 seconds.)

Examine Sample 8. (Pause 2-3 seconds.) Write the number 42 beside the letter B, as in "boy." (Pause 5 seconds.) Write the number 52 beside the letter D, as in "dog." (Pause 5 seconds.) Darken the number-letter combinations you have just made on your answer sheet. (Pause 10 seconds.)

Examine Sample 9. (Pause 2-3 seconds.) Write the letter A, as in "apple," in the circle on the left side. (Pause 5 seconds.) Write the letter D, as in "dog," in the other circle. (Pause 5 seconds). Now, write the number 17 in Circle D, as in "dog," and the number 18 in Circle A, as in "apple." (Pause 10 seconds.) On your answer sheet, darken both number-letter combinations shown in each of the circles. (Pause 10 seconds.)

Examine Sample 9 again. (Pause 2-3 seconds.) If Circle A, as in "apple," and D, as in "dog," are the same size and interconnected, go to number 63 on your answer sheet and darken the letter E, as in "elephant." (Pause 7 seconds.) If the circles are not interconnected, go to number 23 on your answer sheet and darken the letter C, as in "cat." (Pause 7 seconds.)

Examine Sample 10. (Pause 2-3 seconds.) Write the letter A, as in "apple," on the line provided. (Pause 5 seconds.) Select the second highest number from the sequence shown and write it beside the letter you have just written. (Pause 7 seconds.) Darken the resulting number-letter combination on your answer sheet. (Pause 7 seconds.)

Examine Sample 10 again. (Pause 2-3 seconds.) Select the highest number from the sequence shown. Go to that number on your answer sheet. (Pause 5 seconds.) Darken the letter E, as in "elephant." (Pause 5 seconds.)

Examine Sample 11. (Pause 2-3 seconds.) Select the largest number shown, and completely circle it and the letter above it. (Pause 7 seconds.) Examine the last two digits of the number you have circled. Go to that number on your answer sheet. (Pause 5 seconds.) Darken the letter shown in your circle. (Pause 5 seconds.)

Examine Sample 11 again. (Pause 2-3 seconds.) If the number below D, as in "dog," is less than the number below C, as in "cat," go to number 54 on your answer sheet, and darken the letter A, as in "apple." (Pause 10 seconds.) If not, go to 54 on your answer sheet and darken the letter B, as in "boy." (Pause 7 seconds.)

If 5 is greater than 4, but less than 6, darken the letter D, as in "dog," at number 15 of your answer sheet. (Pause 7 seconds.) If not, darken the letter C, as in "cat," at number 55 on your answer sheet. (Pause 7 seconds.)

If 40 is greater than 25 plus 15, go to number 71 on your answer sheet and darken the letter E, as in "elephant." (Pause 7 seconds.) If not, go to number 71 on your answer sheet anyway and darken the letter B, as in "boy." (Pause 7 seconds.)

Examine Sample 10 again. (Pause 2-3 seconds.) If there are more than 5 numbers in the sample, go to number 33 on your answer sheet and darken the letter B, as in "boy." (Pause 7 seconds.) If otherwise, go to number 41 on your answer sheet and darken the letter A, as in "apple." (Pause 7 seconds.)

Examine Sample 1 again. (Pause 2-3 seconds.) If any of the 3 numbers shown is greater than 145, go to number 3 on your answer sheet and darken the letter D, as in "dog." (Pause 7 seconds.) Otherwise, go to number 95 on your answer sheet and darken the letter E, as in "elephant." (Pause 5 seconds.)

-END OF TEST-

FOLLOWING DIRECTIONS/EXERCISE 3 SAMPLES

1. 147   122   130

2. 50_____

3. 0_____A
    0_____C
    0_____E

4.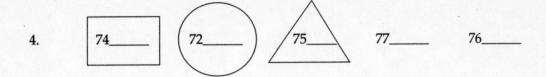

5.   4:05 PM   4:15 PM   4:25 PM   4:35 PM   5:00 PM
       MONDAY   TUESDAY   WEDNESDAY   THURSDAY   FRIDAY

6. _____A

7. _____A   _____X   _____L   _____C   _____F   _____I

8. B_____   D_____

9.

10.   14   28   17   33   _____

11.   A   B   C   D
         .045   .054   .07   .45

ANSWER SHEET TO FOLLOWING DIRECTIONS/EXERCISE 3

1. Ⓐ Ⓑ Ⓒ Ⓓ Ⓔ
2. Ⓐ Ⓑ Ⓒ Ⓓ Ⓔ
3. Ⓐ Ⓑ Ⓒ Ⓓ Ⓔ
4. Ⓐ Ⓑ Ⓒ Ⓓ Ⓔ
5. Ⓐ Ⓑ Ⓒ Ⓓ Ⓔ
6. Ⓐ Ⓑ Ⓒ Ⓓ Ⓔ
7. Ⓐ Ⓑ Ⓒ Ⓓ Ⓔ
8. Ⓐ Ⓑ Ⓒ Ⓓ Ⓔ
9. Ⓐ Ⓑ Ⓒ Ⓓ Ⓔ
10. Ⓐ Ⓑ Ⓒ Ⓓ Ⓔ
11. Ⓐ Ⓑ Ⓒ Ⓓ Ⓔ
12. Ⓐ Ⓑ Ⓒ Ⓓ Ⓔ
13. Ⓐ Ⓑ Ⓒ Ⓓ Ⓔ
14. Ⓐ Ⓑ Ⓒ Ⓓ Ⓔ
15. Ⓐ Ⓑ Ⓒ Ⓓ Ⓔ
16. Ⓐ Ⓑ Ⓒ Ⓓ Ⓔ
17. Ⓐ Ⓑ Ⓒ Ⓓ Ⓔ
18. Ⓐ Ⓑ Ⓒ Ⓓ Ⓔ
19. Ⓐ Ⓑ Ⓒ Ⓓ Ⓔ
20. Ⓐ Ⓑ Ⓒ Ⓓ Ⓔ
21. Ⓐ Ⓑ Ⓒ Ⓓ Ⓔ
22. Ⓐ Ⓑ Ⓒ Ⓓ Ⓔ
23. Ⓐ Ⓑ Ⓒ Ⓓ Ⓔ
24. Ⓐ Ⓑ Ⓒ Ⓓ Ⓔ
25. Ⓐ Ⓑ Ⓒ Ⓓ Ⓔ
26. Ⓐ Ⓑ Ⓒ Ⓓ Ⓔ
27. Ⓐ Ⓑ Ⓒ Ⓓ Ⓔ
28. Ⓐ Ⓑ Ⓒ Ⓓ Ⓔ
29. Ⓐ Ⓑ Ⓒ Ⓓ Ⓔ
30. Ⓐ Ⓑ Ⓒ Ⓓ Ⓔ
31. Ⓐ Ⓑ Ⓒ Ⓓ Ⓔ
32. Ⓐ Ⓑ Ⓒ Ⓓ Ⓔ
33. Ⓐ Ⓑ Ⓒ Ⓓ Ⓔ
34. Ⓐ Ⓑ Ⓒ Ⓓ Ⓔ
35. Ⓐ Ⓑ Ⓒ Ⓓ Ⓔ
36. Ⓐ Ⓑ Ⓒ Ⓓ Ⓔ
37. Ⓐ Ⓑ Ⓒ Ⓓ Ⓔ
38. Ⓐ Ⓑ Ⓒ Ⓓ Ⓔ
39. Ⓐ Ⓑ Ⓒ Ⓓ Ⓔ
40. Ⓐ Ⓑ Ⓒ Ⓓ Ⓔ
41. Ⓐ Ⓑ Ⓒ Ⓓ Ⓔ
42. Ⓐ Ⓑ Ⓒ Ⓓ Ⓔ
43. Ⓐ Ⓑ Ⓒ Ⓓ Ⓔ
44. Ⓐ Ⓑ Ⓒ Ⓓ Ⓔ
45. Ⓐ Ⓑ Ⓒ Ⓓ Ⓔ
46. Ⓐ Ⓑ Ⓒ Ⓓ Ⓔ
47. Ⓐ Ⓑ Ⓒ Ⓓ Ⓔ
48. Ⓐ Ⓑ Ⓒ Ⓓ Ⓔ
49. Ⓐ Ⓑ Ⓒ Ⓓ Ⓔ
50. Ⓐ Ⓑ Ⓒ Ⓓ Ⓔ
51. Ⓐ Ⓑ Ⓒ Ⓓ Ⓔ
52. Ⓐ Ⓑ Ⓒ Ⓓ Ⓔ
53. Ⓐ Ⓑ Ⓒ Ⓓ Ⓔ
54. Ⓐ Ⓑ Ⓒ Ⓓ Ⓔ
55. Ⓐ Ⓑ Ⓒ Ⓓ Ⓔ
56. Ⓐ Ⓑ Ⓒ Ⓓ Ⓔ
57. Ⓐ Ⓑ Ⓒ Ⓓ Ⓔ
58. Ⓐ Ⓑ Ⓒ Ⓓ Ⓔ
59. Ⓐ Ⓑ Ⓒ Ⓓ Ⓔ
60. Ⓐ Ⓑ Ⓒ Ⓓ Ⓔ
61. Ⓐ Ⓑ Ⓒ Ⓓ Ⓔ
62. Ⓐ Ⓑ Ⓒ Ⓓ Ⓔ
63. Ⓐ Ⓑ Ⓒ Ⓓ Ⓔ
64. Ⓐ Ⓑ Ⓒ Ⓓ Ⓔ
65. Ⓐ Ⓑ Ⓒ Ⓓ Ⓔ
66. Ⓐ Ⓑ Ⓒ Ⓓ Ⓔ
67. Ⓐ Ⓑ Ⓒ Ⓓ Ⓔ
68. Ⓐ Ⓑ Ⓒ Ⓓ Ⓔ
69. Ⓐ Ⓑ Ⓒ Ⓓ Ⓔ
70. Ⓐ Ⓑ Ⓒ Ⓓ Ⓔ
71. Ⓐ Ⓑ Ⓒ Ⓓ Ⓔ
72. Ⓐ Ⓑ Ⓒ Ⓓ Ⓔ
73. Ⓐ Ⓑ Ⓒ Ⓓ Ⓔ
74. Ⓐ Ⓑ Ⓒ Ⓓ Ⓔ
75. Ⓐ Ⓑ Ⓒ Ⓓ Ⓔ
76. Ⓐ Ⓑ Ⓒ Ⓓ Ⓔ
77. Ⓐ Ⓑ Ⓒ Ⓓ Ⓔ
78. Ⓐ Ⓑ Ⓒ Ⓓ Ⓔ
79. Ⓐ Ⓑ Ⓒ Ⓓ Ⓔ
80. Ⓐ Ⓑ Ⓒ Ⓓ Ⓔ
81. Ⓐ Ⓑ Ⓒ Ⓓ Ⓔ
82. Ⓐ Ⓑ Ⓒ Ⓓ Ⓔ
83. Ⓐ Ⓑ Ⓒ Ⓓ Ⓔ
84. Ⓐ Ⓑ Ⓒ Ⓓ Ⓔ
85. Ⓐ Ⓑ Ⓒ Ⓓ Ⓔ
86. Ⓐ Ⓑ Ⓒ Ⓓ Ⓔ
87. Ⓐ Ⓑ Ⓒ Ⓓ Ⓔ
88. Ⓐ Ⓑ Ⓒ Ⓓ Ⓔ
89. Ⓐ Ⓑ Ⓒ Ⓓ Ⓔ
90. Ⓐ Ⓑ Ⓒ Ⓓ Ⓔ
91. Ⓐ Ⓑ Ⓒ Ⓓ Ⓔ
92. Ⓐ Ⓑ Ⓒ Ⓓ Ⓔ
93. Ⓐ Ⓑ Ⓒ Ⓓ Ⓔ
94. Ⓐ Ⓑ Ⓒ Ⓓ Ⓔ
95. Ⓐ Ⓑ Ⓒ Ⓓ Ⓔ

(This page may be removed to mark answers.)

ANSWERS TO FOLLOWING DIRECTIONS/EXERCISE 3

1.	22 D	10.	11 D	19.	28 A		
2.	50 E	11.	9 A	20.	33 E		
3.	67 E	12.	57 C	21.	45 D		
4.	68 C	13.	38 D	22.	54 B		
5.	1 A	14.	42 B	23.	15 D		
6.	75 B	15.	52 D	24.	71 B		
7.	77 C	16.	18 A	25.	41 A		
8.	72 D	17.	17 D	26.	3 D		
9.	89 B	18.	23 C				

If you scored:
24 or more correct, you have an excellent score.
22 or 23 correct, you have a good score.
21 or fewer correct, you should practice more.

If you have missed any of the questions in this exercise, review the narrative and identify what you misinterpreted. Most often, applicants make errors in this section because they answer too quickly, and miss key phrases. Remember: Be sure to listen to the entire question.

NOTE: The rest of this study guide has been dedicated to full-length practice exams which incorporate each of the four sections studied earlier. You will need the assistance of someone to time you for each part of the exam as well as narrate the FOLLOWING DIRECTIONS portion of the test. To gain a comprehensive feel for the actual exam, work the entire practice exam (i.e., complete each of the four sections provided) in one session, allowing only a 3–5 minute break between exercises. Be certain not to continue working on an exercise when the allotted time is up. Going beyond the time allotted will only skew your test results. Make it a point to alleviate any potential distractions prior to beginning the exam. Disruptive kids, an inquisitive spouse, telephone calls, etc., can all have a detrimental impact on test preparation.

Try to simulate exam room conditions as best you can. That way, you can approach the real exam with a true sense of confidence and preparation—two factors critical to the achievement of a high test score.

Exam 1

**DO NOT OPEN THIS TEST BOOKLET UNTIL
YOU ARE TOLD TO START BY THE INDIVIDUAL
ASSISTING YOU IN THIS EXERCISE.**

[This page intentionally blank.]

ADDRESS CROSS COMPARISON/EXAM 1   **TIME: 6 MINUTES**

1.	Miami Blvd.	Miami Blvd.
2.	121 Burroughs	112 Burroughs
3.	1489 Van Meter St.	1489 Van Metor St.
4.	789 Holiday Ave.	789 Holliday Ave.
5.	Atlanta, Georgia 35919	Atlanta, Georgia 35919
6.	17666 Shannon ln.	17666 Shanon Ln.
7.	Kingsley Blvd SE	Kinsley Blvd. SE
8.	4456 Lamplight Ct.	4654 Lamplight Ct.
9.	8100 Bonteview St.	8010 Bonteview St.
10.	99-B Moonlight Bay	99-B Moonlight Bay
11.	Las Vegas, Nevada 67088	Las Vegas, Nev. 67088
12.	Tucson, Ariz 85044	Tuscon, Ariz. 85044
13.	Hampton Dr. SW	Hampton Dr. SW
14.	Bonn St. S	Bonn St. N.
15.	418 9th Ave.	481 9th Ave.
16.	1000 Terrace St.	10000 Terrace St.
17.	7478 Wellington	7478 Wellington
18.	Plainsville, NE	Planesville, NE
19.	Faunterloy Rd. NW	Faunterloy Rd. NW
20.	1414 Seaview Place	1414 Seaview Point
21.	Little Rock, Ark. 44807	Little Rock, Ark. 44807
22.	158 Johnathon Ln.	158 Jonathon Ln.
23.	Route 6, Box 4342	Route 6, Box 4342

NORMAN HALL'S *POSTAL EXAM PREPARATION BOOK*

24.	9315 Labador Park	9351 Labador Park
25.	Crysanthanum Place SW	Crysanthinum Place SW
26.	Fullerton, CA	Fullerton, CA
27.	7877 Knotingham Dr.	7877 Knottingham Dr.
28.	323 Warner Ave.	332 Warner Ave.
29.	489 Vermont Pl.	498 Vermont Pl.
30.	Minneapolis, MN 49401	Minneapolis, Minn. 49401
31.	4001 Briginham Rd.	4001 Brigingham Rd.
32.	Constance Bay	Constance Bay
33.	3388 Joplin Blvd.	8833 Joplin Blvd.
34.	684 11th St. NE	684 13th St. NE
35.	210 E Harmont	210 E. Hormont
36.	Tooele, Utah 76900	Tooele, Utah 79600
37.	1717 Carver Dr.	1717 Carver Dr.
38.	546 S. Galveston Ln.	546 W. Galveston Ln.
39.	New York, N.Y. 00723	New Work, N.Y. 00723
40.	3941 Belmont Way	3941 Belmont Way
41.	87-D University Village	87-D Univarsity Village
42.	2815 Monroe Dr.	2815 Monroe Dr.
43.	2211 Northwestern Rd.	2211 Northwestern Pl.
44.	1411 Hawthrone Ct.	1411 Hawthorn Ct.
45.	720 Kellogg	720 Kellogg
46.	2419 S. Douglous	2419 S. Douglous
47.	Holyoke, Mass. 02411	Holyoke, Miss. 02411
48.	707 Pierce Circle	707 Pierce Circle

49.	13251 Harding Dr.	13251 Harding Dr.
50.	2531 Eisenhower	2531 Eisenhower
51.	110 Main St.	110 Main St.
52.	22619 Hayes Point	22619 Heyes Point
53.	435 Wilmoth Ave.	453 Wilmoth Ave.
54.	Bakersville, N.C. 25014	Bakersville, N.C. 25014
55.	334 Lighthouse Pt.	334 Lighthouse Pt.
56.	214 O'Neil Dr. S.	214 O'Neil Dr. SW
57.	4516 Mulberry Blvd.	4516 Mulberry Blvd.
58.	Greenbriar Circle S.	S. Greenbriar Circle
59.	7000 Marston Ct.	70000 Marston Ct.
60.	3501 Jensen Way	3501 Bensen Way
61.	Murfreesboro, TN	Murfreesboro, Tenn.
62.	Paducah, Kentucky 35114	Paducah, Kentucky 35114
63.	10074 Jackson Dr.	10704 Jackson Dr.
64.	330 42nd Ave.	330 42nd Ave.
65.	1111 Bouldergrant Pl.	1117 Bouldergrant Pl.
66.	SW Symington Way	SW Symington Way
67.	3939 Concord Ave.	9393 Concord Ave.
68.	Dubuque, Ia. 52400	Dubuque, Ia. 52400
69.	41 Blanchard Dr.	41-C Blanchard Dr.
70.	901 K. Stables Blvd.	901 K. Stabbles Blvd.
71.	N. Shoshonee Pl.	N. Shoshownee Pl.
72.	222 Welch Ave.	222 Welch Ave.
73.	1515 1st Ave.	1515 1st Ave. S.

74.	103-C King Terrace	103-C King Terrace
75.	4466 Baltic Dr.	4646 Baltic Dr.
76.	Augusta, Maine 00111	Augusta, Maine 01011
77.	New Albany Rd. SW	Old Albany Rd. SW
78.	252 25th Ave. S.	252 22nd Ave. S.
79.	17677 Belfair Square	17677 Belfair Square
80.	111 Washington Blvd.	111 Washinton Blvd.
81.	2029 Isaquah Ln.	2029 Isaquah Ln.
82.	Kansas City, Kansas	Kansas City, Mo
83.	NW Macnally Dr. 1-B	NW Mcnally Dr. 1-B
84.	3078 S. George St.	3078 Saint George Ave.
85.	40473 Paulson Dr.	40473 Paulson Dr.
86.	Jacksonville, FL 46991	Jacksonville, Fla. 46991
87.	2000 Ebeneezor Place	2000 Ebaneezor Place
88.	1212 Ballen Lake Park	1212 Ballon Lake Park
89.	12 Lester Blvd.	21 Lester Blvd.
90.	4392 Crestwood Circle	4392 Crestwood Circle
91.	78990 Norweigan Trail	78990 Norweigen Trail
92.	327 S. Hazel	327 N. Hazel
93.	Cincinnati, Ohio 48921	Cinncinati, Ohio 48921
94.	RR 5, Box 414-S	RR 5, Box 41-4S
95.	Provo, Utah	Provo, Utah

ANSWER SHEET TO ADDRESS CROSS COMPARISON/EXAM 1

1. (A) (D)
2. (A) (D)
3. (A) (D)
4. (A) (D)
5. (A) (D)
6. (A) (D)
7. (A) (D)
8. (A) (D)
9. (A) (D)
10. (A) (D)
11. (A) (D)
12. (A) (D)
13. (A) (D)
14. (A) (D)
15. (A) (D)
16. (A) (D)
17. (A) (D)
18. (A) (D)
19. (A) (D)
20. (A) (D)
21. (A) (D)
22. (A) (D)
23. (A) (D)
24. (A) (D)
25. (A) (D)
26. (A) (D)
27. (A) (D)
28. (A) (D)
29. (A) (D)
30. (A) (D)
31. (A) (D)
32. (A) (D)

33. (A) (D)
34. (A) (D)
35. (A) (D)
36. (A) (D)
37. (A) (D)
38. (A) (D)
39. (A) (D)
40. (A) (D)
41. (A) (D)
42. (A) (D)
43. (A) (D)
44. (A) (D)
45. (A) (D)
46. (A) (D)
47. (A) (D)
48. (A) (D)
49. (A) (D)
50. (A) (D)
51. (A) (D)
52. (A) (D)
53. (A) (D)
54. (A) (D)
55. (A) (D)
56. (A) (D)
57. (A) (D)
58. (A) (D)
59. (A) (D)
60. (A) (D)
61. (A) (D)
62. (A) (D)
63. (A) (D)
64. (A) (D)

65. (A) (D)
66. (A) (D)
67. (A) (D)
68. (A) (D)
69. (A) (D)
70. (A) (D)
71. (A) (D)
72. (A) (D)
73. (A) (D)
74. (A) (D)
75. (A) (D)
76. (A) (D)
77. (A) (D)
78. (A) (D)
79. (A) (D)
80. (A) (D)
81. (A) (D)
82. (A) (D)
83. (A) (D)
84. (A) (D)
85. (A) (D)
86. (A) (D)
87. (A) (D)
88. (A) (D)
89. (A) (D)
90. (A) (D)
91. (A) (D)
92. (A) (D)
93. (A) (D)
94. (A) (D)
95. (A) (D)

(This page may be removed to mark answers.)

[This page intentionally blank.]

MEMORIZATION/EXAM 1

A	B	C	D	E
4800-4899 Brice Covington 6400-6499 Fern Clover Leaf 7300-7399 Amhurst	5300-5399 Brice Plaza Dr. 7300-7399 Fern Granite Dr. 6400-6499 Amhurst	4700-4799 Brice Klondyke 5600-5699 Fern Rainbow Ct. 6000-6099 Amhurst	5100-5199 Brice Cooper Ave. 5500-5599 Fern Harrisburg 5600-5699 Amhurst	4400-4499 Brice Raleigh 6000-6099 Fern Melbourne 5500-5599 Amhurst

NOTE: Follow the same step by step format established for the memorization exercise studied earlier. (See page 41.)

PRACTICE MEMORIZATION/EXAM 1

STEP 2 TIME: 3 MINUTES
STEP 3 TIME: 3 MINUTES (cover key)

A	B	C	D	E
4800-4899 Brice Covington 6400-6499 Fern Clover Leaf 7300-7399 Amhurst	5300-5399 Brice Plaza Dr. 7300-7399 Fern Granite Dr. 6400-6499 Amhurst	4700-4799 Brice Klondyke 5600-5699 Fern Rainbow Ct. 6000-6099 Amhurst	5100-5199 Brice Cooper Ave. 5500-5599 Fern Harrisburg 5600-5699 Amhurst	4400-4499 Brice Raleigh 6000-6099 Fern Melbourne 5500-5599 Amhurst

1. 4800-4899 Brice
2. Granite Dr.
3. 5500-5599 Fern
4. Rainbow Ct.
5. 5100-5199 Brice
6. 5600-5699 Fern
7. Covington
8. Clover Leaf
9. 5300-5399 Brice
10. 7300-7399 Amhurst
11. Klondyke
12. 5600-5699 Amhurst
13. 6000-6099 Fern
14. 4400-4499 Brice
15. Melbourne
16. 6000-6099 Amhurst
17. Harrisburg
18. Cooper Ave.
19. 5500-5599 Amhurst
20. Plaza Dr.
21. Rainbow Ct.
22. Raleigh
23. Melbourne
24. 4700-4799 Brice
25. 6400-6499 Fern
26. Plaza Dr.
27. 5300-5399 Brice
28. 6400-6499 Amhurst
29. 7300-7399 Fern
30. Covington

31. Clover Leaf
32. Granite Dr.
33. Harrisburg
34. Raleigh
35. 5100-5199 Brice
36. 7300-7399 Amhurst
37. Klondyke
38. 4700-4799 Brice
39. 5600-5699 Amhurst
40. 6000-6099 Fern
41. Clover Leaf
42. Cooper Ave.
43. 5300-5399 Brice
44. 7300-7399 Fern
45. Rainbow Ct.
46. 5600-5699 Fern
47. 6400-6499 Amhurst
48. Harrisburg
49. 4800-4899 Brice
50. Covington
51. Plaza Dr.
52. 6400-6499 Fern
53. 7300-7399 Amhurst
54. 5500-5599 Amhurst
55. Granite Dr.
56. Cooper Ave.
57. 5500-5599 Fern
58. 4400-4499 Brice
59. 5500-5599 Amhurst
60. Klondyke

61. 5500-5599 Fern
62. 6400-6499 Amhurst
63. Rainbow Ct.
64. Melbourne
65. 4400-4499 Brice
66. 4800-4899 Brice
67. Klondyke
68. 5500-5599 Fern
69. 6400-6499 Fern
70. 6000-6099 Amhurst
71. Harrisburg
72. Plaza Dr.
73. 5600-5699 Amhurst
74. Cooper Ave.
75. Raleigh
76. 4700-4799 Brice
77. 6000-6099 Fern
78. 6000-6099 Amhurst
79. Granite Dr.
80. Klondyke
81. Covington
82. Raleigh
83. 5100-5199 Brice
84. 7300-7399 Fern
85. Clover Leaf
86. 5600-5699 Fern
87. 4700-4799 Brice
88. Melbourne

PRACTICE ANSWER SHEET TO MEMORIZATION/EXAM 1

1. Ⓐ Ⓑ Ⓒ Ⓓ Ⓔ
2. Ⓐ Ⓑ Ⓒ Ⓓ Ⓔ
3. Ⓐ Ⓑ Ⓒ Ⓓ Ⓔ
4. Ⓐ Ⓑ Ⓒ Ⓓ Ⓔ
5. Ⓐ Ⓑ Ⓒ Ⓓ Ⓔ
6. Ⓐ Ⓑ Ⓒ Ⓓ Ⓔ
7. Ⓐ Ⓑ Ⓒ Ⓓ Ⓔ
8. Ⓐ Ⓑ Ⓒ Ⓓ Ⓔ
9. Ⓐ Ⓑ Ⓒ Ⓓ Ⓔ
10. Ⓐ Ⓑ Ⓒ Ⓓ Ⓔ
11. Ⓐ Ⓑ Ⓒ Ⓓ Ⓔ
12. Ⓐ Ⓑ Ⓒ Ⓓ Ⓔ
13. Ⓐ Ⓑ Ⓒ Ⓓ Ⓔ
14. Ⓐ Ⓑ Ⓒ Ⓓ Ⓔ
15. Ⓐ Ⓑ Ⓒ Ⓓ Ⓔ
16. Ⓐ Ⓑ Ⓒ Ⓓ Ⓔ
17. Ⓐ Ⓑ Ⓒ Ⓓ Ⓔ
18. Ⓐ Ⓑ Ⓒ Ⓓ Ⓔ
19. Ⓐ Ⓑ Ⓒ Ⓓ Ⓔ
20. Ⓐ Ⓑ Ⓒ Ⓓ Ⓔ
21. Ⓐ Ⓑ Ⓒ Ⓓ Ⓔ
22. Ⓐ Ⓑ Ⓒ Ⓓ Ⓔ
23. Ⓐ Ⓑ Ⓒ Ⓓ Ⓔ
24. Ⓐ Ⓑ Ⓒ Ⓓ Ⓔ
25. Ⓐ Ⓑ Ⓒ Ⓓ Ⓔ
26. Ⓐ Ⓑ Ⓒ Ⓓ Ⓔ
27. Ⓐ Ⓑ Ⓒ Ⓓ Ⓔ
28. Ⓐ Ⓑ Ⓒ Ⓓ Ⓔ
29. Ⓐ Ⓑ Ⓒ Ⓓ Ⓔ
30. Ⓐ Ⓑ Ⓒ Ⓓ Ⓔ

31. Ⓐ Ⓑ Ⓒ Ⓓ Ⓔ
32. Ⓐ Ⓑ Ⓒ Ⓓ Ⓔ
33. Ⓐ Ⓑ Ⓒ Ⓓ Ⓔ
34. Ⓐ Ⓑ Ⓒ Ⓓ Ⓔ
35. Ⓐ Ⓑ Ⓒ Ⓓ Ⓔ
36. Ⓐ Ⓑ Ⓒ Ⓓ Ⓔ
37. Ⓐ Ⓑ Ⓒ Ⓓ Ⓔ
38. Ⓐ Ⓑ Ⓒ Ⓓ Ⓔ
39. Ⓐ Ⓑ Ⓒ Ⓓ Ⓔ
40. Ⓐ Ⓑ Ⓒ Ⓓ Ⓔ
41. Ⓐ Ⓑ Ⓒ Ⓓ Ⓔ
42. Ⓐ Ⓑ Ⓒ Ⓓ Ⓔ
43. Ⓐ Ⓑ Ⓒ Ⓓ Ⓔ
44. Ⓐ Ⓑ Ⓒ Ⓓ Ⓔ
45. Ⓐ Ⓑ Ⓒ Ⓓ Ⓔ
46. Ⓐ Ⓑ Ⓒ Ⓓ Ⓔ
47. Ⓐ Ⓑ Ⓒ Ⓓ Ⓔ
48. Ⓐ Ⓑ Ⓒ Ⓓ Ⓔ
49. Ⓐ Ⓑ Ⓒ Ⓓ Ⓔ
50. Ⓐ Ⓑ Ⓒ Ⓓ Ⓔ
51. Ⓐ Ⓑ Ⓒ Ⓓ Ⓔ
52. Ⓐ Ⓑ Ⓒ Ⓓ Ⓔ
53. Ⓐ Ⓑ Ⓒ Ⓓ Ⓔ
54. Ⓐ Ⓑ Ⓒ Ⓓ Ⓔ
55. Ⓐ Ⓑ Ⓒ Ⓓ Ⓔ
56. Ⓐ Ⓑ Ⓒ Ⓓ Ⓔ
57. Ⓐ Ⓑ Ⓒ Ⓓ Ⓔ
58. Ⓐ Ⓑ Ⓒ Ⓓ Ⓔ
59. Ⓐ Ⓑ Ⓒ Ⓓ Ⓔ
60. Ⓐ Ⓑ Ⓒ Ⓓ Ⓔ

61. Ⓐ Ⓑ Ⓒ Ⓓ Ⓔ
62. Ⓐ Ⓑ Ⓒ Ⓓ Ⓔ
63. Ⓐ Ⓑ Ⓒ Ⓓ Ⓔ
64. Ⓐ Ⓑ Ⓒ Ⓓ Ⓔ
65. Ⓐ Ⓑ Ⓒ Ⓓ Ⓔ
66. Ⓐ Ⓑ Ⓒ Ⓓ Ⓔ
67. Ⓐ Ⓑ Ⓒ Ⓓ Ⓔ
68. Ⓐ Ⓑ Ⓒ Ⓓ Ⓔ
69. Ⓐ Ⓑ Ⓒ Ⓓ Ⓔ
70. Ⓐ Ⓑ Ⓒ Ⓓ Ⓔ
71. Ⓐ Ⓑ Ⓒ Ⓓ Ⓔ
72. Ⓐ Ⓑ Ⓒ Ⓓ Ⓔ
73. Ⓐ Ⓑ Ⓒ Ⓓ Ⓔ
74. Ⓐ Ⓑ Ⓒ Ⓓ Ⓔ
75. Ⓐ Ⓑ Ⓒ Ⓓ Ⓔ
76. Ⓐ Ⓑ Ⓒ Ⓓ Ⓔ
77. Ⓐ Ⓑ Ⓒ Ⓓ Ⓔ
78. Ⓐ Ⓑ Ⓒ Ⓓ Ⓔ
79. Ⓐ Ⓑ Ⓒ Ⓓ Ⓔ
80. Ⓐ Ⓑ Ⓒ Ⓓ Ⓔ
81. Ⓐ Ⓑ Ⓒ Ⓓ Ⓔ
82. Ⓐ Ⓑ Ⓒ Ⓓ Ⓔ
83. Ⓐ Ⓑ Ⓒ Ⓓ Ⓔ
84. Ⓐ Ⓑ Ⓒ Ⓓ Ⓔ
85. Ⓐ Ⓑ Ⓒ Ⓓ Ⓔ
86. Ⓐ Ⓑ Ⓒ Ⓓ Ⓔ
87. Ⓐ Ⓑ Ⓒ Ⓓ Ⓔ
88. Ⓐ Ⓑ Ⓒ Ⓓ Ⓔ

1. Covington
2. 5300-5399 Brice
3. 5600-5699 Fern
4. Plaza Dr.
5. Cooper Ave.
6. 7300-7399 Amhurst
7. 5500-5599 Amhurst
8. Granite Dr.
9. 4400-4499 Brice
10. 6400-6499 Fern
11. Clover Leaf
12. Rainbow Ct.
13. Raleigh
14. 4800-4899 Brice
15. 6400-6499 Amhurst
16. 7300-7399 Fern
17. Harrisburg
18. 6000-6099 Fern
19. 4700-4799 Brice
20. Cooper Ave.
21. Klondyke
22. 5500-5599 Fern
23. 5100-5199 Brice
24. 6000-6099 Amhurst
25. Rainbow Ct.
26. 6400-6499 Fern
27. Melbourne
28. 5600-5699 Fern
29. 5300-5399 Brice
30. Covington
31. 5500-5599 Amhurst
32. Raleigh
33. 6400-6499 Amhurst
34. 6400-6499 Fern
35. Plaza Dr.
36. Klondyke
37. Clover Leaf
38. 5500-5599 Fern
39. 7300-7399 Amhurst
40. 4700-4799 Brice
41. Cooper Ave.
42. 4800-4899 Brice
43. Granite Dr.
44. Harrisburg
45. Melbourne
46. 6000-6099 Amhurst
47. 5100-5199 Brice
48. Covington
49. Rainbow Ct.
50. 5500-5599 Amhurst
51. Raleigh
52. 5600-5699 Amhurst
53. Melbourne
54. 5600-5699 Fern
55. 5500-5599 Fern
56. Plaza Dr.
57. 5300-5399 Brice
58. Cooper Ave.
59. 6400-6499 Fern
60. 4800-4899 Brice
61. Klondyke
62. Granite Dr.
63. 7300-7399 Fern
64. 4400-4499 Brice
65. Clover Leaf
66. 5600-5699 Amhurst
67. Rainbow Ct.
68. 7300-7399 Amhurst
69. 5100-5199 Brice
70. 6000-6099 Fern
71. Plaza Dr.
72. Harrisburg
73. 4800-4899 Brice
74. 6000-6099 Amhurst
75. Melbourne
76. Rainbow Ct.
77. Harrisburg
78. 4700-4799 Brice
79. 6000-6099 Fern
80. Klondyke
81. Raleigh
82. 5600-5699 Amhurst
83. Clover Leaf
84. Granite Dr.
85. 6400-6499 Amhurst
86. 7300-7399 Fern
87. Covington
88. 4400-4499 Brice

ANSWER SHEET TO MEMORIZATION/EXAM 1

1. Ⓐ Ⓑ Ⓒ Ⓓ Ⓔ	31. Ⓐ Ⓑ Ⓒ Ⓓ Ⓔ	61. Ⓐ Ⓑ Ⓒ Ⓓ Ⓔ
2. Ⓐ Ⓑ Ⓒ Ⓓ Ⓔ	32. Ⓐ Ⓑ Ⓒ Ⓓ Ⓔ	62. Ⓐ Ⓑ Ⓒ Ⓓ Ⓔ
3. Ⓐ Ⓑ Ⓒ Ⓓ Ⓔ	33. Ⓐ Ⓑ Ⓒ Ⓓ Ⓔ	63. Ⓐ Ⓑ Ⓒ Ⓓ Ⓔ
4. Ⓐ Ⓑ Ⓒ Ⓓ Ⓔ	34. Ⓐ Ⓑ Ⓒ Ⓓ Ⓔ	64. Ⓐ Ⓑ Ⓒ Ⓓ Ⓔ
5. Ⓐ Ⓑ Ⓒ Ⓓ Ⓔ	35. Ⓐ Ⓑ Ⓒ Ⓓ Ⓔ	65. Ⓐ Ⓑ Ⓒ Ⓓ Ⓔ
6. Ⓐ Ⓑ Ⓒ Ⓓ Ⓔ	36. Ⓐ Ⓑ Ⓒ Ⓓ Ⓔ	66. Ⓐ Ⓑ Ⓒ Ⓓ Ⓔ
7. Ⓐ Ⓑ Ⓒ Ⓓ Ⓔ	37. Ⓐ Ⓑ Ⓒ Ⓓ Ⓔ	67. Ⓐ Ⓑ Ⓒ Ⓓ Ⓔ
8. Ⓐ Ⓑ Ⓒ Ⓓ Ⓔ	38. Ⓐ Ⓑ Ⓒ Ⓓ Ⓔ	68. Ⓐ Ⓑ Ⓒ Ⓓ Ⓔ
9. Ⓐ Ⓑ Ⓒ Ⓓ Ⓔ	39. Ⓐ Ⓑ Ⓒ Ⓓ Ⓔ	69. Ⓐ Ⓑ Ⓒ Ⓓ Ⓔ
10. Ⓐ Ⓑ Ⓒ Ⓓ Ⓔ	40. Ⓐ Ⓑ Ⓒ Ⓓ Ⓔ	70. Ⓐ Ⓑ Ⓒ Ⓓ Ⓔ
11. Ⓐ Ⓑ Ⓒ Ⓓ Ⓔ	41. Ⓐ Ⓑ Ⓒ Ⓓ Ⓔ	71. Ⓐ Ⓑ Ⓒ Ⓓ Ⓔ
12. Ⓐ Ⓑ Ⓒ Ⓓ Ⓔ	42. Ⓐ Ⓑ Ⓒ Ⓓ Ⓔ	72. Ⓐ Ⓑ Ⓒ Ⓓ Ⓔ
13. Ⓐ Ⓑ Ⓒ Ⓓ Ⓔ	43. Ⓐ Ⓑ Ⓒ Ⓓ Ⓔ	73. Ⓐ Ⓑ Ⓒ Ⓓ Ⓔ
14. Ⓐ Ⓑ Ⓒ Ⓓ Ⓔ	44. Ⓐ Ⓑ Ⓒ Ⓓ Ⓔ	74. Ⓐ Ⓑ Ⓒ Ⓓ Ⓔ
15. Ⓐ Ⓑ Ⓒ Ⓓ Ⓔ	45. Ⓐ Ⓑ Ⓒ Ⓓ Ⓔ	75. Ⓐ Ⓑ Ⓒ Ⓓ Ⓔ
16. Ⓐ Ⓑ Ⓒ Ⓓ Ⓔ	46. Ⓐ Ⓑ Ⓒ Ⓓ Ⓔ	76. Ⓐ Ⓑ Ⓒ Ⓓ Ⓔ
17. Ⓐ Ⓑ Ⓒ Ⓓ Ⓔ	47. Ⓐ Ⓑ Ⓒ Ⓓ Ⓔ	77. Ⓐ Ⓑ Ⓒ Ⓓ Ⓔ
18. Ⓐ Ⓑ Ⓒ Ⓓ Ⓔ	48. Ⓐ Ⓑ Ⓒ Ⓓ Ⓔ	78. Ⓐ Ⓑ Ⓒ Ⓓ Ⓔ
19. Ⓐ Ⓑ Ⓒ Ⓓ Ⓔ	49. Ⓐ Ⓑ Ⓒ Ⓓ Ⓔ	79. Ⓐ Ⓑ Ⓒ Ⓓ Ⓔ
20. Ⓐ Ⓑ Ⓒ Ⓓ Ⓔ	50. Ⓐ Ⓑ Ⓒ Ⓓ Ⓔ	80. Ⓐ Ⓑ Ⓒ Ⓓ Ⓔ
21. Ⓐ Ⓑ Ⓒ Ⓓ Ⓔ	51. Ⓐ Ⓑ Ⓒ Ⓓ Ⓔ	81. Ⓐ Ⓑ Ⓒ Ⓓ Ⓔ
22. Ⓐ Ⓑ Ⓒ Ⓓ Ⓔ	52. Ⓐ Ⓑ Ⓒ Ⓓ Ⓔ	82. Ⓐ Ⓑ Ⓒ Ⓓ Ⓔ
23. Ⓐ Ⓑ Ⓒ Ⓓ Ⓔ	53. Ⓐ Ⓑ Ⓒ Ⓓ Ⓔ	83. Ⓐ Ⓑ Ⓒ Ⓓ Ⓔ
24. Ⓐ Ⓑ Ⓒ Ⓓ Ⓔ	54. Ⓐ Ⓑ Ⓒ Ⓓ Ⓔ	84. Ⓐ Ⓑ Ⓒ Ⓓ Ⓔ
25. Ⓐ Ⓑ Ⓒ Ⓓ Ⓔ	55. Ⓐ Ⓑ Ⓒ Ⓓ Ⓔ	85. Ⓐ Ⓑ Ⓒ Ⓓ Ⓔ
26. Ⓐ Ⓑ Ⓒ Ⓓ Ⓔ	56. Ⓐ Ⓑ Ⓒ Ⓓ Ⓔ	86. Ⓐ Ⓑ Ⓒ Ⓓ Ⓔ
27. Ⓐ Ⓑ Ⓒ Ⓓ Ⓔ	57. Ⓐ Ⓑ Ⓒ Ⓓ Ⓔ	87. Ⓐ Ⓑ Ⓒ Ⓓ Ⓔ
28. Ⓐ Ⓑ Ⓒ Ⓓ Ⓔ	58. Ⓐ Ⓑ Ⓒ Ⓓ Ⓔ	88. Ⓐ Ⓑ Ⓒ Ⓓ Ⓔ
29. Ⓐ Ⓑ Ⓒ Ⓓ Ⓔ	59. Ⓐ Ⓑ Ⓒ Ⓓ Ⓔ	
30. Ⓐ Ⓑ Ⓒ Ⓓ Ⓔ	60. Ⓐ Ⓑ Ⓒ Ⓓ Ⓔ	

[This page intentionally blank.]

NUMBER SERIES/EXAM 1   TIME: 20 MINUTES

1.   14   5   17   4   20   3   23   ___   ___

- A. 26, 12
- B. 1, 24
- C. 1, 25
- D. 2, 25
- E. 2, 26

2.   9   9   10   15   11   21   ___   ___

- A. 11, 27
- B. 12, 27
- C. 27, 11
- D. 27, 12
- E. 12, 12

3.   3   4   7   9   11   14   15   ___   ___

- A. 19, 19
- B. 13, 19
- C. 11, 19
- D. 12, 18
- E. 18, 18

4.   28   14   21   18   14   22   ___   ___

- A. 20, 15
- B. 16, 20
- C. 7, 26
- D. 21, 23
- E. 26, 7

5.   6   1   12   6   18   36   ___   ___

- A. 24, 261
- B. 24, 216
- C. 42, 216
- D. 42, 48
- E. 48, 58

6.   21   16   17   18   20   19   18   19   20   ___   ___

- A. 21, 18
- B. 20, 17
- C. 19, 18
- D. 21, 17
- E. 18, 20

7.   49   40   36   39   31   22   42   ___   ___

- A. 45, 13
- B. 45, 12
- C. 46, 12
- D. 12, 46
- E. 49, 39

8.   32   39   5   13   46   53   21   ___   ___

     A.   29, 60
     B.   60, 29
     C.   39, 60
     D.   60, 39
     E.   39, 39

9.   3   9   8   3   8   7   3   7   ___   ___

     A.   3, 6
     B.   6, 6
     C.   7, 2
     D.   5, 6
     E.   6, 3

10.   0   0   12   10   24   36   20   48   ___   ___

     A.   56, 26
     B.   60, 30
     C.   56, 30
     D.   30, 60
     E.   62, 26

11.   16   17   19   20   23   24   ___   ___

     A.   29, 30
     B.   29, 28
     C.   28, 29
     D.   27, 28
     E.   28, 27

12.   16   27   27   18   29   29   20   ___   ___

     A.   30, 30
     B.   31, 22
     C.   31, 31
     D.   22, 31
     E.   32, 30

13.   4   6   9   11   14   16   19   ___   ___

     A.   21, 25
     B.   25, 24
     C.   24, 24
     D.   23, 24
     E.   21, 24

14.   81   8   18   28   72   38   48   58   63   68   78   ___   ___

     A.   54, 88
     B.   88, 54
     C.   88, 69
     D.   54, 69
     E.   72, 88

15. 9   3   3   9   4   4   4   9   5   5   __   __

    A. 5, 9
    B. 5, 5
    C. 9, 5
    D. 9, 6
    E. 6, 9

16. 2   2   0   9   9   10   16   16   __   __

    A. 18, 20
    B. 20, 18
    C. 23, 23
    D. 20, 23
    E. 21, 27

17. 1   0   5   3   0   5   9   0   5   __   __

    A. 27, 0
    B. 23, 0
    C. 18, 0
    D. 36, 0
    E. 22, 0

18. 18   16   9   8   14   12   7   __   __

    A. 6, 11
    B. 10, 9
    C. 6, 10
    D. 10, 11
    E. 11, 11

19. 0   5   7   9   1   7   9   11   2   9   11   __   __

    A. 3, 12
    B. 3, 13
    C. 3, 10
    D. 13, 4
    E. 13, 3

20. 9   13   12   11   7   12   11   10   5   11   10   __   __

    A. 9, 4
    B. 9, 3
    C. 9, 9
    D. 8, 3
    E. 8, 4

21. 0   2   4   3   2   4   6   6   2   4   6   8   __   __

    A. 9, 2
    B. 8, 2
    C. 8, 3
    D. 2, 9
    E. 6, 9

22.   2   0   4   4   6   8   8   12   ___   ___

    A.   10, 16
    B.   10, 14
    C.   16, 14
    D.   14, 16
    E.   10, 12

23.   0   1   2   4   1   8   16   32   2   64   128   ___   ___

    A.   252, 3
    B.   256, 3
    C.   250, 4
    D.   4, 256
    E.   3, 252

24.   71   47   63   55   55   63   47   ___   ___

    A.   39, 31
    B.   31, 39
    C.   71, 39
    D.   42, 39
    E.   39, 71

ANSWER SHEET TO NUMBER SERIES/EXAM 1

1. Ⓐ Ⓑ Ⓒ Ⓓ Ⓔ
2. Ⓐ Ⓑ Ⓒ Ⓓ Ⓔ
3. Ⓐ Ⓑ Ⓒ Ⓓ Ⓔ
4. Ⓐ Ⓑ Ⓒ Ⓓ Ⓔ
5. Ⓐ Ⓑ Ⓒ Ⓓ Ⓔ
6. Ⓐ Ⓑ Ⓒ Ⓓ Ⓔ
7. Ⓐ Ⓑ Ⓒ Ⓓ Ⓔ
8. Ⓐ Ⓑ Ⓒ Ⓓ Ⓔ

9. Ⓐ Ⓑ Ⓒ Ⓓ Ⓔ
10. Ⓐ Ⓑ Ⓒ Ⓓ Ⓔ
11. Ⓐ Ⓑ Ⓒ Ⓓ Ⓔ
12. Ⓐ Ⓑ Ⓒ Ⓓ Ⓔ
13. Ⓐ Ⓑ Ⓒ Ⓓ Ⓔ
14. Ⓐ Ⓑ Ⓒ Ⓓ Ⓔ
15. Ⓐ Ⓑ Ⓒ Ⓓ Ⓔ
16. Ⓐ Ⓑ Ⓒ Ⓓ Ⓔ

17. Ⓐ Ⓑ Ⓒ Ⓓ Ⓔ
18. Ⓐ Ⓑ Ⓒ Ⓓ Ⓔ
19. Ⓐ Ⓑ Ⓒ Ⓓ Ⓔ
20. Ⓐ Ⓑ Ⓒ Ⓓ Ⓔ
21. Ⓐ Ⓑ Ⓒ Ⓓ Ⓔ
22. Ⓐ Ⓑ Ⓒ Ⓓ Ⓔ
23. Ⓐ Ⓑ Ⓒ Ⓓ Ⓔ
24. Ⓐ Ⓑ Ⓒ Ⓓ Ⓔ

{This page may be removed to mark answers.)

[This page intentionally blank.]

FOLLOWING DIRECTIONS/EXAM 1

Note To Person Assisting In This Exam:

Remove from this test guide the pages of this exam that comprise the directions to be read out loud. The test applicant should be left with only the sample sheet and answer sheet. Read the following directions out loud at the suggested rate of 75-80 words per minute, pausing only where indicated in parentheses. Speak as clearly as possible: Once a statement has been read, it cannot be repeated.

Examine Sample 1. (Pause 2-3 seconds.) Write the letter E, as in "elephant," beside the fourth highest number of the number series shown. Darken that number-letter combination on your answer sheet. (Pause 5 seconds.)

Examine Sample 1 again. (Pause 2-3 seconds.) If the third number is 10 less than the fourth number and 20 more than the first number, write the letter B, as in "boy," beside the first number shown in the sample. (Pause 2 seconds.) Now darken the number-letter combination you have selected on your answer sheet. (Pause 5 seconds.)

Examine Sample 2. (Pause 2-3 seconds.) Draw a line under the smallest odd number shown if it is greater than the sum of the first two numbers in the series. (Pause 5 seconds.) Otherwise, draw a line under the largest even number shown in the sample. (Pause 2 seconds.) Now, go to the number underlined on your answer sheet and darken the letter A, as in "apple." (Pause 5 seconds.)

Examine Sample 2 again. (Pause 2-3 seconds.) If the numbers 9 and 10 are the largest two even numbers shown in the sample, write the letter D, as in "dog," beside the first number shown in the sample. (Pause 2 seconds.) Otherwise, write the letter D, as in "dog," beside the second number shown in the sample. (Pause 2 seconds.) Now, darken the number-letter combination you have selected on your answer sheet. (Pause 5 seconds.)

Examine Sample 2 one more time. (Pause 2-3 seconds.) If the third number in the sample is less than the sum of the first two numbers, write the letter E, as in "elephant," beside the fifth number. (Pause 2 seconds.) However, if the fourth number is equal to the sum of the first two numbers in the sample, write the letter E, as in "elephant," beside the last number in the sample. (Pause 2 seconds.) Otherwise, write the letter B, as in "boy," beside the first number in the sample. (Pause 2 seconds.) Darken the number-letter combination you chose on your answer sheet. (Pause 5 seconds.)

Examine Sample 3. (Pause 2-3 seconds.) Write the letters D, as in "dog," and C, as in "cat," in the two smallest circles. If the number that you wrote the letter C, as in "cat," is less than the number you wrote the letter D, as in "dog," then write the letter B, as in "boy," beside the number in the last circle in the sample. (Pause 2 seconds.) Otherwise, go to the first circle shown in the sample and write the letter C, as in "cat." (Pause 2 seconds.) Now darken the number-letter combination you have selected on your answer sheet. (Pause 5 seconds.)

Examine Sample 3 again. (Pause 2-3 seconds.) Write the letter E, as in "elephant," in the first and third circle from the left. (Pause 5 seconds.) Between the two circles just mentioned, select the circle with the highest number and mark that number-letter combination on your answer sheet. (Pause 5 seconds.)

Examine Sample 4. (Pause 2-3 seconds.) Write the letter C, as in "cat," in the smaller circle shown if the number in the rectangle is higher than the number in the larger circle. (Pause 2 seconds.) Otherwise, write the letter A, as in "apple," beside the number in the triangle. (Pause 2 seconds.) Darken the number-letter combination you selected on your answer sheet. (Pause 5 seconds.)

Examine Sample 4 again. (Pause 2-3 seconds.) If any of the numbers within the geometric shapes are greater than 43 or less than 24, go to number 13 on your answer sheet and darken the letter B, as in "boy." (Pause 5 seconds.) Otherwise, go to number 12 on your answer sheet and darken the letter D, as in "dog." (Pause 5 seconds.)

Examine Sample 4 one more time. (Pause 2-3 seconds.) Write the letters E, as in "elephant," D, as in "dog," and B, as in "boy," in the larger circle, triangle and square respectively. (Pause 7 seconds.) Now, darken each of those number-letter combinations on your answer sheet. (Pause 10 seconds.)

Examine Sample 5. (Pause 2-3 seconds.) Write the number 61 beside the third letter in the alphabet and darken that number-letter combination on your answer sheet. (Pause 5 seconds.)

Examine Sample 5 again. (Pause 2-3 seconds.) Write the number 71 beside the last letter in the sample if that is the first letter in the alphabet. (Pause 2 seconds.) Otherwise, write the number 86 beside the second letter from the left. (Pause 2 seconds.) Darken the number-letter combination you have selected on your answer sheet. (Pause 5 seconds.)

Examine Sample 6. (Pause 2-3 seconds.) Each pair of numbers shown in the sample represents a route number and its corresponding length in miles. Assume, for now, that the shorter routes comprise business districts, while the longer routes are rural. (Pause 2-3 seconds.) Select the route number that is most likely to be business oriented and go to that same number on your answer sheet. Darken the letter C, as in "cat." (Pause 5 seconds.)

Examine Sample 6 again. (Pause 2-3 seconds.) Using the same guidelines as described in the previous question, select the route number that is the most rural and go to that same number on your answer sheet and darken the letter E, as in "elephant." (Pause 5 seconds.)

Examine Sample 4. (Pause 2-3 seconds.) If the second number is less than the third number, but greater than the fourth number, go to number 92 on your answer sheet and darken the letter A, as in "apple." (Pause 2 seconds.) Otherwise, go to the same number that is shown in the rectangle on your answer sheet and darken the letter D, as in "dog." (Pause 5 seconds.)

Examine Sample 7. (Pause 2-3 seconds.) Each of the letters shown designate postal substations and their respective closing times on Saturdays. (Pause 2-3 seconds.) Go to number 30 on your answer sheet and darken the letter that represents the substation that remains open after 5:00 P.M. (Pause 5 seconds.)

Examine Sample 7 again. (Pause 2-3 seconds.) If substation A, as in "apple," closes before substation D, as in "dog," and substation C, as in "cat," go to number 70 on your answer sheet and darken the letter E, as in "elephant." (Pause 2 seconds.) Otherwise, go to number 1 on your answer sheet and darken the letter E, as in "elephant." (Pause 5 seconds.)

Examine Sample 8. (Pause 2-3 seconds.) Go to the smallest number shown in the sample on your answer sheet and darken the letter B, as in "boy," if the first number in the sample is less than the last number in the sample. (Pause 2 seconds.) Otherwise, go to number 78 on your answer sheet and darken the letter C, as in "cat." (Pause 5 seconds.)

Examine Sample 8 again. (Pause 2-3 seconds.) If the third number from the right is greater than the third number from the left, go to number 82 on your answer sheet and darken the letter E, as in "elephant." Otherwise, go to the same number on your answer sheet that I just mentioned and darken the letter B, as in "boy," instead. (Pause 5 seconds.)

Examine Sample 9. (Pause 2-3 seconds.) Write the letter A, as in "apple," beside both numbers shown in the sample if the first number is less than the second. (Pause 5 seconds.) However, if the opposite is true, write the number 33 beside the letter D, as in "dog," and the number 36 beside the letter A, as in "apple." (Pause 2 seconds.) Now, darken the number-letter combination you have selected on your answer sheet. (Pause 7 seconds.)

Examine Sample 10. (Pause 2-3 seconds.) Each of the numbers shown represents five different Zip Codes. Assume the higher numbered Zip Codes represent destinations that are further west. (Pause 2 seconds.) Go to number 2 on your answer sheet and darken the letter that represents the Zip Code that would be considered the easternmost destination given. (Pause 5 seconds.)

Examine Sample 10 again. (Pause 2-3 seconds.) Now, underline the first two digits of the Zip Code that represents the second most western destination given. Go to that number on your answer sheet and darken the letter that corresponds to the Zip Code selected. (Pause 5 seconds.)

Examine Sample 11. (Pause 2-3 seconds.) If 7 is greater than the sum of 3 plus 3, but less than the product of 3 times 3, write the number 27 beside the letter shown. (Pause 2 seconds.) Otherwise, write the letter E, as in "elephant," beside the number shown. (Pause 2 seconds.) Now darken the number-letter combination you have selected on your answer sheet. (Pause 5 seconds.)

-END OF TEST-

FOLLOWING DIRECTIONS/EXAM 1 SAMPLES

1.　25_____　　　35_____　　　45_____　　　55_____　　　65_____　　　75_____

2.　2　　4　　6　　7　　8　　9　　10

3.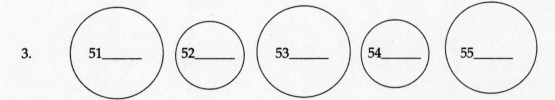

    51_____　　52_____　　53_____　　54_____　　55_____

4.　23_____　　24_____　　29_____　　42_____　　43_____

5.　_____A　　　_____C　　　_____B　　　_____E　　　_____D

6.　　14/30　　　9/15　　　15/8　　　16/2　　　95/14

7.
A	B	C	D
12 NOON	5:30 PM	5:00 PM	3:00 PM

8.　738　　　　645　　　　125　　　　50　　　　892

9.　33_____　　　_____D　　　36_____　　　A_____

10.   A   B   C   D   E

      65322   65311   65221   65111   70500

11.   _____C   17_____

EXAM 1

ANSWER SHEET TO FOLLOWING DIRECTIONS/EXAM 1

1. Ⓐ Ⓑ Ⓒ Ⓓ Ⓔ   33. Ⓐ Ⓑ Ⓒ Ⓓ Ⓔ   65. Ⓐ Ⓑ Ⓒ Ⓓ Ⓔ
2. Ⓐ Ⓑ Ⓒ Ⓓ Ⓔ   34. Ⓐ Ⓑ Ⓒ Ⓓ Ⓔ   66. Ⓐ Ⓑ Ⓒ Ⓓ Ⓔ
3. Ⓐ Ⓑ Ⓒ Ⓓ Ⓔ   35. Ⓐ Ⓑ Ⓒ Ⓓ Ⓔ   67. Ⓐ Ⓑ Ⓒ Ⓓ Ⓔ
4. Ⓐ Ⓑ Ⓒ Ⓓ Ⓔ   36. Ⓐ Ⓑ Ⓒ Ⓓ Ⓔ   68. Ⓐ Ⓑ Ⓒ Ⓓ Ⓔ
5. Ⓐ Ⓑ Ⓒ Ⓓ Ⓔ   37. Ⓐ Ⓑ Ⓒ Ⓓ Ⓔ   69. Ⓐ Ⓑ Ⓒ Ⓓ Ⓔ
6. Ⓐ Ⓑ Ⓒ Ⓓ Ⓔ   38. Ⓐ Ⓑ Ⓒ Ⓓ Ⓔ   70. Ⓐ Ⓑ Ⓒ Ⓓ Ⓔ
7. Ⓐ Ⓑ Ⓒ Ⓓ Ⓔ   39. Ⓐ Ⓑ Ⓒ Ⓓ Ⓔ   71. Ⓐ Ⓑ Ⓒ Ⓓ Ⓔ
8. Ⓐ Ⓑ Ⓒ Ⓓ Ⓔ   40. Ⓐ Ⓑ Ⓒ Ⓓ Ⓔ   72. Ⓐ Ⓑ Ⓒ Ⓓ Ⓔ
9. Ⓐ Ⓑ Ⓒ Ⓓ Ⓔ   41. Ⓐ Ⓑ Ⓒ Ⓓ Ⓔ   73. Ⓐ Ⓑ Ⓒ Ⓓ Ⓔ
10. Ⓐ Ⓑ Ⓒ Ⓓ Ⓔ   42. Ⓐ Ⓑ Ⓒ Ⓓ Ⓔ   74. Ⓐ Ⓑ Ⓒ Ⓓ Ⓔ
11. Ⓐ Ⓑ Ⓒ Ⓓ Ⓔ   43. Ⓐ Ⓑ Ⓒ Ⓓ Ⓔ   75. Ⓐ Ⓑ Ⓒ Ⓓ Ⓔ
12. Ⓐ Ⓑ Ⓒ Ⓓ Ⓔ   44. Ⓐ Ⓑ Ⓒ Ⓓ Ⓔ   76. Ⓐ Ⓑ Ⓒ Ⓓ Ⓔ
13. Ⓐ Ⓑ Ⓒ Ⓓ Ⓔ   45. Ⓐ Ⓑ Ⓒ Ⓓ Ⓔ   77. Ⓐ Ⓑ Ⓒ Ⓓ Ⓔ
14. Ⓐ Ⓑ Ⓒ Ⓓ Ⓔ   46. Ⓐ Ⓑ Ⓒ Ⓓ Ⓔ   78. Ⓐ Ⓑ Ⓒ Ⓓ Ⓔ
15. Ⓐ Ⓑ Ⓒ Ⓓ Ⓔ   47. Ⓐ Ⓑ Ⓒ Ⓓ Ⓔ   79. Ⓐ Ⓑ Ⓒ Ⓓ Ⓔ
16. Ⓐ Ⓑ Ⓒ Ⓓ Ⓔ   48. Ⓐ Ⓑ Ⓒ Ⓓ Ⓔ   80. Ⓐ Ⓑ Ⓒ Ⓓ Ⓔ
17. Ⓐ Ⓑ Ⓒ Ⓓ Ⓔ   49. Ⓐ Ⓑ Ⓒ Ⓓ Ⓔ   81. Ⓐ Ⓑ Ⓒ Ⓓ Ⓔ
18. Ⓐ Ⓑ Ⓒ Ⓓ Ⓔ   50. Ⓐ Ⓑ Ⓒ Ⓓ Ⓔ   82. Ⓐ Ⓑ Ⓒ Ⓓ Ⓔ
19. Ⓐ Ⓑ Ⓒ Ⓓ Ⓔ   51. Ⓐ Ⓑ Ⓒ Ⓓ Ⓔ   83. Ⓐ Ⓑ Ⓒ Ⓓ Ⓔ
20. Ⓐ Ⓑ Ⓒ Ⓓ Ⓔ   52. Ⓐ Ⓑ Ⓒ Ⓓ Ⓔ   84. Ⓐ Ⓑ Ⓒ Ⓓ Ⓔ
21. Ⓐ Ⓑ Ⓒ Ⓓ Ⓔ   53. Ⓐ Ⓑ Ⓒ Ⓓ Ⓔ   85. Ⓐ Ⓑ Ⓒ Ⓓ Ⓔ
22. Ⓐ Ⓑ Ⓒ Ⓓ Ⓔ   54. Ⓐ Ⓑ Ⓒ Ⓓ Ⓔ   86. Ⓐ Ⓑ Ⓒ Ⓓ Ⓔ
23. Ⓐ Ⓑ Ⓒ Ⓓ Ⓔ   55. Ⓐ Ⓑ Ⓒ Ⓓ Ⓔ   87. Ⓐ Ⓑ Ⓒ Ⓓ Ⓔ
24. Ⓐ Ⓑ Ⓒ Ⓓ Ⓔ   56. Ⓐ Ⓑ Ⓒ Ⓓ Ⓔ   88. Ⓐ Ⓑ Ⓒ Ⓓ Ⓔ
25. Ⓐ Ⓑ Ⓒ Ⓓ Ⓔ   57. Ⓐ Ⓑ Ⓒ Ⓓ Ⓔ   89. Ⓐ Ⓑ Ⓒ Ⓓ Ⓔ
26. Ⓐ Ⓑ Ⓒ Ⓓ Ⓔ   58. Ⓐ Ⓑ Ⓒ Ⓓ Ⓔ   90. Ⓐ Ⓑ Ⓒ Ⓓ Ⓔ
27. Ⓐ Ⓑ Ⓒ Ⓓ Ⓔ   59. Ⓐ Ⓑ Ⓒ Ⓓ Ⓔ   91. Ⓐ Ⓑ Ⓒ Ⓓ Ⓔ
28. Ⓐ Ⓑ Ⓒ Ⓓ Ⓔ   60. Ⓐ Ⓑ Ⓒ Ⓓ Ⓔ   92. Ⓐ Ⓑ Ⓒ Ⓓ Ⓔ
29. Ⓐ Ⓑ Ⓒ Ⓓ Ⓔ   61. Ⓐ Ⓑ Ⓒ Ⓓ Ⓔ   93. Ⓐ Ⓑ Ⓒ Ⓓ Ⓔ
30. Ⓐ Ⓑ Ⓒ Ⓓ Ⓔ   62. Ⓐ Ⓑ Ⓒ Ⓓ Ⓔ   94. Ⓐ Ⓑ Ⓒ Ⓓ Ⓔ
31. Ⓐ Ⓑ Ⓒ Ⓓ Ⓔ   63. Ⓐ Ⓑ Ⓒ Ⓓ Ⓔ   95. Ⓐ Ⓑ Ⓒ Ⓓ Ⓔ
32. Ⓐ Ⓑ Ⓒ Ⓓ Ⓔ   64. Ⓐ Ⓑ Ⓒ Ⓓ Ⓔ

(This page may be removed to mark answers.)

[This page intentionally blank.]

ANSWERS TO ADDRESS CROSS COMPARISON/EXAM 1

#		#		#	
1.	A	33.	D	65.	D
2.	D	34.	D	66.	A
3.	D	35.	D	67.	D
4.	D	36.	D	68.	A
5.	A	37.	A	69.	D
6.	D	38.	D	70.	D
7.	D	39.	D	71.	D
8.	D	40.	A	72.	A
9.	D	41.	D	73.	D
10.	A	42.	A	74.	A
11.	D	43.	D	75.	D
12.	D	44.	D	76.	D
13.	A	45.	A	77.	D
14.	D	46.	A	78.	D
15.	D	47.	D	79.	A
16.	D	48.	A	80.	D
17.	A	49.	A	81.	A
18.	D	50.	A	82.	D
19.	A	51.	A	83.	D
20.	D	52.	D	84.	D
21.	A	53.	D	85.	A
22.	D	54.	A	86.	D
23.	A	55.	A	87.	D
24.	D	56.	D	88.	D
25.	D	57.	A	89.	D
26.	A	58.	D	90.	A
27.	D	59.	D	91.	D
28.	D	60.	D	92.	D
29.	D	61.	D	93.	D
30.	D	62.	A	94.	D
31.	D	63.	D	95.	A
32.	A	64.	A		

ANSWERS TO MEMORIZATION/EXAM 1

1.	A	31.	E	61.	C
2.	B	32.	E	62.	B
3.	C	33.	B	63.	B
4.	B	34.	A	64.	E
5.	D	35.	B	65.	A
6.	A	36.	C	66.	D
7.	E	37.	A	67.	C
8.	B	38.	D	68.	A
9.	E	39.	A	69.	D
10.	A	40.	C	70.	E
11.	A	41.	D	71.	B
12.	C	42.	A	72.	D
13.	E	43.	B	73.	A
14.	A	44.	D	74.	C
15.	B	45.	E	75.	E
16.	B	46.	C	76.	C
17.	D	47.	D	77.	D
18.	E	48.	A	78.	C
19.	C	49.	C	79.	E
20.	D	50.	E	80.	C
21.	C	51.	E	81.	E
22.	D	52.	D	82.	D
23.	D	53.	E	83.	A
24.	C	54.	C	84.	B
25.	C	55.	D	85.	B
26.	A	56.	B	86.	B
27.	E	57.	B	87.	A
28.	C	58.	D	88.	E
29.	B	59.	A		
30.	A	60.	A		

ANSWERS TO NUMBER SERIES/EXAM 1

1. E.

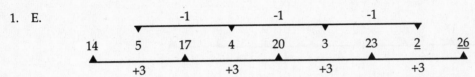

```
        -1        -1        -1
14   5   17   4   20   3   23   2   26
       +3      +3      +3      +3
```

2. B.

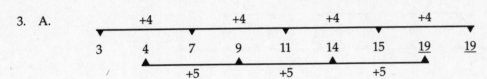

```
       +1        +1        +1
9    9   10   15   11   21   12   27
         +6      +6      +6
```

3. A.

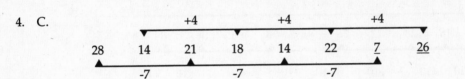

```
      +4       +4       +4       +4
3    4   7   9   11   14   15   19   19
        +5      +5      +5
```

4. C.

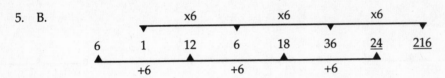

```
       +4       +4       +4
28   14   21   18   14   22   7   26
   -7      -7      -7
```

5. B.

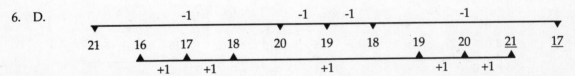

```
       x6       x6       x6
6    1   12   6   18   36   24   216
   +6      +6      +6
```

6. D.

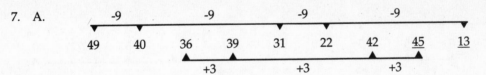

```
       -1        -1  -1        -1
21   16   17   18   20   19   18   19   20   21   17
   +1   +1          +1          +1   +1
```

7. A.

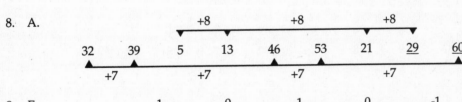

```
    -9        -9        -9        -9
49   40   36   39   31   22   42   45   13
        +3      +3      +3
```

8. A.

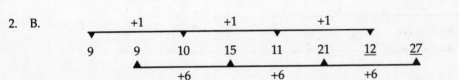

```
          +8        +8        +8
32   39   5   13   46   53   21   29   60
   +7       +7      +7      +7
```

9. E.

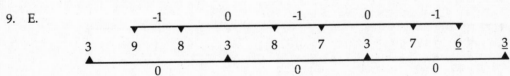

```
      -1      0       -1      0       -1
3    9   8   3   8   7   3   7   6   3
        0           0           0
```

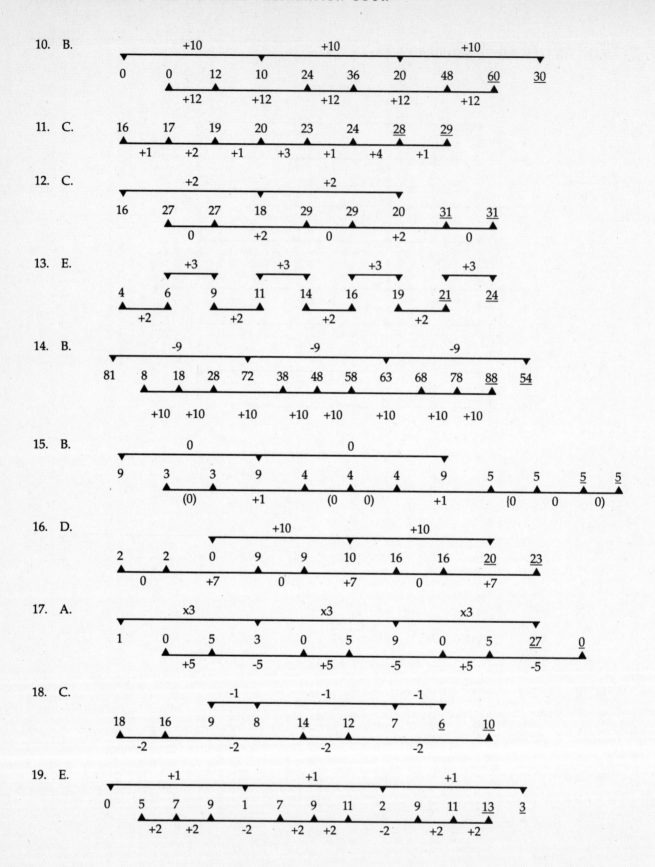

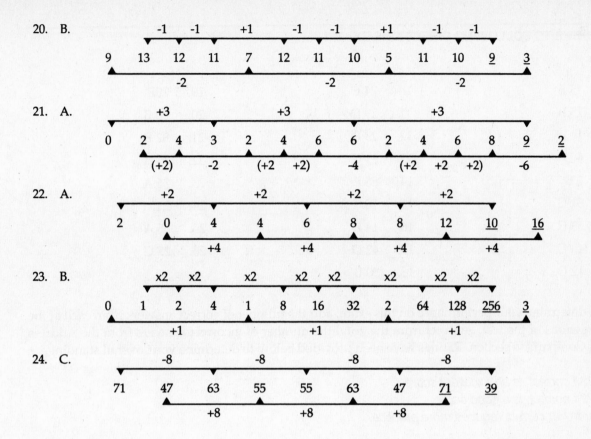

20. B.

	-1	-1		+1	-1	-1		+1	-1	-1	
9	13	12	11	7	12	11	10	5	11	10	<u>9</u>	<u>3</u>

-2   -2   -2

21. A.

+3   +3   +3

0   2   4   3   2   4   6   6   2   4   6   8   <u>9</u>   <u>2</u>

(+2)   -2   (+2   +2)   -4   (+2   +2   +2)   -6

22. A.

+2   +2   +2   +2

2   0   4   4   6   8   8   12   <u>10</u>   <u>16</u>

+4   +4   +4   +4

23. B.

x2   x2   x2   x2   x2   x2   x2   x2

0   1   2   4   1   8   16   32   2   64   128   <u>256</u>   <u>3</u>

+1   +1   +1

24. C.

-8   -8   -8   -8

71   47   63   55   55   63   47   <u>71</u>   <u>39</u>

+8   +8   +8

ANSWERS TO FOLLOWING DIRECTIONS/EXAM 1

1.	45 E	10.	24 E	19.	70E
2.	25 B	11.	29 D	20.	50 B
3.	10 A	12.	23 B	21.	82 B
4.	4 D	13.	61 C	22.	33 A
5.	2 B	14.	86 E	23.	36 A
6.	51 C	15.	16 C	24.	2 D
7.	53 E	16.	14 E	25.	65 A
8.	43 C	17.	42 D	26.	27 C
9.	12 D	18.	30 B		

To determine your performance on this exam, add the number of correct answers from each of the four sections of the test. Subtract from this total the number of incorrect answers from the Address Cross Comparison section. Ratings have been provided below to determine your overall standing.

225-232 correct, is an excellent score.
208-224 correct, is a good score.
207 or fewer correct requires more practice.

NOTE: Don't despair if you ran out of time before completing the first two parts of this exam. These exams are designed to be very time restrictive. However, you can be assured of notable improvement with continued practice.

Exam 2

**DO NOT OPEN THIS TEST BOOKLET UNTIL
YOU ARE TOLD TO START BY THE INDIVIDUAL
ASSISTING YOU IN THIS EXERCISE.**

[This page intentionally blank.]

1.	1502 Tallagson Ln.	1502 Talagson Ln.
2.	1012 Harrison Dr.	1012 Harrison Ave.
3.	102 9th Ave.	102 9th Ave.
4.	18771 Forrest Pl. NW	18771 Forest Pl. NE
5.	E. Pebble Beach	W. Pebble Beach
6.	Poulsbo, Wash. 98370	Poulsbo, Wash. 98370
7.	4213 NE Lincoln Rd.	4123 NE Lincoln Rd.
8.	16345 Tukwilla Rd.	16435 Tukwilla Rd.
9.	Ames, Ia. 50010	Ames, Ia. 50010
10.	Whiteford Rd. SW	Whiteford Rd. SE
11.	Alturas, Calif. 90081	Alturas, Calf. 90081
12.	Beacon Fall, Conn. 00378	Bacon Falls, Conn. 00378
13.	841 W. Liberty Rd.	814 W. Liberty Rd.
14.	1646 Lassie Ln.	1646 Lassie Lane
15.	29580 Mt. View Dr.	29850 Mt. View Dr.
16.	47751 Orseth Circle	47751 Orseth Circle
17.	Kaumakani, Hawaii	Kaumokani, Hawaii
18.	14189 Frontier Dr.	14198 Frontier Dr.
19.	Keyport, Wash.	Keyport, Wash.
20.	13455 NW Spirit Crt.	13455 NW Sirit Crt.
21.	Cass, Illinois	Cass, Ilinois
22.	Nesika Bay Rd.	Nesika Bay Rd.
23.	20895 Melson Dr.	20095 Melson Dr.

24.	Shelby, New York	Shelby, New York
25.	Cedar Heights, Ark.	Cedar Heights, Ark.
26.	Hernando, Florida 11212	Hernando, Florida 11221
27.	453 Canyon Dr.	435 Canyon Ave.
28.	Yuma, Arizona	Yuma, Arizona
29.	11B Shadow Ct. Apts.	113 Shadow Ct. Apts.
30.	77127 Briar Cliff	77127 Briter Cliff
31.	10101 Blackberry Ln.	10101 Blackberry Ln.
32.	105-C Trevor Pl. SW	105-C Trevor Pl. NE
33.	Billings, Mont.	Billings, Mont.
34.	707 Clover Park	707 Clover Park
35.	Trail Ridge, Mo. 58511	Trail Ridge, Ma. 58511
36.	Tombstone, New Mexico	Tombstone, New Mexico
37.	Edgewater Ct. SW	Edgewater Circle SW
38.	11541 Suquamish Dr.	11541 Suqamish Dr.
39.	809 Lemolo Square	908 Lemolo Square
40.	1798 Mulholland SE	1798 Mullholland SE
41.	Quakersville, Penn 10044	Quakersville, Penn 10404
42.	244 Johnston Rd.	2441 Johnston Rd.
43.	185 Division Dr.	185 Division Ave.
44.	10071 Pacific Blvd.	10071 Atlantic Blvd.
45.	Crestview Ct-98	Crestview Ct-98
46.	154 Rindal St.	154 Rindall St.
47.	22252 Woodward Way	22225 Woodward Way
48.	15733 Virginia Pt. Rd.	15733 Virginia Pl. Rd.

49.	903 Knollward Circle	903 Nollward Circle
50.	San Juan Island	San Juan Islands
51.	2350 Sawdust Trail	2350 Sawdust Trail
52.	Bloomingdale, GA 30081	Bloomingdale, GA 30018
53.	Bridgeview, Del. 05811	Bridgeview Dr. SE
54.	21st Street NE	21st Ave. NE
55.	169340 Peterson Blvd.	169340 Petersun Blvd.
56.	995 Indianola Pl.	985 Indianola Pl.
57.	H.M. Asgard Apt. C	H.M. Atgard Apt. C
58.	Brownsville, Texas 77811	Brownsville, Texas 77811
59.	Apache Jct., Ariz.	Apache Jct., Ariz.
60.	Denver, Colo. 89036	Denver, Colorado
61.	236 Lisir Circle	236 Lisir Circle
62.	33810 Melody Lane	33810 Meludy Lane
63.	13102 Dogwood Ave.	13012 Dogwood Ave.
64.	Butte, Mont.	Butte, Mont.
65.	Des Moines, Ia. 50010	Des Moines, Ia. 50011
66.	Down Rapids, Mich.	Down Stream, Mich.
67.	101-D Hoover St. NE	101-D Hoover Dr. NE
68.	48444 Lakeside Shore	48454 Lakeside Shore
69.	2121 8th Ave. N	2121 8th Ave. N
70.	Clay, North Carolina	Clay, South Carolina
71.	Sunnydale, Calif.	Sunnydale, Calif.
72.	Albany, N.Y. 09337	Albany, N.M. 09337
73.	Bloomington, Ill.	Blomington, Ill.

74.	East Ely, Nevada	West Ely, Nevada
75.	Bonscillica, WY 77811	Bonscillica, WY 77811
76.	107-C Wingsong Apts.	107-C Windsong Apts.
77.	Brighton, NH 08813	Brighton NM 08814
78.	Snoqualamine Pass, WA	Snoqualamine Pass, Wash.
79.	223411 Wavecrest Ave.	223416 Wavecrest Ave.
80.	Forest Creek Pk.	Forest Ck. Park
81.	59983 Stottlemeyer Rd.	59983 Stottlemeyer Rd.
82.	333 Chesnut Blvd.	888 Chestnut Blvd.
83.	Silverton Bay, CA	Silverdale Bay, CA
84.	Admirality Pt. Or.	Admirality Point, OR
85.	1656 Sherman Hill Rd.	1656 Sherman Hill Rd.
86.	Vista Center, OK 66711	Vista Canter, OK 66711
87.	Brockton, square S.	Brockson Square S.
88.	119 Lincolnside Apts.	119 Linconside Apts.
89.	71333 Bayberry Ct.	71333 Bayberry Ct.
90.	35556 Sunde Rd.	35556 Sundae Rd.
91.	431 Arizona Ave.	431 Arizona Ave.
92.	276598 Loveland Dr.	27659 Loveland Dr.
93.	Bridle Pt. NE	Briddle Pt. NE
94.	126 8th Ave. SW	126 8th Ave SW
95.	78441 Oyster Bay Rd.	78414 Oyster Bay Rd.

ANSWER SHEET TO ADDRESS CROSS COMPARISON/EXAM 2

1. (A) (D)
2. (A) (D)
3. (A) (D)
4. (A) (D)
5. (A) (D)
6. (A) (D)
7. (A) (D)
8. (A) (D)
9. (A) (D)
10. (A) (D)
11. (A) (D)
12. (A) (D)
13. (A) (D)
14. (A) (D)
15. (A) (D)
16. (A) (D)
17. (A) (D)
18. (A) (D)
19. (A) (D)
20. (A) (D)
21. (A) (D)
22. (A) (D)
23. (A) (D)
24. (A) (D)
25. (A) (D)
26. (A) (D)
27. (A) (D)
28. (A) (D)
29. (A) (D)
30. (A) (D)
31. (A) (D)
32. (A) (D)

33. (A) (D)
34. (A) (D)
35. (A) (D)
36. (A) (D)
37. (A) (D)
38. (A) (D)
39. (A) (D)
40. (A) (D)
41. (A) (D)
42. (A) (D)
43. (A) (D)
44. (A) (D)
45. (A) (D)
46. (A) (D)
47. (A) (D)
48. (A) (D)
49. (A) (D)
50. (A) (D)
51. (A) (D)
52. (A) (D)
53. (A) (D)
54. (A) (D)
55. (A) (D)
56. (A) (D)
57. (A) (D)
58. (A) (D)
59. (A) (D)
60. (A) (D)
61. (A) (D)
62. (A) (D)
63. (A) (D)
64. (A) (D)

65. (A) (D)
66. (A) (D)
67. (A) (D)
68. (A) (D)
69. (A) (D)
70. (A) (D)
71. (A) (D)
72. (A) (D)
73. (A) (D)
74. (A) (D)
75. (A) (D)
76. (A) (D)
77. (A) (D)
78. (A) (D)
79. (A) (D)
80. (A) (D)
81. (A) (D)
82. (A) (D)
83. (A) (D)
84. (A) (D)
85. (A) (D)
86. (A) (D)
87. (A) (D)
88. (A) (D)
89. (A) (D)
90. (A) (D)
91. (A) (D)
92. (A) (D)
93. (A) (D)
94. (A) (D)
95. (A) (D)

(This page may be removed to mark answers.)

[This page intentionally blank.]

MEMORIZATION/EXAM 2

STEP 1 TIME: 3 MINUTES
STEP 4 TIME: 5 MINUTES

A	B	C	D	E
6700-6799 Flint Armstrong Dr. 6700-6799 Simon Bender Way 1200-1299 Grant	6400-6499 Flint Bridgeview 7200-7299 Simon Jackson 3100-3199 Grant	5200-5299 Flint Knoll Rd. 7000-7099 Simon Ford Ave. 2900-2999 Grant	7200-7299 Flint Bingham 6400-6499 Simon Averley Dr. 0300-0399 Grant	7000-7099 Flint Pinecone Ave. 5200-5299 Simon Walnut Grove 1300-1399 Grant

NOTE: Follow the same step by step format established for the memorization exercises studied earlier. (See page 41.)

PRACTICE MEMORIZATION/EXAM 2

STEP 2 TIME: 3 MINUTES
STEP 3 TIME: 3 MINUTES (cover key)

A	B	C	D	E
6700-6799 Flint	6400-6499 Flint	5200-5299 Flint	7200-7299 Flint	7000-7099 Flint
Armstrong Dr.	Bridgeview	Knoll Rd.	Bingham	Pinecone Ave.
6700-6799 Simon	7200-7299 Simon	7000-7099 Simon	6400-6499 Simon	5200-5299 Simon
Bender Way	Jackson	Ford Ave.	Averley Dr.	Walnut Grove
1200-1299 Grant	3100-3199 Grant	2900-2999 Grant	0300-0399 Grant	1300-1399 Grant

1. Walnut Grove
2. 1200-1299 Grant
3. 6400-6499 Simon
4. Bender Way
5. Jackson
6. 2900-2999 Grant
7. 6700-6799 Flint
8. Ford Ave.
9. Averley Dr.
10. Bridgeview
11. 5200-5299 Flint
12. 7200-7299 Simon
13. Bingham
14. 3100-3199 Grant
15. 6400-6499 Simon
16. Knoll Rd.
17. .7000-7099 Flint
18. Jackson
19. 1300-1399 Grant
20. Walnut Grove
21. Armstrong Dr.
22. 6700-6799 Simon
23. Averley Dr.
24. 6700-6799 Flint
25. 0300-0399 Grant
26. Pinecone Ave.
27. Bender Way
28. Pinecone Ave.
29. 1200-1299 Grant
30. 2900-2999 Grant

31. 7000-7099 Simon
32. Bridgeview
33. Jackson
34. 6400-6499 Simon
35. 1300-1399 Grant
36. Walnut Grove
37. 6400-6499 Flint
38. 7200-7299 Flint
39. 7200-7299 Simon
40. Pinecone Ave.
41. Jackson
42. 6400-6499 Simon
43. Armstrong Dr.
44. 1300-1399 Grant
45. 7000-7099 Flint
46. 6700-6799 Flint
47. Knoll Rd.
48. Ford Ave.
49. 5200-5299 Flint
50. 5200-5299 Simon
51. 7200-7299 Flint
52. Averley Dr.
53. Bridgeview
54. Knoll Rd.
55. 3100-3199 Grant
56. 7200-7299 Simon
57. 6400-6499 Flint
58. 2900-2999 Grant
59. 7000-7099 Simon
60. Pinecone Ave.

61. 6700-6799 Simon
62. Ford Ave.
63. Walnut Grove
64. Knoll Rd.
65. Bingham
66. 1200-1299 Grant
67. 6700-6799 Simon
68. 0300-0399 Grant
69. Bender Way
70. Armstrong Dr.
71. 6400-6499 Flint
72. 5200-5299 Simon
73. Bingham
74. 7000-7099 Flint
75. 5200-5299 Flint
76. Averley Dr.
77. 7200-7299 Simon
78. 7000-7099 Simon
79. 7200-7299 Flint
80. Bridgeview
81. 0300-0399 Grant
82. Bender Way
83. 3100-3199 Grant
84. Armstrong Dr.
85. 2900-2999 Grant
86. Ford Ave.
87. Bingham
88. 5200-5299 Simon

PRACTICE ANSWER SHEET TO MEMORIZATION/EXAM 2

1. Ⓐ Ⓑ Ⓒ Ⓓ Ⓔ
2. Ⓐ Ⓑ Ⓒ Ⓓ Ⓔ
3. Ⓐ Ⓑ Ⓒ Ⓓ Ⓔ
4. Ⓐ Ⓑ Ⓒ Ⓓ Ⓔ
5. Ⓐ Ⓑ Ⓒ Ⓓ Ⓔ
6. Ⓐ Ⓑ Ⓒ Ⓓ Ⓔ
7. Ⓐ Ⓑ Ⓒ Ⓓ Ⓔ
8. Ⓐ Ⓑ Ⓒ Ⓓ Ⓔ
9. Ⓐ Ⓑ Ⓒ Ⓓ Ⓔ
10. Ⓐ Ⓑ Ⓒ Ⓓ Ⓔ
11. Ⓐ Ⓑ Ⓒ Ⓓ Ⓔ
12. Ⓐ Ⓑ Ⓒ Ⓓ Ⓔ
13. Ⓐ Ⓑ Ⓒ Ⓓ Ⓔ
14. Ⓐ Ⓑ Ⓒ Ⓓ Ⓔ
15. Ⓐ Ⓑ Ⓒ Ⓓ Ⓔ
16. Ⓐ Ⓑ Ⓒ Ⓓ Ⓔ
17. Ⓐ Ⓑ Ⓒ Ⓓ Ⓔ
18. Ⓐ Ⓑ Ⓒ Ⓓ Ⓔ
19. Ⓐ Ⓑ Ⓒ Ⓓ Ⓔ
20. Ⓐ Ⓑ Ⓒ Ⓓ Ⓔ
21. Ⓐ Ⓑ Ⓒ Ⓓ Ⓔ
22. Ⓐ Ⓑ Ⓒ Ⓓ Ⓔ
23. Ⓐ Ⓑ Ⓒ Ⓓ Ⓔ
24. Ⓐ Ⓑ Ⓒ Ⓓ Ⓔ
25. Ⓐ Ⓑ Ⓒ Ⓓ Ⓔ
26. Ⓐ Ⓑ Ⓒ Ⓓ Ⓔ
27. Ⓐ Ⓑ Ⓒ Ⓓ Ⓔ
28. Ⓐ Ⓑ Ⓒ Ⓓ Ⓔ
29. Ⓐ Ⓑ Ⓒ Ⓓ Ⓔ
30. Ⓐ Ⓑ Ⓒ Ⓓ Ⓔ

31. Ⓐ Ⓑ Ⓒ Ⓓ Ⓔ
32. Ⓐ Ⓑ Ⓒ Ⓓ Ⓔ
33. Ⓐ Ⓑ Ⓒ Ⓓ Ⓔ
34. Ⓐ Ⓑ Ⓒ Ⓓ Ⓔ
35. Ⓐ Ⓑ Ⓒ Ⓓ Ⓔ
36. Ⓐ Ⓑ Ⓒ Ⓓ Ⓔ
37. Ⓐ Ⓑ Ⓒ Ⓓ Ⓔ
38. Ⓐ Ⓑ Ⓒ Ⓓ Ⓔ
39. Ⓐ Ⓑ Ⓒ Ⓓ Ⓔ
40. Ⓐ Ⓑ Ⓒ Ⓓ Ⓔ
41. Ⓐ Ⓑ Ⓒ Ⓓ Ⓔ
42. Ⓐ Ⓑ Ⓒ Ⓓ Ⓔ
43. Ⓐ Ⓑ Ⓒ Ⓓ Ⓔ
44. Ⓐ Ⓑ Ⓒ Ⓓ Ⓔ
45. Ⓐ Ⓑ Ⓒ Ⓓ Ⓔ
46. Ⓐ Ⓑ Ⓒ Ⓓ Ⓔ
47. Ⓐ Ⓑ Ⓒ Ⓓ Ⓔ
48. Ⓐ Ⓑ Ⓒ Ⓓ Ⓔ
49. Ⓐ Ⓑ Ⓒ Ⓓ Ⓔ
50. Ⓐ Ⓑ Ⓒ Ⓓ Ⓔ
51. Ⓐ Ⓑ Ⓒ Ⓓ Ⓔ
52. Ⓐ Ⓑ Ⓒ Ⓓ Ⓔ
53. Ⓐ Ⓑ Ⓒ Ⓓ Ⓔ
54. Ⓐ Ⓑ Ⓒ Ⓓ Ⓔ
55. Ⓐ Ⓑ Ⓒ Ⓓ Ⓔ
56. Ⓐ Ⓑ Ⓒ Ⓓ Ⓔ
57. Ⓐ Ⓑ Ⓒ Ⓓ Ⓔ
58. Ⓐ Ⓑ Ⓒ Ⓓ Ⓔ
59. Ⓐ Ⓑ Ⓒ Ⓓ Ⓔ
60. Ⓐ Ⓑ Ⓒ Ⓓ Ⓔ

61. Ⓐ Ⓑ Ⓒ Ⓓ Ⓔ
62. Ⓐ Ⓑ Ⓒ Ⓓ Ⓔ
63. Ⓐ Ⓑ Ⓒ Ⓓ Ⓔ
64. Ⓐ Ⓑ Ⓒ Ⓓ Ⓔ
65. Ⓐ Ⓑ Ⓒ Ⓓ Ⓔ
66. Ⓐ Ⓑ Ⓒ Ⓓ Ⓔ
67. Ⓐ Ⓑ Ⓒ Ⓓ Ⓔ
68. Ⓐ Ⓑ Ⓒ Ⓓ Ⓔ
69. Ⓐ Ⓑ Ⓒ Ⓓ Ⓔ
70. Ⓐ Ⓑ Ⓒ Ⓓ Ⓔ
71. Ⓐ Ⓑ Ⓒ Ⓓ Ⓔ
72. Ⓐ Ⓑ Ⓒ Ⓓ Ⓔ
73. Ⓐ Ⓑ Ⓒ Ⓓ Ⓔ
74. Ⓐ Ⓑ Ⓒ Ⓓ Ⓔ
75. Ⓐ Ⓑ Ⓒ Ⓓ Ⓔ
76. Ⓐ Ⓑ Ⓒ Ⓓ Ⓔ
77. Ⓐ Ⓑ Ⓒ Ⓓ Ⓔ
78. Ⓐ Ⓑ Ⓒ Ⓓ Ⓔ
79. Ⓐ Ⓑ Ⓒ Ⓓ Ⓔ
80. Ⓐ Ⓑ Ⓒ Ⓓ Ⓔ
81. Ⓐ Ⓑ Ⓒ Ⓓ Ⓔ
82. Ⓐ Ⓑ Ⓒ Ⓓ Ⓔ
83. Ⓐ Ⓑ Ⓒ Ⓓ Ⓔ
84. Ⓐ Ⓑ Ⓒ Ⓓ Ⓔ
85. Ⓐ Ⓑ Ⓒ Ⓓ Ⓔ
86. Ⓐ Ⓑ Ⓒ Ⓓ Ⓔ
87. Ⓐ Ⓑ Ⓒ Ⓓ Ⓔ
88. Ⓐ Ⓑ Ⓒ Ⓓ Ⓔ

1. Pinecone Ave.	31. 6700-6799 Simon	61. 3100-3199 Grant
2. 6700-6799 Flint	32. 6700-6799 Flint	62. Bender Way
3. 2900-2999 Grant	33. 2900-2999 Grant	63. Bridgeview
4. Armstrong Dr.	34. 7200-7299 Flint	64. 1300-1399 Grant
5. Averley Dr.	35. Armstrong Dr.	65. 6700-6799 Flint
6. 6700-6799 Simon	36. Bridgeview	66. 7200-7299 Simon
7. 0300-0399 Grant	37. Knoll Rd.	67. 2900-2999 Grant
8. Knoll Rd.	38. Ford Ave.	68. Knoll Rd.
9. Walnut Grove	39. 5200-5299 Flint	69. Pinecone Ave.
10. 5200-5299 Flint	40. 7200-7299 Flint	70. Walnut Grove
11. 7000-7099 Flint	41. 5200-5299 Simon	71. 5200-5299 Simon
12. 6400-6499 Simon	42. Bingham	72. 1200-1299 Grant
13. Bridgeview	43. 0300-0399 Grant	73. 1300-1399 Grant
14. 7200-7299 Flint	44. 6400-6499 Flint	74. Averley Dr.
15. 7000-7099 Simon	45. Bender Way	75. Ford Ave.
16. Bingham	46. Walnut Grove	76. 6400-6499 Simon
17. Bender Way	47. 7200-7299 Flint	77. 3100-3199 Grant
18. Ford Ave.	48. 1200-1299 Grant	78. Pinecone Ave.
19. 1200-1299 Grant	49. 7200-7299 Simon	79. Bingham
20. 5200-5299 Simon	50. Pinecone Ave.	80. Bender Way
21. Jackson	51. Ford Ave.	81. 5200-5299 Flint
22. 6400-6499 Flint	52. 1300-1399 Grant	82. Bridgeview
23. 7200-7299 Simon	53. Armstrong Dr.	83. Jackson
24. 0300-0399 Grant	54. 7000-7099 Simon	84. 7000-7099 Flint
25. Averley Dr.	55. 0300-0399 Grant	85. Armstrong Dr.
26. Walnut Grove	56. Jackson	86. 7000-7099 Simon
27. 6400-6499 Simon	57. Bingham	87. 6400-6499 Flint
28. 3100-3199 Grant	58. Averley Dr.	88. Knoll Rd.
29. Jackson	59. 7000-7099 Flint	
30. Averley Dr.	60. 6700-6799 Simon	

ANSWER SHEET TO MEMORIZATION/EXAM 2

1. Ⓐ Ⓑ Ⓒ Ⓓ Ⓔ
2. Ⓐ Ⓑ Ⓒ Ⓓ Ⓔ
3. Ⓐ Ⓑ Ⓒ Ⓓ Ⓔ
4. Ⓐ Ⓑ Ⓒ Ⓓ Ⓔ
5. Ⓐ Ⓑ Ⓒ Ⓓ Ⓔ
6. Ⓐ Ⓑ Ⓒ Ⓓ Ⓔ
7. Ⓐ Ⓑ Ⓒ Ⓓ Ⓔ
8. Ⓐ Ⓑ Ⓒ Ⓓ Ⓔ
9. Ⓐ Ⓑ Ⓒ Ⓓ Ⓔ
10. Ⓐ Ⓑ Ⓒ Ⓓ Ⓔ
11. Ⓐ Ⓑ Ⓒ Ⓓ Ⓔ
12. Ⓐ Ⓑ Ⓒ Ⓓ Ⓔ
13. Ⓐ Ⓑ Ⓒ Ⓓ Ⓔ
14. Ⓐ Ⓑ Ⓒ Ⓓ Ⓔ
15. Ⓐ Ⓑ Ⓒ Ⓓ Ⓔ
16. Ⓐ Ⓑ Ⓒ Ⓓ Ⓔ
17. Ⓐ Ⓑ Ⓒ Ⓓ Ⓔ
18. Ⓐ Ⓑ Ⓒ Ⓓ Ⓔ
19. Ⓐ Ⓑ Ⓒ Ⓓ Ⓔ
20. Ⓐ Ⓑ Ⓒ Ⓓ Ⓔ
21. Ⓐ Ⓑ Ⓒ Ⓓ Ⓔ
22. Ⓐ Ⓑ Ⓒ Ⓓ Ⓔ
23. Ⓐ Ⓑ Ⓒ Ⓓ Ⓔ
24. Ⓐ Ⓑ Ⓒ Ⓓ Ⓔ
25. Ⓐ Ⓑ Ⓒ Ⓓ Ⓔ
26. Ⓐ Ⓑ Ⓒ Ⓓ Ⓔ
27. Ⓐ Ⓑ Ⓒ Ⓓ Ⓔ
28. Ⓐ Ⓑ Ⓒ Ⓓ Ⓔ
29. Ⓐ Ⓑ Ⓒ Ⓓ Ⓔ
30. Ⓐ Ⓑ Ⓒ Ⓓ Ⓔ

31. Ⓐ Ⓑ Ⓒ Ⓓ Ⓔ
32. Ⓐ Ⓑ Ⓒ Ⓓ Ⓔ
33. Ⓐ Ⓑ Ⓒ Ⓓ Ⓔ
34. Ⓐ Ⓑ Ⓒ Ⓓ Ⓔ
35. Ⓐ Ⓑ Ⓒ Ⓓ Ⓔ
36. Ⓐ Ⓑ Ⓒ Ⓓ Ⓔ
37. Ⓐ Ⓑ Ⓒ Ⓓ Ⓔ
38. Ⓐ Ⓑ Ⓒ Ⓓ Ⓔ
39. Ⓐ Ⓑ Ⓒ Ⓓ Ⓔ
40. Ⓐ Ⓑ Ⓒ Ⓓ Ⓔ
41. Ⓐ Ⓑ Ⓒ Ⓓ Ⓔ
42. Ⓐ Ⓑ Ⓒ Ⓓ Ⓔ
43. Ⓐ Ⓑ Ⓒ Ⓓ Ⓔ
44. Ⓐ Ⓑ Ⓒ Ⓓ Ⓔ
45. Ⓐ Ⓑ Ⓒ Ⓓ Ⓔ
46. Ⓐ Ⓑ Ⓒ Ⓓ Ⓔ
47. Ⓐ Ⓑ Ⓒ Ⓓ Ⓔ
48. Ⓐ Ⓑ Ⓒ Ⓓ Ⓔ
49. Ⓐ Ⓑ Ⓒ Ⓓ Ⓔ
50. Ⓐ Ⓑ Ⓒ Ⓓ Ⓔ
51. Ⓐ Ⓑ Ⓒ Ⓓ Ⓔ
52. Ⓐ Ⓑ Ⓒ Ⓓ Ⓔ
53. Ⓐ Ⓑ Ⓒ Ⓓ Ⓔ
54. Ⓐ Ⓑ Ⓒ Ⓓ Ⓔ
55. Ⓐ Ⓑ Ⓒ Ⓓ Ⓔ
56. Ⓐ Ⓑ Ⓒ Ⓓ Ⓔ
57. Ⓐ Ⓑ Ⓒ Ⓓ Ⓔ
58. Ⓐ Ⓑ Ⓒ Ⓓ Ⓔ
59. Ⓐ Ⓑ Ⓒ Ⓓ Ⓔ
60. Ⓐ Ⓑ Ⓒ Ⓓ Ⓔ

61. Ⓐ Ⓑ Ⓒ Ⓓ Ⓔ
62. Ⓐ Ⓑ Ⓒ Ⓓ Ⓔ
63. Ⓐ Ⓑ Ⓒ Ⓓ Ⓔ
64. Ⓐ Ⓑ Ⓒ Ⓓ Ⓔ
65. Ⓐ Ⓑ Ⓒ Ⓓ Ⓔ
66. Ⓐ Ⓑ Ⓒ Ⓓ Ⓔ
67. Ⓐ Ⓑ Ⓒ Ⓓ Ⓔ
68. Ⓐ Ⓑ Ⓒ Ⓓ Ⓔ
69. Ⓐ Ⓑ Ⓒ Ⓓ Ⓔ
70. Ⓐ Ⓑ Ⓒ Ⓓ Ⓔ
71. Ⓐ Ⓑ Ⓒ Ⓓ Ⓔ
72. Ⓐ Ⓑ Ⓒ Ⓓ Ⓔ
73. Ⓐ Ⓑ Ⓒ Ⓓ Ⓔ
74. Ⓐ Ⓑ Ⓒ Ⓓ Ⓔ
75. Ⓐ Ⓑ Ⓒ Ⓓ Ⓔ
76. Ⓐ Ⓑ Ⓒ Ⓓ Ⓔ
77. Ⓐ Ⓑ Ⓒ Ⓓ Ⓔ
78. Ⓐ Ⓑ Ⓒ Ⓓ Ⓔ
79. Ⓐ Ⓑ Ⓒ Ⓓ Ⓔ
80. Ⓐ Ⓑ Ⓒ Ⓓ Ⓔ
81. Ⓐ Ⓑ Ⓒ Ⓓ Ⓔ
82. Ⓐ Ⓑ Ⓒ Ⓓ Ⓔ
83. Ⓐ Ⓑ Ⓒ Ⓓ Ⓔ
84. Ⓐ Ⓑ Ⓒ Ⓓ Ⓔ
85. Ⓐ Ⓑ Ⓒ Ⓓ Ⓔ
86. Ⓐ Ⓑ Ⓒ Ⓓ Ⓔ
87. Ⓐ Ⓑ Ⓒ Ⓓ Ⓔ
88. Ⓐ Ⓑ Ⓒ Ⓓ Ⓔ

[This page intentionally blank.]

NUMBER SERIES/EXAM 2   **TIME: 20 MINUTES**

1. 5   15   30   10   45   60   15   75   ___   ___
    A. 80, 20
    B. 90, 20
    C. 20, 85
    D. 90, 30
    E. 85, 30

2. 2   4   6   6   9   12   12   16   ___   ___
    A. 16, 20
    B. 16, 16
    C. 20, 20
    D. 16, 18
    E. 18, 18

3. 9   26   13   7   13   26   5   26   13   3   13   ___   ___
    A. 26, 1
    B. 13, 26
    C. 26, 13
    D. 26, 3
    E. 26, 0

4. 5   10   10   9   15   20   8   7   ___   ___
    A. 6, 25
    B. 25, 6
    C. 25, 10
    D. 25, 30
    E. 6, 30

5. 33   26   28   30   23   34   ___   ___
    A. 17, 38
    B. 18, 37
    C. 20, 28
    D. 38, 18
    E. 18, 38

6. 27   1   1   30   1   2   34   1   3   39   1   ___   ___
    A. 45, 1
    B. 45, 4
    C. 44, 4
    D. 43, 4
    E. 4, 45

7. 1   2   2   3   4   4   8   5   ___   ___
    A. 12, 6
    B. 10, 4
    C. 16, 6
    D. 20, 4
    E. 12, 18

8. 1   1   4   5   16   25   __   __
    A. 64, 125
    B. 62, 120
    C. 54, 125
    D. 52, 120
    E. 74, 115

9. 14   3   3   12   6   6   10   9   __   __
    A. 9, 9
    B. 9, 8
    C. 8, 8
    D. 10, 10
    E. 9, 11

10. 41   40   39   37   40   34   30   25   39   19   __   __
    A. 12, 4
    B. 12, 38
    C. 38, 12
    D. 13, 3
    E. 3, 13

11. 4   6   10   12   16   18   __   __
    A. 20, 24
    B. 23, 23
    C. 20, 22
    D. 22, 24
    E. 22, 22

12. 32   40   1   37   39   1   42   38   1   __   __
    A. 47, 1
    B. 47, 37
    C. 1, 47
    D. 40, 1
    E. 40, 42

13. 22   5   6   7   23   5   6   7   24   __   __
    A. 6, 7
    B. 6, 25
    C. 5, 6
    D. 7, 25
    E. 5, 7

14. 60   63   55   60   46   36   60   25   __   __
    A. 60, 13
    B. 12, 60
    C. 13, 60
    D. 14, 60
    E. 60, 14

15. 70   44   48   67   64   52   56   61   58   60   ___   ___

    A.   55, 60
    B.   64, 55
    C.   60, 55
    D.   62, 53
    E.   62, 55

16. 9   2   2   2   12   10   9   3   3   3   12   10   ___   ___

    A.   9, 3
    B.   8, 4
    C.   9, 5
    D.   9, 4
    E.   9, 10

17. 1   0   5   3   0   6   9   0   7   27   0   ___   ___

    A.   8, 72
    B.   81, 0
    C.   72, 0
    D.   8, 80
    E.   8, 81

18. 42   37   40   37   38   38   37   38   39   36   37   38   39   ___   ___

    A.   40, 34
    B.   39, 34
    C.   38, 33
    D.   38, 34
    E.   37, 36

19. 12   14   15   14   14   15   16   15   16   16   17   ___   ___

    A.   16, 17
    B.   17, 19
    C.   17, 20
    D.   16, 18
    E.   18, 16

20. 2   4   4   6   6   6   8   8   ___   ___

    A.   8, 8
    B.   8, 10
    C.   10, 8
    D.   8, 12
    E.   12, 12

21. 0   55   57   60   10   64   69   75   ___   ___

    A.   82, 89
    B.   89, 82
    C.   20, 82
    D.   82, 22
    E.   82, 84

22. 25   26   23   23   18   15   21   10   ___ ___

    A.   19, 7
    B.   7, 20
    C.   8, 19
    D.   8, 20
    E.   7, 19

23. 21   7   7   14   14   14   7   21   ___ ___

    A.   21, 7
    B.   20, 0
    C.   14, 0
    D.   14, 14
    E.   21, 0

24. 12   30   32   28   12   40   42   38   12   50   52   48   12   60   ___ ___

    A.   62, 58
    B.   62, 12
    C.   58, 12
    D.   12, 62
    E.   12, 58

ANSWER SHEET TO NUMBER SERIES/EXAM 2

1. Ⓐ Ⓑ Ⓒ Ⓓ Ⓔ
2. Ⓐ Ⓑ Ⓒ Ⓓ Ⓔ
3. Ⓐ Ⓑ Ⓒ Ⓓ Ⓔ
4. Ⓐ Ⓑ Ⓒ Ⓓ Ⓔ
5. Ⓐ Ⓑ Ⓒ Ⓓ Ⓔ
6. Ⓐ Ⓑ Ⓒ Ⓓ Ⓔ
7. Ⓐ Ⓑ Ⓒ Ⓓ Ⓔ
8. Ⓐ Ⓑ Ⓒ Ⓓ Ⓔ

9. Ⓐ Ⓑ Ⓒ Ⓓ Ⓔ
10. Ⓐ Ⓑ Ⓒ Ⓓ Ⓔ
11. Ⓐ Ⓑ Ⓒ Ⓓ Ⓔ
12. Ⓐ Ⓑ Ⓒ Ⓓ Ⓔ
13. Ⓐ Ⓑ Ⓒ Ⓓ Ⓔ
14. Ⓐ Ⓑ Ⓒ Ⓓ Ⓔ
15. Ⓐ Ⓑ Ⓒ Ⓓ Ⓔ
16. Ⓐ Ⓑ Ⓒ Ⓓ Ⓔ

17. Ⓐ Ⓑ Ⓒ Ⓓ Ⓔ
18. Ⓐ Ⓑ Ⓒ Ⓓ Ⓔ
19. Ⓐ Ⓑ Ⓒ Ⓓ Ⓔ
20. Ⓐ Ⓑ Ⓒ Ⓓ Ⓔ
21. Ⓐ Ⓑ Ⓒ Ⓓ Ⓔ
22. Ⓐ Ⓑ Ⓒ Ⓓ Ⓔ
23. Ⓐ Ⓑ Ⓒ Ⓓ Ⓔ
24. Ⓐ Ⓑ Ⓒ Ⓓ Ⓔ

(This page may be removed to mark answers.)

[This page intentionally blank.]

FOLLOWING DIRECTIONS/EXAM 2

Note To Person Assisting In This Exam:

Remove from this test guide the pages of this exam that comprise the directions to be read out loud. The test applicant should be left with only the sample sheet and answer sheet. Read the following directions out loud at the suggested rate of 75-80 words per minute, pausing only where indicated in parentheses. Speak as clearly as possible: Once a statement has been read, it cannot be repeated.

Examine Sample 1. (Pause 2-3 seconds.) If 14 is less than the sum of 7 plus 7, write the letter D, as in "dog," beside the number shown. (Pause 2 seconds.) If 14 is greater than or equal to the sum I just mentioned, write the letter E, as in "elephant," beside the number shown. (Pause 2 seconds.) Now, go to your answer sheet and darken the number-letter combination you have chosen for the question. (Pause 5 seconds.)

Examine Sample 2. (Pause 2-3 seconds.) Write the number 22 in the large box and number 23 in the smaller box if the letter C, as in "cat," is in the smaller of the two circles in the sample. (Pause 5 seconds.) Otherwise, write the number 8 in the smaller circle shown and the number 80 in the larger circle. (Pause 5 seconds.) Now, go to your answer sheet and mark both number-letter combinations selected. (Pause 10 seconds.)

Examine Sample 2 again. (Pause 2-3 seconds.) If the letter A, as in "apple," is in a smaller box than the letter B, as in "boy," is in, and the letter D, as in "dog," is in the smaller circle, go to number 72 on your answer sheet and darken the letter E, as in "elephant." (Pause 5 seconds.) Otherwise, go to number 71 on your answer sheet and darken the letter E, as in "elephant." (Pause 5 seconds.)

Examine Sample 3. (Pause 2-3 seconds.) If the third number in the sample is the second largest and the last number is the smallest, write the letter B, as in "boy," beside the number 2. (Pause 2 seconds.) If not, write the letter D, as in "dog," beside the number 2. (Pause 2 seconds.) Darken the number-letter combination selected on your answer sheet. (Pause 5 seconds.)

Examine Sample 3 again. (Pause 2-3 seconds.) If the three smallest numbers add up to be less than the first number shown, go to number 27 on your answer sheet and darken the letter B, as in "boy." (Pause 5 seconds.) Otherwise, go to that same number on your answer sheet and darken the letter A, as in "apple." (Pause 5 seconds.)

Examine Sample 3 one more time. (Pause 2-3 seconds.) Draw a circle, square and triangle around the numbers 3, 30, and 1 respectively. (Pause 5 seconds.) Go to the same number that is within the square on your answer sheet and darken the letter C, as in "cat." (Pause 5 seconds.) Now, go to the same number that is within the triangle on your answer sheet and darken the letter D, as in "dog." (Pause 5 seconds.)

Examine Sample 4. (Pause 2-3 seconds.) Write the letter E, as in "elephant," beside the highest number shown if the fourth number is the lowest in the sample. (Pause 2 seconds.) Otherwise, write the letter A, as in "apple," beside the first number given. (Pause 2 seconds.) Now, go to your answer sheet and darken the number-letter combination chosen. (Pause 5 seconds.)

Examine Sample 5. (Pause 2-3 seconds.) Go to number 73 on your answer sheet and darken the only letter in this sample that is not enclosed in a geometric shape. (Pause 5 seconds.)

Examine Sample 5 again. (Pause 2-3 seconds.) If the letters B, E, and A are enclosed by a square, triangle, and circle respectively, go to number 12 on your answer sheet and darken the letter A, as in "apple." (Pause 5 seconds.) Otherwise, go to number 19 on your answer sheet and darken the letter shown in the triangle. (Pause 5 seconds.)

Examine Sample 6. (Pause 2-3 seconds.) Write the letter B, as in "boy," beside the first and last numbers. (Pause 5 seconds.) Write the letter C, as in "cat," beside the middle number. (Pause 2 seconds.) Now, go to your answer sheet and darken the letter D, as in "dog," on number 63. (Pause 5 seconds.)

Examine Sample 6 again. (Pause 2-3 seconds.) If the letter E, as in "elephant," is the fifth letter in the alphabet, write the number 56 beside the letter D, as in "dog." (Pause 2 seconds.) Otherwise, write the number 55 beside the letter E, as in "elephant." (Pause 2 seconds.) Now, go to your answer sheet and darken the number-letter combination you just made. (Pause 5 seconds.)

Examine Sample 7. (Pause 2-3 seconds.) The first two digits of each number represents a given mail route. If the number is 50 or higher, it represents a city route; 49 or less represents rural delivery. (Pause 2 seconds.) The last three digits of each number designate the number of households served by each route. (Pause 2 seconds.) If there are more than two city routes in the sample, go to number 86 on your answer sheet and darken the letter D, as in "dog." (Pause 5 seconds.) If there are only two rural routes shown in the sample, go to number 39 on your answer sheet and darken the letter B, as in "boy." (Pause 5 seconds.)

Examine Sample 7 again. (Pause 2-3 seconds.) Write the letters A, as in "apple," B, as in "boy," C, as in "cat," and E, as in "elephant," under the four numbers shown in the sample respectively. (Pause 5 seconds.) Go to number 38 on your answer sheet and darken the letter that corresponds to the route having the largest number of deliveries. (Pause 5 seconds.) Now, go to number 93 on your answer sheet and darken the letter that corresponds to the route having the second highest number of deliveries. (Pause 5 seconds.)

Examine Sample 8. (Pause 2-3 seconds.) Write the number 7 in the largest box that does not have an enclosed letter designation. (Pause 2 seconds.) Darken that number-letter combination on your answer sheet. (Pause 5 seconds.) Now, write the number 16 in the largest box and the number 91 in the smaller triangle. (Pause 2 seconds.) Darken both of these number-letter combinations on your answer sheet. (Pause 10 seconds.)

Examine Sample 9. (Pause 2-3 seconds.) Each of the figures shown represents the average time required of five different carriers to sort 1 foot of mail into letters or flats. (Pause 2 seconds.) Go to number 88 on your answer sheet and darken the letter that corresponds to the most efficient carrier. (Pause 5 seconds.) Now, determine which carrier is the slowest and go to number 43 on your answer sheet and darken the corresponding letter. (Pause 5 seconds.)

Examine Sample 10. (Pause 2-3 seconds.) Write the letter A, as in "apple," beneath the second earliest time shown. (Pause 2 seconds.) Look at the minutes after the hour of the same selection, and go to the same number on your answer sheet and darken the same letter you wrote on your sample sheet. (Pause 5 seconds.)

Examine Sample 10 again. (Pause 2-3 seconds.) Write the letter D, as in "dog," beneath the latest time shown. (Pause 2 seconds.) If there is more than an hour's difference between this time and the second latest time given, go to number 61 on your answer sheet and darken the letter C, as in "cat." (Pause 5 seconds.) Otherwise, go to number 3 on your answer sheet and darken the same letter you wrote beneath the latest time sample. (Pause 5 seconds.)

If 13 is less than 12 and 3 is greater than 4, go to number 77 on your answer sheet and darken the letter A, as in "apple." (Pause 5 seconds.) If the preceding statement was only half-true, go to number 74 on your answer sheet and darken the letter D, as in "dog." (Pause 5 seconds.) Otherwise, go to number 77 on your answer sheet and darken the letter E, as in "elephant." (Pause 5 seconds.)

If Monday precedes Sunday, and Tuesday precedes Wednesday, go to number 46 on your answer sheet and darken the letter A, as in "apple." (Pause 5 seconds.) If the statement made was only half-true, go to number 47 on your answer sheet and darken the letter E, as in "elephant." (Pause 5 seconds.) Otherwise, go to number 46 on your answer sheet and darken the letter B, as in "boy." (Pause 5 seconds.)

-END OF TEST-

FOLLOWING DIRECTIONS/EXAM 2 SAMPLES

1. 13_____

2.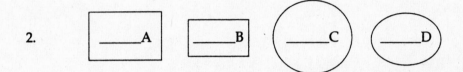

3. 15_____   3_____   30_____   2_____   45_____   1_____

4. 59_____   61_____   69_____   56_____   65_____

5. A   C   E   D   B

6. 47_____,   _____E,   53_____,   _____D,   62_____

7. 95723   10751   14210   87440

8. E   C   D   A   B

9.   E   D   C   B   A
      18.25   15.72   9.67   24.03   12.60

10. 8:15 AM   9:10 PM   8:15 PM   7:40 PM   7:15 AM
    _____   _____   _____   _____   _____

[This page intentionally blank.]

ANSWER SHEET TO FOLLOWING DIRECTIONS/EXAM 2

#						#						#					
1.	A	B	C	D	E	33.	A	B	C	D	E	65.	A	B	C	D	E
2.	A	B	C	D	E	34.	A	B	C	D	E	66.	A	B	C	D	E
3.	A	B	C	D	E	35.	A	B	C	D	E	67.	A	B	C	D	E
4.	A	B	C	D	E	36.	A	B	C	D	E	68.	A	B	C	D	E
5.	A	B	C	D	E	37.	A	B	C	D	E	69.	A	B	C	D	E
6.	A	B	C	D	E	38.	A	B	C	D	E	70.	A	B	C	D	E
7.	A	B	C	D	E	39.	A	B	C	D	E	71.	A	B	C	D	E
8.	A	B	C	D	E	40.	A	B	C	D	E	72.	A	B	C	D	E
9.	A	B	C	D	E	41.	A	B	C	D	E	73.	A	B	C	D	E
10.	A	B	C	D	E	42.	A	B	C	D	E	74.	A	B	C	D	E
11.	A	B	C	D	E	43.	A	B	C	D	E	75.	A	B	C	D	E
12.	A	B	C	D	E	44.	A	B	C	D	E	76.	A	B	C	D	E
13.	A	B	C	D	E	45.	A	B	C	D	E	77.	A	B	C	D	E
14.	A	B	C	D	E	46.	A	B	C	D	E	78.	A	B	C	D	E
15.	A	B	C	D	E	47.	A	B	C	D	E	79.	A	B	C	D	E
16.	A	B	C	D	E	48.	A	B	C	D	E	80.	A	B	C	D	E
17.	A	B	C	D	E	49.	A	B	C	D	E	81.	A	B	C	D	E
18.	A	B	C	D	E	50.	A	B	C	D	E	82.	A	B	C	D	E
19.	A	B	C	D	E	51.	A	B	C	D	E	83.	A	B	C	D	E
20.	A	B	C	D	E	52.	A	B	C	D	E	84.	A	B	C	D	E
21.	A	B	C	D	E	53.	A	B	C	D	E	85.	A	B	C	D	E
22.	A	B	C	D	E	54.	A	B	C	D	E	86.	A	B	C	D	E
23.	A	B	C	D	E	55.	A	B	C	D	E	87.	A	B	C	D	E
24.	A	B	C	D	E	56.	A	B	C	D	E	88.	A	B	C	D	E
25.	A	B	C	D	E	57.	A	B	C	D	E	89.	A	B	C	D	E
26.	A	B	C	D	E	58.	A	B	C	D	E	90.	A	B	C	D	E
27.	A	B	C	D	E	59.	A	B	C	D	E	91.	A	B	C	D	E
28.	A	B	C	D	E	60.	A	B	C	D	E	92.	A	B	C	D	E
29.	A	B	C	D	E	61.	A	B	C	D	E	93.	A	B	C	D	E
30.	A	B	C	D	E	62.	A	B	C	D	E	94.	A	B	C	D	E
31.	A	B	C	D	E	63.	A	B	C	D	E	95.	A	B	C	D	E
32.	A	B	C	D	E	64.	A	B	C	D	E						

(This page may be removed to mark answers.)

[This page intentionally blank.]

ANSWERS TO ADDRESS CROSS COMPARISON/EXAM 2

1.	D	33.	A	65.	D
2.	D	34.	A	66.	D
3.	A	35.	D	67.	D
4.	D	36.	A	68.	D
5.	D	37.	D	69.	A
6.	A	38.	D	70.	D
7.	D	39.	D	71.	A
8.	D	40.	D	72.	D
9.	A	41.	D	73.	D
10.	D	42.	D	74.	D
11.	D	43.	D	75.	A
12.	D	44.	D	76.	D
13.	D	45.	A	77.	D
14.	D	46.	D	78.	D
15.	D	47.	D	79.	D
16.	A	48.	D	80.	D
17.	D	49.	D	81.	A
18.	D	50.	D	82.	D
19.	A	51.	A	83.	D
20.	D	52.	D	84.	D
21.	D	53.	D	85.	A
22.	A	54.	D	86.	D
23.	D	55.	D	87.	D
24.	A	56.	D	88.	D
25.	A	57.	D	89.	A
26.	D	58.	A	90.	D
27.	D	59.	A	91.	A
28.	A	60.	D	92.	D
29.	D	61.	A	93.	D
30.	D	62.	D	94.	A
31.	A	63.	D	95.	D
32.	D	64.	A		

ANSWERS TO MEMORIZATION/EXAM 2

1.	E	31.	A	61.	B
2.	A	32.	A	62.	A
3.	C	33.	C	63.	B
4.	A	34.	D	64.	E
5.	D	35.	A	65.	A
6.	A	36.	B	66.	B
7.	D	37.	C	67.	C
8.	C	38.	C	68.	C
9.	E	39.	C	69.	E
10.	C	40.	D	70.	E
11.	E	41.	E	71.	E
12.	D	42.	D	72.	A
13.	B	43.	D	73.	E
14.	D	44.	B	74.	D
15.	C	45.	A	75.	C
16.	D	46.	E	76.	D
17.	A	47.	D	77.	B
18.	C	48.	A	78.	E
19.	A	49.	B	79.	D
20.	E	50.	E	80.	A
21.	B	51.	C	81.	C
22.	B	52.	E	82.	B
23.	B	53.	A	83.	B
24.	D	54.	C	84.	E
25.	D	55.	D	85.	A
26.	E	56.	B	86.	C
27.	D	57.	D	87.	B
28.	B	58.	D	88.	C
29.	B	59.	E		
30.	D	60.	A		

ANSWERS TO NUMBER SERIES/EXAM 2

1. B.
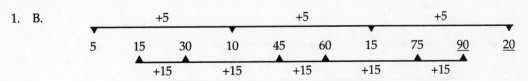

2. C.
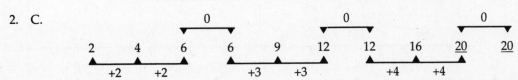

3. A.
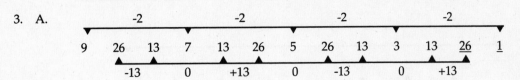

4. D.
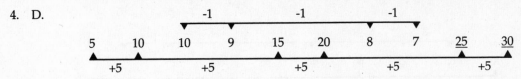

5. E.
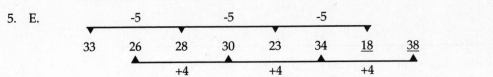

6. E.
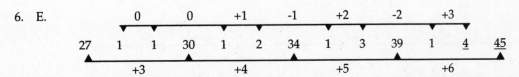

7. C.
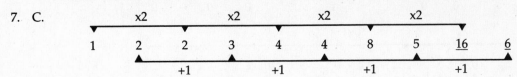

8. A.
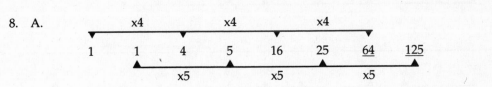

9. B.
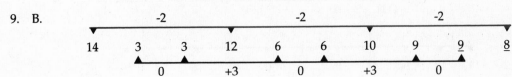

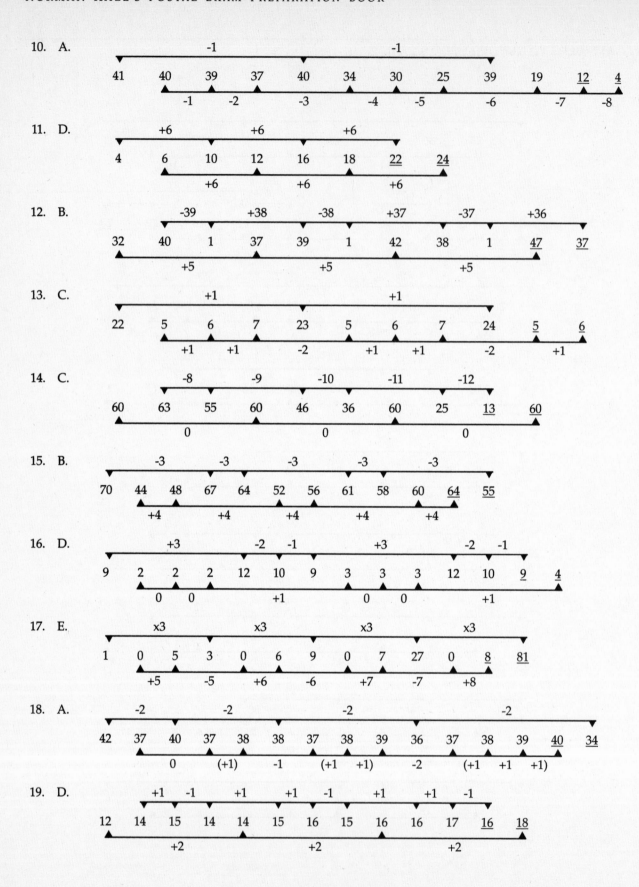

20. A.

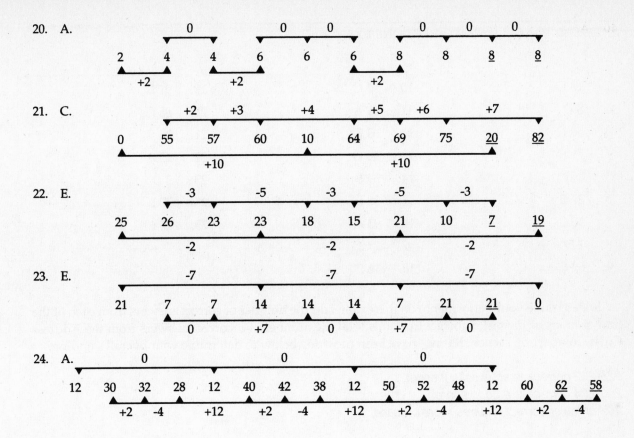

21. C.

22. E.

23. E.

24. A.

ANSWERS TO FOLLOWING DIRECTIONS/EXAM 2

1.	13 E	10.	73 C	19.	91 B
2.	8 D	11.	19 A	20.	88 C
3.	80 C	12.	63 D	21.	43 B
4.	71 E	13.	56 D	22.	15 A
5.	2 B	14.	39 B	23.	3 D
6.	27 B	15.	38 B	24.	77 E
7.	30 C	16.	93 A	25.	47 E
8.	1 D	17.	7 C		
9.	69 E	18.	16 E		

To determine your performance on this exam, add the number of correct answers from each of the four sections of the test. Subtract from this total the number of incorrect answers from the Address Cross Comparison section. Ratings have been provided below to determine your overall standing.

225-232 correct, is an excellent score.
208-224 correct, is a good score.
207 or fewer correct requires more practice.

Exam 3

**DO NOT OPEN THIS TEST BOOKLET UNTIL
YOU ARE TOLD TO START BY THE INDIVIDUAL
ASSISTING YOU IN THIS EXERCISE.**

[This page intentionally blank.]

1.	Franklin Ave. SW	Franklin Dr. SW
2.	1011 Tripp St.	1011 Trip St.
3.	Chickasaw, MS 43506	Chickasaw, MS 43506
4.	Bonneville Road S.	Boneville Road S.
5.	Pleasant Dr. SE	Pleasant Dr. SE
6.	111-D Beatrice Apts.	777-D Beatrice Apts.
7.	Aurora, KY 25344	Aurora, KY 25844
8.	65783 Baton Rouge Ave.	65783 Baton Rogue Ave.
9.	2095 Serenade Way	2095 Serenade Way
10.	129 Sunset Lane	129 Sunset Lane
11.	Lake Minetonka, MN	Lake Minnetonka, MN
12.	8760 State Hiway 303	8760 State Hiway 303
13.	147 Wycoff S.	147 Wycoff S.
14.	1913 Gregory Blvd.	1913 Gregory Lane
15.	Star Rt. 2, Box 2144	Star Rt. 2, Box 2414
16.	13058 Olalla Valley Dr.	13058 Olalla Valley Dr.
17.	4189 NE Papoose Pt.	4819 NE Papoose Pt.
18.	Portland, Ore. 87483	Portland, Ore. 87783
19.	Oroville, Calif.	Oroville, Calif.
20.	2222 Schley Blvd.	2222 Shley Blvd.
21.	3315 Olympus Ave.	3315 Olympus Ave.
22.	630 N. Towne Pl.	630 N. Town Pl.
23.	1130 Gattling Dr.	1113 Gattling Dr.

24.	Sioux City, Ia. 54050	Sioux City, Ia. 54050
25.	245 4th Ave.	245 4th Ave.
26.	84-D Turnquist Ave.	84-D Turnquist Ave.
27.	808 Brashem Way	880 Brashem Way
28.	Saskatoon, Canada	Sascatoon, Canada
29.	North Platte, Neb.	North Platte, NE
30.	Twin Falls, ID 83091	Twin Falls, ID 83091
31.	Corpus Christi, TX	Corpus Christi, Texas
32.	San Bernadino, CA	San Bernadine, CA
33.	Phoenix, Ariz. 85020	Phoenix, Ariz. 85020
34.	3012 Ridgeview Dr.	3012 Ridgeview Dr.
35.	631 Charlette Rd.	631 Charlotte Rd.
36.	101-E Buckthorn	101-D Buckthorn
37.	324 Constitution Ln.	324 Constetution Ln.
38.	Yreka, CA	Yreka, CA
39.	383 Pinecone Ct.	838 Pinecone Ct.
40.	Powhaton Point, Ohio	Powhaton Point, Ohio
41.	10011 Richmond Rd.	100111 Richmond Rd.
42.	Zanesville, Ohio 53420	Zanesvile, Ohio 53420
43.	Madison, WI 49509	Madeson, WI 49509
44.	Eastview Dr. SW	Eastveiw Ave. SW
45.	9955 Fredrickson Ln.	5599 Fredrickson Ln.
46.	Enumclaw, Wash. 98177	Enumclaw, Wash. 48577
47.	1352 Lafayette N.	1352 Lafayette N.
48.	77-B Hemlock Pl.	77-B Hemlock Pl.

49.	29443 Clover Blossom Rd.	29443 Clover Blossum Rd.
50.	5050 Dibb	5050 Dibb
51.	Multnomah, ORE 91507	Multnomah, ORE 91570
52.	Perrysburg, Penn 12744	Perysburg, Penn 12744
53.	Oakwood Dr. NE	Oakwood Dr. NE
54.	S. Bentwer Way	S. Benter Way
55.	111 Caldwell Ct.	111 Caldwell Ct.
56.	Almonesson, New Jersey	Almoneson, New Jersey
57.	6699 Falner Dr.	6699 Falkner Dr.
58.	222 Utica Place	222 Utica Place
59.	Ballantine, Mont. 54533	Ballantine, Mont. 54533
60.	S. Michigan Ave.	N. Michigan Ave.
61.	Bay Springs, Miss.	Bay Springs, Miss.
62.	Cedar Rapids, Ia.	Cedar Rapids, Iowa
63.	122 Cambrian SW	122 Cambrean SW
64.	3217 Perry	3217 Perry
65.	16-A Sunset Beach	16-A Sunset Beach
66.	4288 Russell Rd.	4288 Russell Rd.
67.	3007 Kennedy St.	3007 Kennedy St.
68.	7774 Altar Vista	7747 Altar Vista
69.	Missionary Pt., NM	Missionary Pt., NM
70.	Aberdeen, MD 04883	Aberden, MD 04883
71.	2814 Sierra Rd.	2814 Sierra Rd.
72.	444 Aegean Blvd.	4444 Aegean Blvd.
73.	7911 Manchester	7911 Manchester

#		
74.	Aleknagnik, Alaska	Aleknagic, Alaska
75.	147 Sereno Cr. Dr.	147 Cereno Cr. Dr.
76.	806 High St.	806 High St.
77.	202 Hoover Pl.	222 Hoover Pl.
78.	Ahwahnee, Calif.	Ahwohnee, Calif.
79.	Payton Ave. NE	Payton Ave. NE
80.	702 Cline	702 Kline
81.	154 Cherrywood Ln.	154 Cherrywood Ln.
82.	1240 8th Ave.	1240 8th St.
83.	Beautford Way E.	Beautford Way E.
84.	444 4th St.	44 44th St.
85.	1699-1/2 Corning Ct.	1699-1/2 Cornning Ct.
86.	1818 Belmont	1818 Belmont
87.	Bennett, Colo. 67011	Benett, Colo. 67011
88.	3060 N. McWilliams	3060 S. McWilliams
89.	11 Goldenrod Cr.	12 Goldenrod Cr.
90.	SW Lakehurst Dr.	SW Lakehurst Dr.
91.	Boncher Way	Boncher Way
92.	910 Sidney	901 Sidney
93.	33481 Jocobsen Blvd.	33481 Jacobson Blvd.
94.	Waimanalo Beach HI	Waimanalo Beach HI
95.	209 Hobb St.	209 Hobb St.

ANSWER SHEET TO ADDRESS CROSS COMPARISON/EXAM 3

1. (A) (D)		33. (A) (D)		65. (A) (D)	
2. (A) (D)		34. (A) (D)		66. (A) (D)	
3. (A) (D)		35. (A) (D)		67. (A) (D)	
4. (A) (D)		36. (A) (D)		68. (A) (D)	
5. (A) (D)		37. (A) (D)		69. (A) (D)	
6. (A) (D)		38. (A) (D)		70. (A) (D)	
7. (A) (D)		39. (A) (D)		71. (A) (D)	
8. (A) (D)		40. (A) (D)		72. (A) (D)	
9. (A) (D)		41. (A) (D)		73. (A) (D)	
10. (A) (D)		42. (A) (D)		74. (A) (D)	
11. (A) (D)		43. (A) (D)		75. (A) (D)	
12. (A) (D)		44. (A) (D)		76. (A) (D)	
13. (A) (D)		45. (A) (D)		77. (A) (D)	
14. (A) (D)		46. (A) (D)		78. (A) (D)	
15. (A) (D)		47. (A) (D)		79. (A) (D)	
16. (A) (D)		48. (A) (D)		80. (A) (D)	
17. (A) (D)		49. (A) (D)		81. (A) (D)	
18. (A) (D)		50. (A) (D)		82. (A) (D)	
19. (A) (D)		51. (A) (D)		83. (A) (D)	
20. (A) (D)		52. (A) (D)		84. (A) (D)	
21. (A) (D)		53. (A) (D)		85. (A) (D)	
22. (A) (D)		54. (A) (D)		86. (A) (D)	
23. (A) (D)		55. (A) (D)		87. (A) (D)	
24. (A) (D)		56. (A) (D)		88. (A) (D)	
25. (A) (D)		57. (A) (D)		89. (A) (D)	
26. (A) (D)		58. (A) (D)		90. (A) (D)	
27. (A) (D)		59. (A) (D)		91. (A) (D)	
28. (A) (D)		60. (A) (D)		92. (A) (D)	
29. (A) (D)		61. (A) (D)		93. (A) (D)	
30. (A) (D)		62. (A) (D)		94. (A) (D)	
31. (A) (D)		63. (A) (D)		95. (A) (D)	
32. (A) (D)		64. (A) (D)			

(This page may be removed to mark answers.)

[This page intentionally blank.]

MEMORIZATION/EXAM 3

A	B	C	D	E
1700-1799 Straton	2500-2599 Straton	2200-2299 Straton	1400-1499 Straton	1100-1199 Straton
Northern Dr.	Belmont Ln.	Meadowbrook	Lowry Ave.	Buckner
2500-2599 King	1700-1799 King	1400-1499 King	1100-1199 King	2200-2299 King
Prairie Dr.	Conifer Ct.	Juniper	Wright Ave.	Snyder Blvd.
2200-2299 Knox	1400-1499 Knox	1100-1199 Knox	1700-1799 Knox	2500-2599 Knox

NOTE: Follow the same step by step format established for the memorization exercises studied earlier. (See page 41.)

PRACTICE MEMORIZATION/EXAM 3

STEP 2 TIME: 3 MINUTES
STEP 3 TIME: 3 MINUTES (cover key)

A	B	C	D	E
1700-1799 Straton Northern Dr. 2500-2599 King Prairie Dr. 2200-2299 Knox	2500-2599 Straton Belmont Ln. 1700-1799 King Conifer Ct. 1400-1499 Knox	2200-2299 Straton Meadowbrook 1400-1499 King Juniper 1100-1199 Knox	1400-1499 Straton Lowry Ave. 1100-1199 King Wright Ave. 1700-1799 Knox	1100-1199 Straton Buckner 2200-2299 King Snyder Blvd. 2500-2599 Knox

1. 1700-1799 King
2. 1700-1799 Straton
3. 1100-1199 Knox
4. Northern Dr.
5. Belmont Ln.
6. Conifer Ct.
7. 1400-1499 Straton
8. 2500-2599 King
9. Prairie Dr.
10. Meadowbrook
11. 2500-2599 Straton
12. 2200-2299 King
13. Buckner
14. Juniper
15. 2500-2599 Knox
16. 1400-1499 King
17. Lowry Ave.
18. 2500-2599 Knox
19. 1100-1199 Straton
20. Conifer Ct.
21. Buckner
22. 2200-2299 King
23. Prairie Dr.
24. Juniper
25. Snyder Blvd.
26. 1100-1199 Knox
27. 1700-1799 Straton
28. Meadowbrook
29. 2200-2299 Straton
30. 2500-2599 King

31. Northern Dr.
32. 1400-1499 Knox
33. 2500-2599 Straton
34. Lowry Ave.
35. 2200-2299 King
36. Belmont Ln.
37. Wright Ave.
38. 1400-1499 King
39. 1700-1799 Knox
40. 1400-1499 Straton
41. Snyder Blvd.
42. Northern Dr.
43. 1100-1199 Straton
44. 2200-2299 Knox
45. 1700-1799 King
46. Belmont Ln.
47. Prairie Dr.
48. Wright Ave.
49. 1400-1499 King
50. 2500-2599 Straton
51. 1100-1199 Knox
52. Meadowbrook
53. Lowry Ave.
54. Conifer Ct.
55. 1400-1499 Knox
56. Buckner
57. 1100-1199 King
58. 2500-2599 Knox
59. 1700-1799 Straton
60. 2200-2299 Knox

61. Wright Ave.
62. 1400-1499 King
63. 2200-2299 Straton
64. Meadowbrook
65. Snyder Blvd.
66. 2500-2599 King
67. 2200-2299 Knox
68. 1700-1799 Straton
69. Belmont Ln.
70. Juniper
71. 1100-1199 Straton
72. 1700-1799 Knox
73. 1100-1199 King
74. Prairie Dr.
75. Conifer Ct.
76. 2500-2599 Knox
77. 1400-1499 Straton
78. 1400-1499 Knox
79. 2200-2299 Knox
80. Wright Ave.
81. Juniper
82. Snyder Blvd.
83. 1700-1799 King
84. Northern Dr.
85. Lowry Ave.
86. 1100-1199 King
87. 2200-2299 Straton
88. Buckner

PRACTICE ANSWER SHEET TO MEMORIZATION/EXAM 3

1. Ⓐ Ⓑ Ⓒ Ⓓ Ⓔ	31. Ⓐ Ⓑ Ⓒ Ⓓ Ⓔ	61. Ⓐ Ⓑ Ⓒ Ⓓ Ⓔ
2. Ⓐ Ⓑ Ⓒ Ⓓ Ⓔ	32. Ⓐ Ⓑ Ⓒ Ⓓ Ⓔ	62. Ⓐ Ⓑ Ⓒ Ⓓ Ⓔ
3. Ⓐ Ⓑ Ⓒ Ⓓ Ⓔ	33. Ⓐ Ⓑ Ⓒ Ⓓ Ⓔ	63. Ⓐ Ⓑ Ⓒ Ⓓ Ⓔ
4. Ⓐ Ⓑ Ⓒ Ⓓ Ⓔ	34. Ⓐ Ⓑ Ⓒ Ⓓ Ⓔ	64. Ⓐ Ⓑ Ⓒ Ⓓ Ⓔ
5. Ⓐ Ⓑ Ⓒ Ⓓ Ⓔ	35. Ⓐ Ⓑ Ⓒ Ⓓ Ⓔ	65. Ⓐ Ⓑ Ⓒ Ⓓ Ⓔ
6. Ⓐ Ⓑ Ⓒ Ⓓ Ⓔ	36. Ⓐ Ⓑ Ⓒ Ⓓ Ⓔ	66. Ⓐ Ⓑ Ⓒ Ⓓ Ⓔ
7. Ⓐ Ⓑ Ⓒ Ⓓ Ⓔ	37. Ⓐ Ⓑ Ⓒ Ⓓ Ⓔ	67. Ⓐ Ⓑ Ⓒ Ⓓ Ⓔ
8. Ⓐ Ⓑ Ⓒ Ⓓ Ⓔ	38. Ⓐ Ⓑ Ⓒ Ⓓ Ⓔ	68. Ⓐ Ⓑ Ⓒ Ⓓ Ⓔ
9. Ⓐ Ⓑ Ⓒ Ⓓ Ⓔ	39. Ⓐ Ⓑ Ⓒ Ⓓ Ⓔ	69. Ⓐ Ⓑ Ⓒ Ⓓ Ⓔ
10. Ⓐ Ⓑ Ⓒ Ⓓ Ⓔ	40. Ⓐ Ⓑ Ⓒ Ⓓ Ⓔ	70. Ⓐ Ⓑ Ⓒ Ⓓ Ⓔ
11. Ⓐ Ⓑ Ⓒ Ⓓ Ⓔ	41. Ⓐ Ⓑ Ⓒ Ⓓ Ⓔ	71. Ⓐ Ⓑ Ⓒ Ⓓ Ⓔ
12. Ⓐ Ⓑ Ⓒ Ⓓ Ⓔ	42. Ⓐ Ⓑ Ⓒ Ⓓ Ⓔ	72. Ⓐ Ⓑ Ⓒ Ⓓ Ⓔ
13. Ⓐ Ⓑ Ⓒ Ⓓ Ⓔ	43. Ⓐ Ⓑ Ⓒ Ⓓ Ⓔ	73. Ⓐ Ⓑ Ⓒ Ⓓ Ⓔ
14. Ⓐ Ⓑ Ⓒ Ⓓ Ⓔ	44. Ⓐ Ⓑ Ⓒ Ⓓ Ⓔ	74. Ⓐ Ⓑ Ⓒ Ⓓ Ⓔ
15. Ⓐ Ⓑ Ⓒ Ⓓ Ⓔ	45. Ⓐ Ⓑ Ⓒ Ⓓ Ⓔ	75. Ⓐ Ⓑ Ⓒ Ⓓ Ⓔ
16. Ⓐ Ⓑ Ⓒ Ⓓ Ⓔ	46. Ⓐ Ⓑ Ⓒ Ⓓ Ⓔ	76. Ⓐ Ⓑ Ⓒ Ⓓ Ⓔ
17. Ⓐ Ⓑ Ⓒ Ⓓ Ⓔ	47. Ⓐ Ⓑ Ⓒ Ⓓ Ⓔ	77. Ⓐ Ⓑ Ⓒ Ⓓ Ⓔ
18. Ⓐ Ⓑ Ⓒ Ⓓ Ⓔ	48. Ⓐ Ⓑ Ⓒ Ⓓ Ⓔ	78. Ⓐ Ⓑ Ⓒ Ⓓ Ⓔ
19. Ⓐ Ⓑ Ⓒ Ⓓ Ⓔ	49. Ⓐ Ⓑ Ⓒ Ⓓ Ⓔ	79. Ⓐ Ⓑ Ⓒ Ⓓ Ⓔ
20. Ⓐ Ⓑ Ⓒ Ⓓ Ⓔ	50. Ⓐ Ⓑ Ⓒ Ⓓ Ⓔ	80. Ⓐ Ⓑ Ⓒ Ⓓ Ⓔ
21. Ⓐ Ⓑ Ⓒ Ⓓ Ⓔ	51. Ⓐ Ⓑ Ⓒ Ⓓ Ⓔ	81. Ⓐ Ⓑ Ⓒ Ⓓ Ⓔ
22. Ⓐ Ⓑ Ⓒ Ⓓ Ⓔ	52. Ⓐ Ⓑ Ⓒ Ⓓ Ⓔ	82. Ⓐ Ⓑ Ⓒ Ⓓ Ⓔ
23. Ⓐ Ⓑ Ⓒ Ⓓ Ⓔ	53. Ⓐ Ⓑ Ⓒ Ⓓ Ⓔ	83. Ⓐ Ⓑ Ⓒ Ⓓ Ⓔ
24. Ⓐ Ⓑ Ⓒ Ⓓ Ⓔ	54. Ⓐ Ⓑ Ⓒ Ⓓ Ⓔ	84. Ⓐ Ⓑ Ⓒ Ⓓ Ⓔ
25. Ⓐ Ⓑ Ⓒ Ⓓ Ⓔ	55. Ⓐ Ⓑ Ⓒ Ⓓ Ⓔ	85. Ⓐ Ⓑ Ⓒ Ⓓ Ⓔ
26. Ⓐ Ⓑ Ⓒ Ⓓ Ⓔ	56. Ⓐ Ⓑ Ⓒ Ⓓ Ⓔ	86. Ⓐ Ⓑ Ⓒ Ⓓ Ⓔ
27. Ⓐ Ⓑ Ⓒ Ⓓ Ⓔ	57. Ⓐ Ⓑ Ⓒ Ⓓ Ⓔ	87. Ⓐ Ⓑ Ⓒ Ⓓ Ⓔ
28. Ⓐ Ⓑ Ⓒ Ⓓ Ⓔ	58. Ⓐ Ⓑ Ⓒ Ⓓ Ⓔ	88. Ⓐ Ⓑ Ⓒ Ⓓ Ⓔ
29. Ⓐ Ⓑ Ⓒ Ⓓ Ⓔ	59. Ⓐ Ⓑ Ⓒ Ⓓ Ⓔ	
30. Ⓐ Ⓑ Ⓒ Ⓓ Ⓔ	60. Ⓐ Ⓑ Ⓒ Ⓓ Ⓔ	

1. Meadowbrook	31. 1100-1199 Knox	61. 1700-1799 King
2. 1700-1799 Straton	32. Belmont Ln.	62. 2500-2599 Knox
3. 1700-1799 King	33. 2200-2299 Straton	63. Meadowbrook
4. Lowry Ave.	34. 1100-1199 King	64. Lowry Ave.
5. Belmont Ln.	35. Lowry Ave.	65. Juniper
6. 2200-2299 Knox	36. Buckner	66. 2500-2599 Straton
7. 2500-2599 Knox	37. 1700-1799 Straton	67. Prairie Dr.
8. Buckner	38. Prairie Dr.	68. 2200-2299 King
9. 1400-1499 Straton	39. Wright Ave.	69. Snyder Blvd.
10. 1100-1199 King	40. 2200-2299 King	70. 1400-1499 Knox
11. 1400-1499 Knox	41. 1400-1499 Knox	71. 1400-1499 King
12. Northern Dr.	42. Northern Dr.	72. 1400-1499 Straton
13. 2500-2599 King	43. 1700-1799 Knox	73. Meadowbrook
14. Prairie Dr.	44. 2200-2299 Straton	74. Juniper
15. Conifer Ct.	45. 1100-1199 King	75. 2500-2599 Straton
16. 2200-2299 Straton	46. 2500-2599 King	76. Buckner
17. 1100-1199 Knox	47. Juniper	77. Wright Ave.
18. 2200-2299 King	48. 2500-2599 Knox	78. 2500-2599 King
19. Snyder Blvd.	49. 1400-1499 King	79. 1100-1199 Knox
20. Meadowbrook	50. 1100-1199 Straton	80. Belmont Ln.
21. 1700-1799 Knox	51. Belmont Ln.	81. Prairie Dr.
22. 1100-1199 Straton	52. 2200-2299 Knox	82. Lowry Ave.
23. 1400-1499 King	53. 2500-2599 Straton	83. 1700-1799 Straton
24. 1400-1499 Knox	54. 1700-1799 Knox	84. 2500-2599 Knox
25. Wright Ave.	55. Northern Dr.	85. Northern Dr.
26. Conifer Ct.	56. 1100-1199 King	86. Snyder Blvd.
27. Juniper	57. Buckner	87. 2200-2299 Knox
28. 2500-2599 Straton	58. Conifer Ct.	88. Conifer Ct.
29. Snyder Blvd.	59. Wright Ave.	
30. 1700-1799 King	60. 1100-1199 Straton	

ANSWER SHEET TO MEMORIZATION/EXAM 3

1. A B C D E	31. A B C D E	61. A B C D E
2. A B C D E	32. A B C D E	62. A B C D E
3. A B C D E	33. A B C D E	63. A B C D E
4. A B C D E	34. A B C D E	64. A B C D E
5. A B C D E	35. A B C D E	65. A B C D E
6. A B C D E	36. A B C D E	66. A B C D E
7. A B C D E	37. A B C D E	67. A B C D E
8. A B C D E	38. A B C D E	68. A B C D E
9. A B C D E	39. A B C D E	69. A B C D E
10. A B C D E	40. A B C D E	70. A B C D E
11. A B C D E	41. A B C D E	71. A B C D E
12. A B C D E	42. A B C D E	72. A B C D E
13. A B C D E	43. A B C D E	73. A B C D E
14. A B C D E	44. A B C D E	74. A B C D E
15. A B C D E	45. A B C D E	75. A B C D E
16. A B C D E	46. A B C D E	76. A B C D E
17. A B C D E	47. A B C D E	77. A B C D E
18. A B C D E	48. A B C D E	78. A B C D E
19. A B C D E	49. A B C D E	79. A B C D E
20. A B C D E	50. A B C D E	80. A B C D E
21. A B C D E	51. A B C D E	81. A B C D E
22. A B C D E	52. A B C D E	82. A B C D E
23. A B C D E	53. A B C D E	83. A B C D E
24. A B C D E	54. A B C D E	84. A B C D E
25. A B C D E	55. A B C D E	85. A B C D E
26. A B C D E	56. A B C D E	86. A B C D E
27. A B C D E	57. A B C D E	87. A B C D E
28. A B C D E	58. A B C D E	88. A B C D E
29. A B C D E	59. A B C D E	
30. A B C D E	60. A B C D E	

[This page intentionally blank.]

NUMBER SERIES/EXAM 3   **TIME: 20 MINUTES**

---

1. 2   2   5   5   9   9   ___   ___
    A. 12, 12
    B. 13, 13
    C. 10, 10
    D. 15, 15
    E. 14, 14

2. 12   15   20   20   28   25   36   ___   ___
    A. 36, 44
    B. 30, 44
    C. 40, 42
    D. 40, 44
    E. 44, 44

3. 0   62   50   16   32   38   26   48   ___   ___
    A. 58, 14
    B. 64, 12
    C. 64, 14
    D. 14, 64
    E. 68, 20

4. 90   76   85   77   78   80   79   80   81   75   82   83   84   ___   ___
    A. 70, 85
    B. 85, 85
    C. 85, 70
    D. 75, 85
    E. 75, 75

5. 8   1   3   16   9   27   24   81   ___   ___
    A. 32, 243
    B. 240, 32
    C. 256, 30
    D. 256, 36
    E. 243, 32

6. 21   28   26   20   24   21   19   19   15   ___   ___
    A. 18, 13
    B. 13, 18
    C. 18, 18
    D. 17, 18
    E. 16, 17

7. 16   5   6   12   7   8   8   9   ___   ___
    A. 9, 4
    B. 4, 9
    C. 10, 5
    D. 10, 4
    E. 11, 6

---

8.   62   60   63   65   60   67   70   72   58   __   __

    A.   73, 75
    B.   75, 73
    C.   74, 76
    D.   74, 77
    E.   76, 76

9.   37   40   45   52   61   __   __

    A.   68, 78
    B.   69, 78
    C.   68, 80
    D.   72, 85
    E.   67, 77

10.   1   8   8   5   10   10   9   13   13   __   __

    A.   14, 17
    B.   13, 17
    C.   17, 17
    D.   15, 17
    E.   13, 15

11.   3   4   8   6   16   32   12   64   __   __

    A.   24, 128
    B.   18, 120
    C.   18, 64
    D.   128, 20
    E.   128, 24

12.   9   8   5   9   8   6   9   8   7   9   8   __   __

    A.   9, 8
    B.   8, 9
    C.   10, 9
    D.   9, 10
    E.   11, 10

13.   80   99   83   95   87   91   92   87   __   __

    A.   83, 96
    B.   96, 85
    C.   98, 83
    D.   97, 83
    E.   85, 85

14.   23   40   32   40   39   40   44   __   __

    A.   40, 47
    B.   47, 40
    C.   42, 47
    D.   46, 40
    E.   40, 48

15. 80 70 75 75 80 70 90 65 65 100 60 ___ ___
    A. 100, 55
    B. 110, 50
    C. 60, 55
    D. 100, 50
    E. 110, 55

16. 10 11 22 22 33 44 34 55 ___ ___
    A. 60, 50
    B. 60, 46
    C. 66, 44
    D. 65, 46
    E. 66, 46

17. 45 38 1 36 37 2 27 36 3 ___ ___
    A. 18, 4
    B. 18, 35
    C. 4, 18
    D. 16, 35
    E. 17, 35

18. 52 48 5 43 40 6 34 32 7 ___ ___
    A. 23, 24
    B. 25, 24
    C. 24, 25
    D. 26, 24
    E. 25, 25

19. 18 14 15 17 21 20 21 23 24 26 27 ___ ___
    A. 28, 27
    B. 29, 28
    C. 29, 27
    D. 28, 30
    E. 30, 32

20. 3 4 2 4 5 3 5 6 ___ ___
    A. 4, 6
    B. 6, 4
    C. 6, 5
    D. 5, 6
    E. 6, 7

21. 1 5 10 3 10 5 9 5 10 ___ ___
    A. 27, 10
    B. 27, 5
    C. 5, 27
    D. 27, 15
    E. 29, 10

22. 40   80   60   30   70   50   20   __   __

    A. 40, 60
    B. 50, 50
    C. 50, 60
    D. 60, 30
    E. 60, 40

23. 30   0   29   1   28   2   __   __

    A. 3, 27
    B. 30, 5
    C. 29, 1
    D. 27, 3
    E. 1, 29

24. 67   73   70   67   70   64   61   58   73   55   52   __   __

    A. 49, 52
    B. 52, 49
    C. 49, 76
    D. 50, 76
    E. 50. 75

ANSWER SHEET TO NUMBER SERIES/EXAM 3

1. Ⓐ Ⓑ Ⓒ Ⓓ Ⓔ
2. Ⓐ Ⓑ Ⓒ Ⓓ Ⓔ
3. Ⓐ Ⓑ Ⓒ Ⓓ Ⓔ
4. Ⓐ Ⓑ Ⓒ Ⓓ Ⓔ
5. Ⓐ Ⓑ Ⓒ Ⓓ Ⓔ
6. Ⓐ Ⓑ Ⓒ Ⓓ Ⓔ
7. Ⓐ Ⓑ Ⓒ Ⓓ Ⓔ
8. Ⓐ Ⓑ Ⓒ Ⓓ Ⓔ

9. Ⓐ Ⓑ Ⓒ Ⓓ Ⓔ
10. Ⓐ Ⓑ Ⓒ Ⓓ Ⓔ
11. Ⓐ Ⓑ Ⓒ Ⓓ Ⓔ
12. Ⓐ Ⓑ Ⓒ Ⓓ Ⓔ
13. Ⓐ Ⓑ Ⓒ Ⓓ Ⓔ
14. Ⓐ Ⓑ Ⓒ Ⓓ Ⓔ
15. Ⓐ Ⓑ Ⓒ Ⓓ Ⓔ
16. Ⓐ Ⓑ Ⓒ Ⓓ Ⓔ

17. Ⓐ Ⓑ Ⓒ Ⓓ Ⓔ
18. Ⓐ Ⓑ Ⓒ Ⓓ Ⓔ
19. Ⓐ Ⓑ Ⓒ Ⓓ Ⓔ
20. Ⓐ Ⓑ Ⓒ Ⓓ Ⓔ
21. Ⓐ Ⓑ Ⓒ Ⓓ Ⓔ
22. Ⓐ Ⓑ Ⓒ Ⓓ Ⓔ
23. Ⓐ Ⓑ Ⓒ Ⓓ Ⓔ
24. Ⓐ Ⓑ Ⓒ Ⓓ Ⓔ

(This page may be removed to mark answers.)

[This page intentionally blank.]

FOLLOWING DIRECTIONS/EXAM 3

Note To Person Assisting In This Exam:

Remove from this test guide the pages of this exam that comprise the directions to be read out loud. The test applicant should be left with only the sample sheet and answer sheet. Read the following directions our loud at the suggested rate of 75-80 words per minute, pausing only where indicated in parentheses. Speak as clearly as possible: Once a statement has been read, it cannot be repeated.

Examine Sample 1. (Pause 2-3 seconds.) Write the letter A, as in "apple," beside the fourth number if it has a line beside it and the preceding number does not. (Pause 2 seconds.) Otherwise, write the letter B, as in "boy," beside the fifth number in the sample. (Pause 2 seconds.) Darken this number-letter combination on your answer sheet. (Pause 5 seconds.)

Examine Sample 1 again. (Pause 2-3 seconds.) Write the letter C, as in "cat," beside the third highest number shown. (Pause 2-3 seconds.) If that number is less than or equal to 40, darken that same number-letter combination on your answer sheet. (Pause 5 seconds.) Otherwise, go to the second highest number shown in the sample and on that same number on your answer sheet, darken the letter E, as in "elephant." (Pause 5 seconds.)

Examine Sample 2. (Pause 2-3 seconds.) Write the letter D, as in "dog," beside the middle number shown in the sample if the preceding number is less and the number that immediately follows is greater. (Pause 2 seconds.) Otherwise, write the letter E, as in "elephant," beside the last number in the sample. (Pause 2 seconds.) Now, darken the number-letter combination you selected on your answer sheet. (Pause 5 seconds.)

Examine Sample 1. (Pause 2-3 seconds.) If the sixth number is less than the fifth number, go to number 18 on your answer sheet and darken the letter E, as in "elephant." (Pause 5 seconds.) If the opposite is true, go to number 40 on your answer sheet and darken the letter C, as in "cat." (Pause 5 seconds.)

Examine Sample 3. (Pause 2-3 seconds.) Each letter in this sample designates one of five different routes and its area of coverage. (Pause 2 seconds.) Go to number 86 on your answer sheet and darken the same letter of the route that has 1490 KINGSLEY AVE. as a delivery stop. (Pause 10 seconds.) Now, go to number 68 on your answer sheet and darken the same letter of the route that has 1500 KINGSLEY ST. as a delivery stop. (Pause 10 seconds.)

Examine Sample 3 again. (Pause 2-3 seconds.) Go to number 54 on your answer sheet and darken the letter that represents 1750-1825 KINGSLEY ST. (Pause 5 seconds.)

Examine Sample 2. (Pause 2-3 seconds.) If the second number is less than the first number and the third number is less than the fourth number, go to number 5 on your answer sheet and darken the letter A, as in "apple." (Pause 5 seconds.) Otherwise, go to number 6 on your answer sheet and darken the letter B, as in "boy." (Pause 5 seconds.)

Examine Sample 4. (Pause 2-3 seconds.) Write the number 65 in the smaller box shown in the sample. (Pause 2 seconds.) Write the number 91 in the largest circle. (Pause 2 seconds.) Now, darken both of these number-letter combinations on your answer sheet. (Pause 10 seconds.)

Examine Sample 4 again. (Pause 2-3 seconds.) If the month of January precedes the month of February, and the month of May follows April, write the number 15 in the smaller circle. (Pause 2 seconds.) If not, write the number 35 in the larger box. (Pause 2 seconds.) Now, go to your answer sheet and darken the number-letter combination selected. (Pause 5 seconds.)

Examine Sample 5. (Pause 2-3 seconds.) If the fourth letter in this sample precedes the second letter in the alphabet, go to number 58 on your answer sheet and darken the letter C, as in "cat." (Pause 5 seconds.) If not, go to number 59 on your answer sheet and darken the letter D, as in "dog." (Pause 5 seconds.)

Examine Sample 6. (Pause 2-3 seconds.) Three letter carriers, represented by the letters X, Y, and Z are shown here along with the time each began and finished his/her work day. (Pause 2 seconds.) If

Carrier Z has a later starting time than Carrier Y, go to number 34 on your answer sheet and darken the letter A, as in "apple." (Pause 5 seconds.) Otherwise, go to number 53 on your answer sheet and darken the letter C, as in "cat." (Pause 5 seconds.)

Examine Sample 6 again. (Pause 2-3 seconds.) If Carrier X worked longer than Carrier Z, go to number 47 on your answer sheet and darken the letter B, as in "boy." (Pause 5 seconds.) If not, go to number 33 on your answer sheet and darken the letter D, as in "dog." (Pause 5 seconds.)

Examine Sample 1. (Pause 2-3 seconds.) If the product of two times the second number shown in the sample is less than the first number shown in the sample, go to number 1 on your answer sheet and darken the letter E, as in "elephant." (Pause 5 seconds.) If not, go to number 93 on your answer sheet and darken the letter A, as in "apple." (Pause 5 seconds.)

Examine Sample 6 again. (Pause 2-3 seconds.) If Carrier Z, Y, and X ended their work day at 4:45 PM, 4:30 PM, and 6:00 PM respectively, go to number 12 on your answer sheet and darken the letter B, as in "boy." (Pause 5 seconds.) Otherwise, go to number 12 on your answer sheet and mark the letter C, as in "cat," instead. (Pause 5 seconds.)

Examine Sample 7. (Pause 2-3 seconds.) The five numbers shown represent various Zip Codes. If the lowest numbered Zip Code has been underlined, go to number 19 on your answer sheet and darken the letter C, as in "cat." (Pause 5 seconds.) If the highest numbered Zip Code has been underlined, go to number 19 on your answer sheet and darken the letter A, as in "apple." (Pause 5 seconds.) Otherwise, go to number 16 on your answer sheet and darken the letter B, as in "boy." (Pause 5 seconds.)

Examine Sample 7 again. (Pause 2-3 seconds.) If the last two digits in the second highest numbered Zip Code are 1 and 3 respectively, go to number 13 on your answer sheet and darken the letter E, as in "elephant." (Pause 5 seconds.) Otherwise, go to number 31 on your answer sheet and darken the letter D, as in "dog." (Pause 5 seconds.)

Examine Sample 2. (Pause 2-3 seconds.) Darken the letter E, as in "elephant" for number 75 on your answer sheet if the last number shown in the sample is greater than the preceding number. (Pause 5 seconds.) Otherwise, go to number 8 on your answer sheet and darken the letter E, as in "elephant." (Pause 5 seconds.)

Examine Sample 3. (Pause 2-3 seconds.) Go to number 82 on your answer sheet and darken the letter that corresponds with the route that delivers the 1650-1725 KINGSLEY AVENUE area. (Pause 5 seconds.)

Examine Sample 8. (Pause 2-3 seconds.) If the second number shown is less than the first, write the letter B, as in "boy," beside the first number and A, as in "apple," beside the second number. (Pause 10 seconds.) If not, do exactly the opposite of what was just instructed. (Pause 5 seconds.) Now, darken both of the number-letter combinations selected on your answer sheet. (Pause 10 seconds.)

Examine Sample 9. (Pause 2-3 seconds.) Write the letter B, as in "boy," beside the smallest number shown. (Pause 2 seconds.) Write the letter C, as in "cat," beside the second highest number shown. (Pause 2 seconds.) Write the letter E, as in "elephant," beside the highest number shown. (Pause 2 seconds.) Now, darken these three number-letter combinations on your answer sheet. (Pause 15 seconds.)

-END OF TEST-

FOLLOWING DIRECTIONS/EXAM 3 SAMPLES

1. 27_____ 13_____ 37_____ 14_____ 67_____ 18_____ 40_____

2. 15_____ 14_____ 12_____ 20_____ 22_____ 25_____ 29_____

3. A. 1650-1725 KINGSLEY AVE.
    B. 1475-1575 KINGSLEY ST,
    C. 1425-1500 KINGSLEY AVE.
    D. 1750-1825 KINGSLEY ST.
    E. 1505-1645 KINGSLEY AVE.

4. _____B   _____E   _____C   _____D

5. A   D   C   B   E

6.

X	Y	Z
8:00 AM	8:30 AM	7:50 AM
4:30 PM	6:00 PM	4:45 PM

7. 98500   06511   82713   32577   42113

8. 8_____   10_____

9. 17_____   71_____   7_____

[This page intentionally blank.]

ANSWER SHEET TO FOLLOWING DIRECTIONS/EXAM 3

1. (A) (B) (C) (D) (E)
2. (A) (B) (C) (D) (E)
3. (A) (B) (C) (D) (E)
4. (A) (B) (C) (D) (E)
5. (A) (B) (C) (D) (E)
6. (A) (B) (C) (D) (E)
7. (A) (B) (C) (D) (E)
8. (A) (B) (C) (D) (E)
9. (A) (B) (C) (D) (E)
10. (A) (B) (C) (D) (E)
11. (A) (B) (C) (D) (E)
12. (A) (B) (C) (D) (E)
13. (A) (B) (C) (D) (E)
14. (A) (B) (C) (D) (E)
15. (A) (B) (C) (D) (E)
16. (A) (B) (C) (D) (E)
17. (A) (B) (C) (D) (E)
18. (A) (B) (C) (D) (E)
19. (A) (B) (C) (D) (E)
20. (A) (B) (C) (D) (E)
21. (A) (B) (C) (D) (E)
22. (A) (B) (C) (D) (E)
23. (A) (B) (C) (D) (E)
24. (A) (B) (C) (D) (E)
25. (A) (B) (C) (D) (E)
26. (A) (B) (C) (D) (E)
27. (A) (B) (C) (D) (E)
28. (A) (B) (C) (D) (E)
29. (A) (B) (C) (D) (E)
30. (A) (B) (C) (D) (E)
31. (A) (B) (C) (D) (E)
32. (A) (B) (C) (D) (E)

33. (A) (B) (C) (D) (E)
34. (A) (B) (C) (D) (E)
35. (A) (B) (C) (D) (E)
36. (A) (B) (C) (D) (E)
37. (A) (B) (C) (D) (E)
38. (A) (B) (C) (D) (E)
39. (A) (B) (C) (D) (E)
40. (A) (B) (C) (D) (E)
41. (A) (B) (C) (D) (E)
42. (A) (B) (C) (D) (E)
43. (A) (B) (C) (D) (E)
44. (A) (B) (C) (D) (E)
45. (A) (B) (C) (D) (E)
46. (A) (B) (C) (D) (E)
47. (A) (B) (C) (D) (E)
48. (A) (B) (C) (D) (E)
49. (A) (B) (C) (D) (E)
50. (A) (B) (C) (D) (E)
51. (A) (B) (C) (D) (E)
52. (A) (B) (C) (D) (E)
53. (A) (B) (C) (D) (E)
54. (A) (B) (C) (D) (E)
55. (A) (B) (C) (D) (E)
56. (A) (B) (C) (D) (E)
57. (A) (B) (C) (D) (E)
58. (A) (B) (C) (D) (E)
59. (A) (B) (C) (D) (E)
60. (A) (B) (C) (D) (E)
61. (A) (B) (C) (D) (E)
62. (A) (B) (C) (D) (E)
63. (A) (B) (C) (D) (E)
64. (A) (B) (C) (D) (E)

65. (A) (B) (C) (D) (E)
66. (A) (B) (C) (D) (E)
67. (A) (B) (C) (D) (E)
68. (A) (B) (C) (D) (E)
69. (A) (B) (C) (D) (E)
70. (A) (B) (C) (D) (E)
71. (A) (B) (C) (D) (E)
72. (A) (B) (C) (D) (E)
73. (A) (B) (C) (D) (E)
74. (A) (B) (C) (D) (E)
75. (A) (B) (C) (D) (E)
76. (A) (B) (C) (D) (E)
77. (A) (B) (C) (D) (E)
78. (A) (B) (C) (D) (E)
79. (A) (B) (C) (D) (E)
80. (A) (B) (C) (D) (E)
81. (A) (B) (C) (D) (E)
82. (A) (B) (C) (D) (E)
83. (A) (B) (C) (D) (E)
84. (A) (B) (C) (D) (E)
85. (A) (B) (C) (D) (E)
86. (A) (B) (C) (D) (E)
87. (A) (B) (C) (D) (E)
88. (A) (B) (C) (D) (E)
89. (A) (B) (C) (D) (E)
90. (A) (B) (C) (D) (E)
91. (A) (B) (C) (D) (E)
92. (A) (B) (C) (D) (E)
93. (A) (B) (C) (D) (E)
94. (A) (B) (C) (D) (E)
95. (A) (B) (C) (D) (E)

(This page may be removed to mark answers.)

[This page intentionally blank.]

ANSWERS TO ADDRESS CROSS COMPARISON/EXAM 3

1.	D	33.	A	65.	A
2.	D	34.	A	66.	A
3.	A	35.	D	67.	A
4.	D	36.	D	68.	D
5.	A	37.	D	69.	A
6.	D	38.	A	70.	D
7.	D	39.	D	71.	A
8.	D	40.	A	72.	D
9.	A	41.	D	73.	A
10.	A	42.	D	74.	D
11.	D	43.	D	75.	D
12.	A	44.	D	76.	A
13.	A	45.	D	77.	D
14.	D	46.	D	78.	D
15.	D	47.	A	79.	A
16.	A	48.	A	80.	D
17.	D	49.	D	81.	A
18.	D	50.	A	82.	D
19.	A	51.	D	83.	A
20.	D	52.	D	84.	D
21.	A	53.	A	85.	D
22.	D	54.	D	86.	A
23.	D	55.	A	87.	D
24.	A	56.	D	88.	D
25.	A	57.	D	89.	D
26.	A	58.	A	90.	A
27.	D	59.	A	91.	A
28.	D	60.	D	92.	D
29.	D	61.	A	93.	D
30.	A	62.	D	94.	A
31.	D	63.	D	95.	A
32.	D	64.	A		

ANSWERS TO MEMORIZATION/EXAM 3

1.	C	31.	C	61.	B
2.	A	31.	B	62.	E
3.	B	33.	C	63.	C
4.	D	34.	D	64.	D
5.	B	35.	D	65.	C
6.	A	36.	E	66.	B
7.	E	37.	A	67.	A
8.	E	38.	A	68.	E
9.	D	39.	D	69.	E
10.	D	40.	E	70.	B
11.	B	41.	B	71.	C
12.	A	42.	A	72.	D
13.	A	43.	D	73.	C
14.	A	44.	C	74.	C
15.	B	45.	D	75.	B
16.	C	46.	A	76.	E
17.	C	47.	C	77.	D
18.	E	48.	E	78.	A
19.	E	49.	C	79.	C
20.	C	50.	E	80.	B
21.	D	51.	B	81.	A
22.	E	52.	A	82.	D
23.	C	53.	B	83.	A
24.	B	54.	D	84.	E
25.	D	55.	A	85.	A
26.	B	56.	D	86.	E
27.	C	57.	E	87.	A
28.	B	58.	B	88.	B
29.	E	59.	D		
30.	B	60.	E		

ANSWERS TO NUMBER SERIES/EXAM 3

1. E.
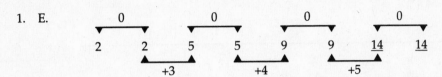

2. B.
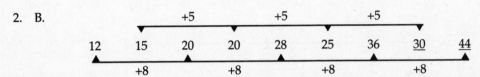

3. C.
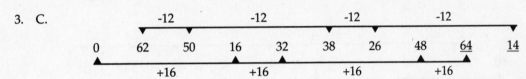

4. C.
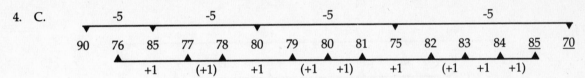

5. E.
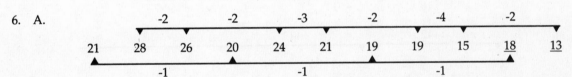

6. A.
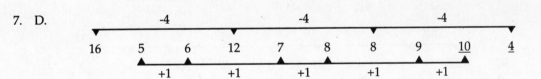

7. D.
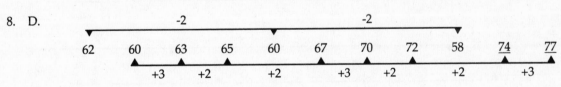

8. D.
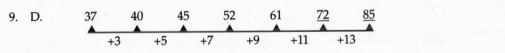

9. D.
37   40   45   52   61   72   85
  +3   +5   +7   +9   +11   +13

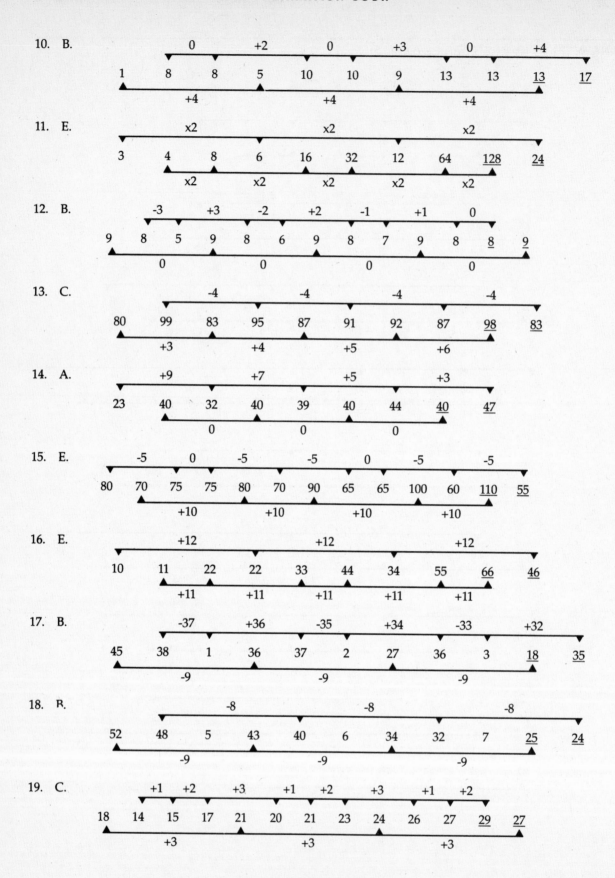

10. B.

```
              0        +2        0        +3        0        +4
      1     8     8     5    10    10     9    13    13    13      17
                +4              +4              +4
```

11. E.

```
              x2                x2                x2
      3     4     8     6    16    32    12    64    128      24
            x2        x2        x2        x2        x2
```

12. B.

```
            -3        +3       -2        +2       -1        +1       0
      9    8    5    9    8    6    9    8    7    9    8    8      9
           0              0              0              0
```

13. C.

```
                -4              -4              -4              -4
      80    99    83    95    87    91    92    87    98      83
              +3              +4              +5              +6
```

14. A.

```
            +9              +7              +5              +3
      23    40    32    40    39    40    44    40      47
            0              0              0
```

15. E.

```
           -5        0       -5       -5       0       -5       -5
      80   70   75   75   80   70   90   65   65  100   60   110    55
               +10            +10            +10            +10
```

16. E.

```
            +12              +12              +12
      10    11    22    22    33    44    34    55    66      46
            +11        +11        +11        +11        +11
```

17. B.

```
            -37        +36       -35        +34       -33        +32
      45    38    1    36    37    2    27    36    3    18      35
               -9              -9              -9
```

18. B.

```
                -8                -8                -8
      52    48    5    43    40    6    34    32    7    25      24
               -9              -9              -9
```

19. C.

```
          +1   +2    +3    +1   +2    +3    +1   +2
      18   14   15   17   21   20   21   23   24   26   27   29    27
           +3              +3              +3
```

20. A.

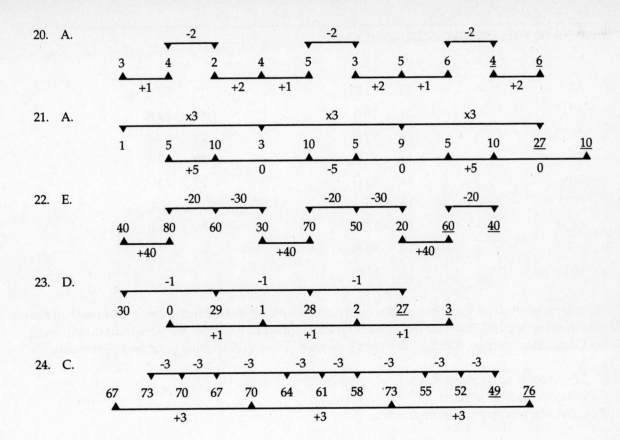

21. A.

22. E.

23. D.

24. C.

ANSWERS TO FOLLOWING DIRECTIONS/EXAM 3

1.	67 B	10.	91 E	19.	75 E
2.	37 C	11.	15 B	20.	82 A
3.	20 D	12.	59 D	21.	8 A
4.	18 E	13.	53 C	22.	10 B
5.	86 C	14.	33 D	23.	7 B
6.	68 B	15.	1 E	24.	17 C
7.	54 D	16.	12 C	25.	71 E
8.	5 A	17.	16 B		
9.	65 C	18.	13 E		

To determine your performance on this exam, add the number of correct answers from each of the four sections of the test. Subtract from this total the number of incorrect answers from the Address Cross Comparison section. Ratings have been provided below to determine your overall standing.

225-232 correct is an excellent score.
208-224 correct is a good score.
207 or fewer correct requires more practice.

Exam 4

**DO NOT OPEN THIS TEST BOOKLET UNTIL
YOU ARE TOLD TO START BY THE INDIVIDUAL
ASSISTING YOU IN THIS EXERCISE**

[This page intentionally blank.]

1.	421 Briarwood Pl.	421 Briarwood Pl.
2.	2524 Torry Pines Dr.	2523 Torry Pines Dr.
3.	688 John Hoptkins St.	688 John Hopkins St.
4.	Palm Springs, CA 94611	Palm Springs, CA 94611
5.	Bon Vista Industrial Park	Bon Vista Industrial Park
6.	667 66th Ave. SW	667 67th Ave. SW
7.	400431 Monteray Lane	404031 Monteray Lane
8.	15-D Bolstad Blvd.	15-D Bolstad Blvd.
9.	160 South Dakota St.	160 South Dakota St.
10.	150-A Schilleter Village	150-A Schileter Village
11.	Waterbury, Connecticut 22411	Waterbury, Conn. 22411
12.	1419 Wheeler Dr. SE	1419 Wheeler Dr. SE
13.	1711 Meadowlane	1171 Meadowland
14.	330 Harcomb Ct. N.	330 Harcomb Ct. N.
15.	88-1/2 Walnut Place	88-1/4 Walnut Place
16.	Emerald Bay Apts. 11C	Emerald Bay Apts. 11C
17.	Carson City, Nev. 55811	Carson City, Nev. 55811
18.	126491 Garfield Ave.	126419 Garfield Ave.
19.	240 Quigley Blvd.	240 Quigley Blvd.
20.	Honolulu, Hawaii 99894	Honalulu, Hawaii 99894
21.	50010 Doctrine Place	5010 Doctrine Place
22.	411 Hystead Ave.	411 Histead Ave.
23.	69731 Ferndale Pkwy.	69731 Perdale Park

24.	N. Palo Alto Dr.	N. Palo Alto Dr.
25.	1451 SW Spannus Dr.	1451 SW Spannus Dr.
26.	Severance Canyon Rd.	Severence Canyon Rd.
27.	4410 Phoenix St.	4410 Phoenix St.
28.	11-B Deer Antler Cr.	11-B Deer Antler Circle
29.	8435 Orchard Grove S.	8435 Orchard Grove S.
30.	Northwest Orient Blvd.	Northwest Orient Blvd.
31.	441 Stanford Ave.	441 Stanford Ave.
32.	67351 Opalamine Circle	67351 Opal Circle
33.	837 Harding Way NE	837 Harding Way
34.	New Orleans, LA 77501	New Orleans, LA 75701
35.	Citronelle, Ala, 67891	Citronelle, Ala. 67891
36.	320 Four Seasons Apts.	302 Four Seasons Apts.
37.	4115 Ontario Dr.	4115 Ontario Dr.
38.	58423 Lincoln Ct.	58423 Lincoln Place
39.	RR 2, Boone, Ia 50123	RR 2, Boone, ID 50123
40.	Point Defiance, Wash.	Point Defiance, Wash.
41.	221 16th St.	221 16th St.
42.	Norfolk, Neb. 68744	Norfolk, Neb. 68474
43.	108 E. Lime St.	108 W. Lime St.
44.	1707 Amherst Blvd.	1707 Amhurst Blvd.
45.	310 Mathews Dr.	301 Mathews Dr.
46.	Middlebourne, W.V. 05691	Middleborne, W.V. 05691
47.	1461 Madison Ave.	1461 Madison Ave.
48.	Oshkosh, Wisc. 54420	Oshkosh, Wisc. 54420

49.	N. Manitowac Dr.	N. Manatowac Dr.
50.	1599 Bothell Lane SW	1599 Bothell Lane SW
51.	5743 Whiney Park	5734 Whitney Park
52.	711 SW Richardson Pl.	711 SW Richardson Pl.
53.	Port Bolivar, Tex. 67019	Port Bolivar, Tex. 67019
54.	763241 Columbia Ave.	763241 Columbia Ave.
55.	707-C West Minster Park	707-C West Minster Park
56.	Beecher Falls, VT. 08917	Beacher Falls, VT. 08917
57.	4440 Chester Ave.	4440 Chester Ave.
58.	8980 Fauquier Square	8980 Fauquier Square
59.	Duchesne, Utah 79818	Duchesnee, Utah 79818
60.	30045 Montgomery	30045 Montgomery
61.	SE Carroll St.	SE 111 Carroll St.
62.	1477 Newbury Place	1477 Newbury Place
63.	Bryn Mawr, Wash. 78113	Bryn Mawr, Wash. 78113
64.	343 S. Wendover Ave.	343 S. Wendover Ave.
65.	140 W. St. Patrick	140 W. Saint Patrick
66.	1515 Elsinore Dr.	5151 Elsinore Dr.
67.	Centrahoma, Okla. 65077	Centrahoma, Okla. 65077
68.	400-401 Essex Ct.	400-401 Esex Ct.
69.	7581 Box Elder Pkwy	7581 Box Alder Pkwy
70.	7600 Mount Vernon Rd.	7600 Mt. Vernon Road
71.	651 Trinity St.	651 Trinity St.
72.	Chiloquin, ORE 90403	Chiloquin, ORE 90403
73.	3777 Comanche Ct.	3773 Comanche Ct.

74.	404 Hamilton Place	404 Hamilton Place
75.	Philadelphia Dr. SW	Philadelphia Dr. SW
76.	701 Canton Dr.	701 Canton Ave.
77.	11130 Joesephine St.	11130 Joseephine St.
78.	488 Kenwood	488 Kenwood
79.	9080 Lansing Pl.	9080 Lansing Pk.
80.	1501-D Cleveland Hts.	1501-D Cleveland Hts.
81.	2575 Covington Dr.	2575 Covington Dr.
82.	Northumberland, Penn. 09432	Northumberland, Penn. 09432
83.	1616 Drexal	1616 Drexel
84.	705 Tuscarawas Point	705 Tuscarawas Point
85.	54330 Haskins Dr. S.	54338 Haskins Dr. S.
86.	1221 Cortland Way	2112 Cortland Way
87.	100 Preble Beach	100 Preeble Beach
88.	8595 Perry Ave.	8595 Perry Ave.
89.	7734 Clayton Blvd. NW	7734 Clayton Blvd. NW
90.	22441 Lancaster Dr.	22441 Lancaster Dr.
91.	Campbellsburg, Ind. 54013	Campbelsburg, Ind. 54013
92.	Pickneyville, Ill. 52388	Pinckneyville, Ill. 52388
93.	515 Olmstead Pl.	515 Olmstead Pl.
94.	4016 Thomson	4016 Thomson
95.	Cape Elizabeth, Maine	Cape Elizebeth, Maine

ANSWER SHEET TO ADDRESS CROSS COMPARISON/EXAM 4

1. (A) (D)
2. (A) (D)
3. (A) (D)
4. (A) (D)
5. (A) (D)
6. (A) (D)
7. (A) (D)
8. (A) (D)
9. (A) (D)
10. (A) (D)
11. (A) (D)
12. (A) (D)
13. (A) (D)
14. (A) (D)
15. (A) (D)
16. (A) (D)
17. (A) (D)
18. (A) (D)
19. (A) (D)
20. (A) (D)
21. (A) (D)
22. (A) (D)
23. (A) (D)
24. (A) (D)
25. (A) (D)
26. (A) (D)
27. (A) (D)
28. (A) (D)
29. (A) (D)
30. (A) (D)
31. (A) (D)
32. (A) (D)

33. (A) (D)
34. (A) (D)
35. (A) (D)
36. (A) (D)
37. (A) (D)
38. (A) (D)
39. (A) (D)
40. (A) (D)
41. (A) (D)
42. (A) (D)
43. (A) (D)
44. (A) (D)
45. (A) (D)
46. (A) (D)
47. (A) (D)
48. (A) (D)
49. (A) (D)
50. (A) (D)
51. (A) (D)
52. (A) (D)
53. (A) (D)
54. (A) (D)
55. (A) (D)
56. (A) (D)
57. (A) (D)
58. (A) (D)
59. (A) (D)
60. (A) (D)
61. (A) (D)
62. (A) (D)
63. (A) (D)
64. (A) (D)

65. (A) (D)
66. (A) (D)
67. (A) (D)
68. (A) (D)
69. (A) (D)
70. (A) (D)
71. (A) (D)
72. (A) (D)
73. (A) (D)
74. (A) (D)
75. (A) (D)
76. (A) (D)
77. (A) (D)
78. (A) (D)
79. (A) (D)
80. (A) (D)
81. (A) (D)
82. (A) (D)
83. (A) (D)
84. (A) (D)
85. (A) (D)
86. (A) (D)
87. (A) (D)
88. (A) (D)
89. (A) (D)
90. (A) (D)
91. (A) (D)
92. (A) (D)
93. (A) (D)
94. (A) (D)
95. (A) (D)

(This page may be removed to mark answers.)

[This page intentionally blank.]

MEMORIZATION/EXAM 4

A	B	C	D	E
7000-7099 Bell	8000-8099 Bell	7100-7199 Bell	8400-8499 Bell	7700-7799 Bell
Belfair	Knottingham	Springer Ave.	Jersey St.	Silverton Ct.
7700-7799 Boyson	8000-8099 Boyson	8400-8499 Boyson	7100-7199 Boyson	7000-7099 Boyson
Eldorado Blvd.	Summit Ave.	Marine Dr.	Burwell	Almira Dr.
7700-7799 Foster	8400-8499 Foster	7100-7199 Foster	7000-7099 Foster	8000-8099 Foster

NOTE: Follow the same step by step format established for the memorization exercises studied earlier. (See page 41.)

PRACTICE MEMORIZATION/EXAM 4

STEP 2 TIME: 3 MINUTES
STEP 3 TIME: 3 MINUTES (cover key)

A	B	C	D	E
7000-7099 Bell Belfair 7700-7799 Boyson Eldorado Blvd. 7700-7799 Foster	8000-8099 Bell Knottingham 8000-8099 Boyson Summit Ave. 8400-8499 Foster	7100-7199 Bell Springer Ave. 8400-8499 Boyson Marine Dr. 7100-7199 Foster	8400-8499 Bell Jersey St. 7100-7199 Boyson Burwell 7000-7099 Foster	7700-7799 Bell Silverton Ct. 7000-7099 Boyson Almira Dr. 8000-8099 Foster

1. Summit Ave.
2. 8400-8499 Bell
3. 8000-8099 Boyson
4. Belfair
5. Marine Dr.
6. 7000-7099 Bell
7. 7100-7199 Boyson
8. Knottingham
9. Jersey St.
10. Springer Ave.
11. Almira Dr.
12. 8000-8099 Bell
13. 7700-7799 Foster
14. 8000-8099 Foster
15. Eldorado Blvd.
16. 8400-8499 Foster
17. 8400-8499 Bell
18. 7000-7099 Foster
19. 7100-7199 Boyson
20. Summit Ave.
21. Silverton Ct.
22. Almira Dr.
23. 7700-7799 Boyson
24. Marine Dr.
25. 8000-8099 Bell
26. 7100-7199 Foster
27. Belfair
28. Springer Ave.
29. Eldorado Blvd.
30. 7000-7099 Bell

31. Burwell
32. 7700-7799 Foster
33. 7700-7799 Boyson
34. 7000-7099 Foster
35. Jersey St.
36. 7100-7199 Bell
37. 8000-8099 Boyson
38. 8000-8099 Foster
39. Burwell
40. 8400-8499 Foster
41. Knottingham
42. Almira Dr.
43. 8400-8499 Boyson
44. Springer Ave.
45. 7700-7799 Foster
46. 7100-7199 Boyson
47. Jersey St.
48. Eldorado Blvd.
49. 8000-8099 Boyson
50. Springer Ave.
51. 7100-7199 Bell
52. Silverton Ct.
53. 7100-7199 Foster
54. 8400-8499 Boyson
55. Marine Dr.
56. 8000-8099 Foster
57. 8400-8499 Bell
58. 7700-7799 Bell
59. 8400-8499 Foster
60. Summit Ave.

61. Belfair
62. 7100-7199 Bell
63. 7000-7099 Boyson
64. Knottingham
65. Burwell
66. 8400-8499 Boyson
67. 7000-7099 Bell
68. 8000-8099 Bell
69. Silverton Ct.
70. 7000-7099 Foster
71. Springer Ave.
72. Summit Ave.
73. 7700-7799 Bell
74. Marine Dr.
75. 7000-7099 Boyson
76. 7100-7199 Foster
77. Knottingham
78. 7700-7799 Boyson
79. 7700-7799 Foster
80. Eldorado Blvd.
81. Silverton Ct.
82. Burwell
83. 7700-7799 Bell
84. Belfair
85. Jersey St.
86. 7000-7099 Boyson
87. 8400-8499 Boyson
88. Almira Dr.

PRACTICE ANSWER SHEET TO MEMORIZATION/EXAM 4

1. A B C D E
2. A B C D E
3. A B C D E
4. A B C D E
5. A B C D E
6. A B C D E
7. A B C D E
8. A B C D E
9. A B C D E
10. A B C D E
11. A B C D E
12. A B C D E
13. A B C D E
14. A B C D E
15. A B C D E
16. A B C D E
17. A B C D E
18. A B C D E
19. A B C D E
20. A B C D E
21. A B C D E
22. A B C D E
23. A B C D E
24. A B C D E
25. A B C D E
26. A B C D E
27. A B C D E
28. A B C D E
29. A B C D E
30. A B C D E

31. A B C D E
32. A B C D E
33. A B C D E
34. A B C D E
35. A B C D E
36. A B C D E
37. A B C D E
38. A B C D E
39. A B C D E
40. A B C D E
41. A B C D E
42. A B C D E
43. A B C D E
44. A B C D E
45. A B C D E
46. A B C D E
47. A B C D E
48. A B C D E
49. A B C D E
50. A B C D E
51. A B C D E
52. A B C D E
53. A B C D E
54. A B C D E
55. A B C D E
56. A B C D E
57. A B C D E
58. A B C D E
59. A B C D E
60. A B C D E

61. A B C D E
62. A B C D E
63. A B C D E
64. A B C D E
65. A B C D E
66. A B C D E
67. A B C D E
68. A B C D E
69. A B C D E
70. A B C D E
71. A B C D E
72. A B C D E
73. A B C D E
74. A B C D E
75. A B C D E
76. A B C D E
77. A B C D E
78. A B C D E
79. A B C D E
80. A B C D E
81. A B C D E
82. A B C D E
83. A B C D E
84. A B C D E
85. A B C D E
86. A B C D E
87. A B C D E
88. A B C D E

1.	Almira Dr.	31.	Jersey St.
2.	Jersey St.	32.	Eldorado Blvd.
3.	7000-7099 Bell	33.	8400-8499 Bell
4.	7100-7199 Boyson	34.	8000-8099 Boyson
5.	Eldorado Blvd.	35.	Knottingham
6.	7700-7799 Boyson	36.	Springer Ave.
7.	8400-8499 Boyson	37.	7700-7799 Bell
8.	Belfair	38.	7100-7199 Boyson
9.	Springer Ave.	39.	Silverton Ct.
10.	Burwell	40.	Summit Ave.
11.	Summit Ave.	41.	7100-7199 Bell
12.	800-8099 Bell	42.	Almira Dr.
13.	7700-7799 Foster	43.	7700-7799 Foster
14.	7000-7099 Boyson	44.	7000-7099 Boyson
15.	Knottingham	45.	Eldorado Blvd.
16.	7100-7199 Bell	46.	8400-8499 Foster
17.	7100-7199 Foster	47.	Marine Dr.
18.	Jersey St.	48.	8400-8499 Boyson
19.	Marine Dr.	49.	7100-7199 Foster
20.	8000-8099 Foster	50.	Almira Dr.
21.	8400-8499 Bell	51.	Burwell
22.	7700-7799 Bell	52.	8000-8099 Boyson
23.	7000-7099 Foster	53.	Knottingham
24.	Silverton Ct.	54.	7100-7199 Boyson
25.	7100-7199 Bell	55.	7000-7099 Bell
26.	Summit Ave.	56.	Springer Ave.
27.	7700-7799 Boyson	57.	Jersey St.
28.	Burwell	58.	7700-7799 Bell
29.	7000-7099 Bell	59.	Silverton Ct.
30.	Belfair	60.	7700-7799 Boyson

61.	8000-8099 Bell
62.	Eldorado Blvd.
63.	7000-7099 Foster
64.	8400-8499 Foster
65.	Belfair
66.	Marine Dr.
67.	8000-8099 Foster
68.	7100-7199 Bell
69.	7100-7199 Foster
70.	Springer Ave.
71.	Jersey St.
72.	7000-7099 Boyson
73.	Almira Dr.
74.	8000-8099 Foster
75.	7000-7099 Foster
76.	Summit Ave.
77.	Burwell
78.	Almira Dr.
79.	8400-8499 Boyson
80.	Belfair
81.	8400-8499 Foster
82.	8400-8499 Bell
83.	Knottingham
84.	Marine Dr.
85.	Silverton Ct.
86.	7700-7799 Foster
87.	8000-8099 Boyson
88.	8000-8099 Bell

ANSWER SHEET TO MEMORIZATION/EXAM 4

1. Ⓐ Ⓑ Ⓒ Ⓓ Ⓔ
2. Ⓐ Ⓑ Ⓒ Ⓓ Ⓔ
3. Ⓐ Ⓑ Ⓒ Ⓓ Ⓔ
4. Ⓐ Ⓑ Ⓒ Ⓓ Ⓔ
5. Ⓐ Ⓑ Ⓒ Ⓓ Ⓔ
6. Ⓐ Ⓑ Ⓒ Ⓓ Ⓔ
7. Ⓐ Ⓑ Ⓒ Ⓓ Ⓔ
8. Ⓐ Ⓑ Ⓒ Ⓓ Ⓔ
9. Ⓐ Ⓑ Ⓒ Ⓓ Ⓔ
10. Ⓐ Ⓑ Ⓒ Ⓓ Ⓔ
11. Ⓐ Ⓑ Ⓒ Ⓓ Ⓔ
12. Ⓐ Ⓑ Ⓒ Ⓓ Ⓔ
13. Ⓐ Ⓑ Ⓒ Ⓓ Ⓔ
14. Ⓐ Ⓑ Ⓒ Ⓓ Ⓔ
15. Ⓐ Ⓑ Ⓒ Ⓓ Ⓔ
16. Ⓐ Ⓑ Ⓒ Ⓓ Ⓔ
17. Ⓐ Ⓑ Ⓒ Ⓓ Ⓔ
18. Ⓐ Ⓑ Ⓒ Ⓓ Ⓔ
19. Ⓐ Ⓑ Ⓒ Ⓓ Ⓔ
20. Ⓐ Ⓑ Ⓒ Ⓓ Ⓔ
21. Ⓐ Ⓑ Ⓒ Ⓓ Ⓔ
22. Ⓐ Ⓑ Ⓒ Ⓓ Ⓔ
23. Ⓐ Ⓑ Ⓒ Ⓓ Ⓔ
24. Ⓐ Ⓑ Ⓒ Ⓓ Ⓔ
25. Ⓐ Ⓑ Ⓒ Ⓓ Ⓔ
26. Ⓐ Ⓑ Ⓒ Ⓓ Ⓔ
27. Ⓐ Ⓑ Ⓒ Ⓓ Ⓔ
28. Ⓐ Ⓑ Ⓒ Ⓓ Ⓔ
29. Ⓐ Ⓑ Ⓒ Ⓓ Ⓔ
30. Ⓐ Ⓑ Ⓒ Ⓓ Ⓔ

31. Ⓐ Ⓑ Ⓒ Ⓓ Ⓔ
32. Ⓐ Ⓑ Ⓒ Ⓓ Ⓔ
33. Ⓐ Ⓑ Ⓒ Ⓓ Ⓔ
34. Ⓐ Ⓑ Ⓒ Ⓓ Ⓔ
35. Ⓐ Ⓑ Ⓒ Ⓓ Ⓔ
36. Ⓐ Ⓑ Ⓒ Ⓓ Ⓔ
37. Ⓐ Ⓑ Ⓒ Ⓓ Ⓔ
38. Ⓐ Ⓑ Ⓒ Ⓓ Ⓔ
39. Ⓐ Ⓑ Ⓒ Ⓓ Ⓔ
40. Ⓐ Ⓑ Ⓒ Ⓓ Ⓔ
41. Ⓐ Ⓑ Ⓒ Ⓓ Ⓔ
42. Ⓐ Ⓑ Ⓒ Ⓓ Ⓔ
43. Ⓐ Ⓑ Ⓒ Ⓓ Ⓔ
44. Ⓐ Ⓑ Ⓒ Ⓓ Ⓔ
45. Ⓐ Ⓑ Ⓒ Ⓓ Ⓔ
46. Ⓐ Ⓑ Ⓒ Ⓓ Ⓔ
47. Ⓐ Ⓑ Ⓒ Ⓓ Ⓔ
48. Ⓐ Ⓑ Ⓒ Ⓓ Ⓔ
49. Ⓐ Ⓑ Ⓒ Ⓓ Ⓔ
50. Ⓐ Ⓑ Ⓒ Ⓓ Ⓔ
51. Ⓐ Ⓑ Ⓒ Ⓓ Ⓔ
52. Ⓐ Ⓑ Ⓒ Ⓓ Ⓔ
53. Ⓐ Ⓑ Ⓒ Ⓓ Ⓔ
54. Ⓐ Ⓑ Ⓒ Ⓓ Ⓔ
55. Ⓐ Ⓑ Ⓒ Ⓓ Ⓔ
56. Ⓐ Ⓑ Ⓒ Ⓓ Ⓔ
57. Ⓐ Ⓑ Ⓒ Ⓓ Ⓔ
58. Ⓐ Ⓑ Ⓒ Ⓓ Ⓔ
59. Ⓐ Ⓑ Ⓒ Ⓓ Ⓔ
60. Ⓐ Ⓑ Ⓒ Ⓓ Ⓔ

61. Ⓐ Ⓑ Ⓒ Ⓓ Ⓔ
62. Ⓐ Ⓑ Ⓒ Ⓓ Ⓔ
63. Ⓐ Ⓑ Ⓒ Ⓓ Ⓔ
64. Ⓐ Ⓑ Ⓒ Ⓓ Ⓔ
65. Ⓐ Ⓑ Ⓒ Ⓓ Ⓔ
66. Ⓐ Ⓑ Ⓒ Ⓓ Ⓔ
67. Ⓐ Ⓑ Ⓒ Ⓓ Ⓔ
68. Ⓐ Ⓑ Ⓒ Ⓓ Ⓔ
69. Ⓐ Ⓑ Ⓒ Ⓓ Ⓔ
70. Ⓐ Ⓑ Ⓒ Ⓓ Ⓔ
71. Ⓐ Ⓑ Ⓒ Ⓓ Ⓔ
72. Ⓐ Ⓑ Ⓒ Ⓓ Ⓔ
73. Ⓐ Ⓑ Ⓒ Ⓓ Ⓔ
74. Ⓐ Ⓑ Ⓒ Ⓓ Ⓔ
75. Ⓐ Ⓑ Ⓒ Ⓓ Ⓔ
76. Ⓐ Ⓑ Ⓒ Ⓓ Ⓔ
77. Ⓐ Ⓑ Ⓒ Ⓓ Ⓔ
78. Ⓐ Ⓑ Ⓒ Ⓓ Ⓔ
79. Ⓐ Ⓑ Ⓒ Ⓓ Ⓔ
80. Ⓐ Ⓑ Ⓒ Ⓓ Ⓔ
81. Ⓐ Ⓑ Ⓒ Ⓓ Ⓔ
82. Ⓐ Ⓑ Ⓒ Ⓓ Ⓔ
83. Ⓐ Ⓑ Ⓒ Ⓓ Ⓔ
84. Ⓐ Ⓑ Ⓒ Ⓓ Ⓔ
85. Ⓐ Ⓑ Ⓒ Ⓓ Ⓔ
86. Ⓐ Ⓑ Ⓒ Ⓓ Ⓔ
87. Ⓐ Ⓑ Ⓒ Ⓓ Ⓔ
88. Ⓐ Ⓑ Ⓒ Ⓓ Ⓔ

[This page intentionally blank.]

1. 5   5   5   10   6   6   15   7   7   ___   ___

    A. 20, 8
    B. 20, 9
    C. 8, 25
    D. 25, 8
    E. 8, 8

2. 34   36   40   43   46   50   52   57   ___   ___

    A. 57, 64
    B. 59, 62
    C. 60, 64
    D. 64, 64
    E. 58, 64

3. 3   1   7   5   1   6   7   1   5   9   1   ___   ___

    A. 5, 11
    B. 10, 12
    C. 4, 11
    D. 11, 5
    E. 9, 8

4. 1   1   4   3   16   9   ___   ___

    A. 27, 36
    B. 36, 27
    C. 27, 64
    D. 64, 27
    E. 36, 64

5. 13   10   15   20   17   22   27   ___   ___

    A. 24, 30
    B. 25, 28
    C. 28, 29
    D. 24, 29
    E. 26, 30

6. 23   28   22   31   36   30   39   ___   ___

    A. 42, 42
    B. 44, 37
    C. 43, 37
    D. 38, 44
    E. 44, 38

7. 49   38   37   35   40   32   28   23   31   17   10   ___   ___

    A. 0, 12
    B. 2, 22
    C. 2, 20
    D. 1, 18
    E. 2, 16

8. 60   35   65   63   40   70   66   45   75   __   __

    A. 50, 69
    B. 72, 55
    C. 69, 50
    D. 55, 72
    E. 70, 50

9. 1   5   0   0   5   7   0   0   9   9   0   0   __   __

    A. 13, 11
    B. 10, 10
    C. 10, 11
    D. 12, 11
    E. 13, 13

10. 9   7   9   6   7   9   5   6   7   9   4   5   6   7   __   __

    A. 6, 2
    B. 6, 3
    C. 3, 3
    D. 7, 9
    E. 9, 3

11. 16   15   20   17   24   20   28   24   __   __

    A. 32, 29
    B. 30, 28
    C. 30, 29
    D. 29, 29
    E. 32, 28

12. 33   29   26   30   26   23   27   23   __   __

    A. 21, 24
    B. 20, 24
    C. 23, 24
    D. 24, 23
    E. 26, 23

13. 25   28   30   26   20   23   25   19   15   14   20   __   __

    A. 16, 10
    B. 8, 12
    C. 8, 6
    D. 8, 8
    E. 8, 10

14. 0   1   2   8   4   8   16   16   __   __

    A. 20, 24
    B. 32, 24
    C. 30, 20
    D. 32, 34
    E. 28, 26

15.	19	15	20	16	14	20	13	13	20	10	___ ___

      A. 10, 20
      B. 14, 18
      C. 18, 14
      D. 12, 20
      E. 8, 12

16.	13	17	12	16	11	___ ___

      A. 15, 11
      B. 13, 10
      C. 14, 10
      D. 15, 10
      E. 14, 14

17.	68	71	80	60	60	69	52	49	58 ___ ___

      A. 42, 40
      B. 38, 44
      C. 44, 38
      D. 46, 36
      E. 60, 56

18.	2	15	4	14	6	12	8	9	___ ___

      A. 10, 5
      B. 5, 8
      C. 9, 5
      D. 9, 4
      E. 9, 7

19.	91	89	79	79	67	69	55	___ ___

      A. 43, 59
      B. 57, 41
      C. 57, 42
      D. 57, 54
      E. 59, 43

20.	41	42	41	37	35	31	35	24 ___ ___

      A. 30, 16
      B. 32, 18
      C. 26, 18
      D. 25, 16
      E. 29, 16

21.	30	16	28	28	40	26	38	38 ___ ___

      A. 50, 50
      B. 36, 50
      C. 50, 40
      D. 48, 38
      E. 50, 36

22.　15　　12　　12　　20　　14　　14　　25　　16　　16　　___　　___

    A.　35, 16
    B.　35, 18
    C.　30, 18
    D.　30, 16
    E.　30, 30

23.　8　　1　　3　　12　　9　　27　　16　　81　　___　　___

    A.　243, 18
    B.　243, 20
    C.　240, 23
    D.　240, 16
    E.　162, 20

24.　40　　43　　48　　55　　___　　___

    A.　65, 74
    B.　62, 71
    C.　60, 65
    D.　64, 75
    E.　64, 74

ANSWER SHEET TO NUMBER SERIES/EXAM 4

1. Ⓐ Ⓑ Ⓒ Ⓓ Ⓔ   9. Ⓐ Ⓑ Ⓒ Ⓓ Ⓔ   17. Ⓐ Ⓑ Ⓒ Ⓓ Ⓔ
2. Ⓐ Ⓑ Ⓒ Ⓓ Ⓔ   10. Ⓐ Ⓑ Ⓒ Ⓓ Ⓔ   18. Ⓐ Ⓑ Ⓒ Ⓓ Ⓔ
3. Ⓐ Ⓑ Ⓒ Ⓓ Ⓔ   11. Ⓐ Ⓑ Ⓒ Ⓓ Ⓔ   19. Ⓐ Ⓑ Ⓒ Ⓓ Ⓔ
4. Ⓐ Ⓑ Ⓒ Ⓓ Ⓔ   12. Ⓐ Ⓑ Ⓒ Ⓓ Ⓔ   20. Ⓐ Ⓑ Ⓒ Ⓓ Ⓔ
5. Ⓐ Ⓑ Ⓒ Ⓓ Ⓔ   13. Ⓐ Ⓑ Ⓒ Ⓓ Ⓔ   21. Ⓐ Ⓑ Ⓒ Ⓓ Ⓔ
6. Ⓐ Ⓑ Ⓒ Ⓓ Ⓔ   14. Ⓐ Ⓑ Ⓒ Ⓓ Ⓔ   22. Ⓐ Ⓑ Ⓒ Ⓓ Ⓔ
7. Ⓐ Ⓑ Ⓒ Ⓓ Ⓔ   15. Ⓐ Ⓑ Ⓒ Ⓓ Ⓔ   23. Ⓐ Ⓑ Ⓒ Ⓓ Ⓔ
8. Ⓐ Ⓑ Ⓒ Ⓓ Ⓔ   16. Ⓐ Ⓑ Ⓒ Ⓓ Ⓔ   24. Ⓐ Ⓑ Ⓒ Ⓓ Ⓔ

(This page may be removed to mark answers.)

[This page intentionally blank.]

FOLLOWING DIRECTIONS/EXAM 4

Note To Person Assisting In This Exam:

Remove from this test guide those pages of the exam that comprise the directions to be read out loud. The test applicant should be left with only the sample sheet and answer sheet. Read the following directions out loud at the suggested rate of 75-80 words per minute, pausing only where indicated in parentheses. Speak as clearly as possible: Once a statement has been read, it cannot be repeated.

Examine Sample 1. (Pause 2-3 seconds.) If the second number is less than the first number, but greater than the third number, write the letter B, as in "boy," beside the first number in the sample. (Pause 2 seconds.) Otherwise, write the letter C, as in "cat," beside the third number in the sample. (Pause 2 seconds.) Now, darken the number-letter combination you selected on your answer sheet. (Pause 5 seconds.)

Examine Sample 1 again. (Pause 2-3 seconds.) If the first number is 3 less than the second number, and one less than the third number, write the letter D, as in "dog," beside the first number. (Pause 2 seconds.) Otherwise, write the letter A, as in "apple," beside the first number. (Pause 2 seconds.) Now, darken the number-letter combination selected on your answer sheet. (Pause 5 seconds.)

Examine Sample 2. (Pause 2-3 seconds.) Go to number 20 on your answer sheet and darken the letter that represents the geometric figure with the fewest sides. (Pause 5 seconds.)

Examine Sample 3. (Pause 2-3 seconds.) Each of the letters in the sample represents one of five different regions with corresponding Postal Customer Satisfaction Indexes, expressed as a percentage. (Pause 2 seconds.) Go to number 13 on your answer sheet and darken the letter that represents the region with the second highest Customer Satisfaction Index. (Pause 5 seconds.) Now, go to number 14 on your answer sheet and darken the letter that represents the region with the second lowest Customer Satisfaction Index. (Pause 5 seconds.)

Examine Sample 2. (Pause 2-3 seconds.) If either Figure C, as in "cat," or Figure D, as in "dog," has fewer sides than Figure B, as in "boy," write the number 39 in Figure C, as in "cat." (Pause 2 seconds.) Otherwise, write the number 38 in Figure A, as in "apple." (Pause 2 seconds.) Now, go to your answer sheet and darken the number-letter combination you selected. (Pause 5 seconds.)

Examine Sample 3. (Pause 2-3 seconds.) Go to number 44 on your answer sheet and darken the letter that represents the lowest Customer Satisfaction Index percentage. (Pause 5 seconds.)

Examine Sample 4. (Pause 2-3 seconds.) Write the numbers 55, 52, and 49 beside the letters D, C, and E respectively. (Pause 7 seconds.) Now, go to your answer sheet and darken each of these number-letter combinations. (Pause 15 seconds.)

Examine Sample 5. (Pause 2-3 seconds.) Write the number 66 in the third box from the right. (Pause 2 seconds.) Write the number 4 in the third circle. (Pause 2 seconds.) Write the number 15 in the middle box. (Pause 2 seconds.) Now, go to your answer sheet and darken only the first two number-letter combinations selected. (Pause 10 seconds.)

Examine Sample 6. (Pause 2-3 seconds.) Select the second highest number in this sample and underline the last two digits. (Pause 2 seconds.) Go to that number on your answer sheet and darken the letter A, as in "apple." (Pause 5 seconds.)

Examine Sample 6 again. (Pause 2-3 seconds.) If the first number is less than the third number and greater than the fourth number, go to number 72 on your answer sheet and darken the letter E, as in "elephant." (Pause 5 seconds.) Otherwise, go to number 72 on your answer sheet anyway and darken the letter D, as in "dog." (Pause 5 seconds.)

Examine Sample 7. (Pause 2-3 seconds.) Letters A through E represent five different curbside mailboxes and their respective collection times. (Pause 2 seconds.) Go to number 19 on your answer sheet and darken the letter that represents the third earliest collection time in the sample. (Pause 5 seconds.)

Examine Sample 7 again. (Pause 2-3 seconds.) If Mailbox B, as in "boy," is collected before Mailbox D, as in "dog," or E, as in "elephant," darken the letter D, as in "dog," on number 10 of your answer sheet. (Pause 5 seconds.) If not, go to number 17 on your answer sheet and darken the letter E, as in "elephant." (Pause 5 seconds.)

Examine Sample 7 one more time. (Pause 2-3 seconds.) Select the letter that represents the first curbside mailbox to be collected after 12 noon and go to number 50 on your answer sheet and darken that same letter. (Pause 5 seconds.)

Examine Sample 8. (Pause 2-3 seconds.) Four city letter carriers, represented by the letters A through D, recently underwent route inspections. The number pairs shown beneath each letter reflect the degree of efficiency with which each carrier sorts mail according to route schemes. The first number in each pair illustrates the average number of letters cased, or sorted, per minute. The second number illustrates the average number of magazines cased per minute. (Pause 5 seconds.) Go to number 28 on your answer sheet and darken the letter that represents the carrier with the fastest letter-casing speed. (Pause 5 seconds.) Now, go to number 29 on your answer sheet and darken the letter that represents the letter carrier with the second slowest casing time of magazines. (Pause 5 seconds.)

Examine Sample 8 again. (Pause 2-3 seconds.) If Carrier B, as in "boy," can sort letter mail faster than Carrier D, as in "dog," and Carrier A, as in "apple," can sort magazines faster than Carrier C, as in "cat," go to number 82 on your answer sheet and darken the letter C, as in "cat." (Pause 5 seconds.) Otherwise, go to number 85 on your answer sheet and darken the letter A, as in "apple." (Pause 5 seconds.)

Examine Sample 9. (Pause 2-3 seconds.) Each of the numbers shown reflects daily delivery volumes which are expressed in linear feet, for three different postal operations. (Pause 2 seconds.) If Wednesday appears to be the lightest day of the week for all three stations, go to number 36 on your answer sheet and darken the letter E, as in "elephant." (Pause 5 seconds.) Otherwise, go to number 33 on your answer sheet and darken the letter A, as in "apple." (Pause 5 seconds.)

Examine Sample 9 again. (Pause 2-3 seconds.) If Postal Station Z gets more mail volume on Thursday than it does either on Monday or Saturday, go to number 63 on your answer sheet and darken the letter C, as in "cat." (Pause 5 seconds.) If not, go to number 67 on your answer sheet and darken the letter E, as in "elephant." (Pause 5 seconds.)

Examine Sample 6. (Pause 2-3 seconds.) If the second number is greater than the fourth number but is less than either the first or third number, darken the letter A, as in "apple," on number 73 on your answer sheet. (Pause 5 seconds.) Otherwise, go to number 26 on your answer sheet and darken the letter C, as in "cat." (Pause 5 seconds.)

Examine Sample 9 again. (Pause 2-3 seconds.) If Postal Station X gets more mail volume on Tuesday than either Postal Station Z or Postal Station Y, go to number 59 on your answer sheet and darken the letter B, as in "boy." (Pause 5 seconds.) If, on the other hand, Postal Station X gets more mail volume on Tuesday than Postal Station Y, go to number 58 on your answer sheet and darken the letter C, as in "cat." (Pause 5 seconds.) Otherwise, go to number 60 on your answer sheet and darken the letter D, as in "dog." (Pause 5 seconds.)

Now, go to number 65 on your answer sheet and darken the letter that represents the octagon in Sample 2. (Pause 5 seconds.)

-END OF TEST-

FOLLOWING DIRECTIONS/EXAM 4 SAMPLES

1.   90_____   87_____   91_____

2.   A   B   C   D

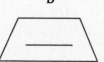

3.   A   B   C   D   E
      .83   .87   .82   .91   .86

4.   _____E   _____D   _____C

5.   (__E) [__B] (__D) [__A] (__C) [__D] (__A)

6.   679   450   890   75

7.   A   B   C   D   E

| 10:00 AM | 1:00 PM | 11:30 AM | 3:30 PM | 2:30 PM |

8.   A   B   C   D
     31/15   28/10   32/12   25/8

9.

	POSTAL STATION X	POSTAL STATION Y	POSTAL STATION Z
Monday:	135	185	133
Tuesday:	167	190	150
Wednesday:	110	126	105
Thursday:	152	173	128
Friday:	131	146	125
Saturday:	147	169	113

ANSWER SHEET TO FOLLOWING DIRECTIONS/EXAM 4

1. Ⓐ Ⓑ Ⓒ Ⓓ Ⓔ
2. Ⓐ Ⓑ Ⓒ Ⓓ Ⓔ
3. Ⓐ Ⓑ Ⓒ Ⓓ Ⓔ
4. Ⓐ Ⓑ Ⓒ Ⓓ Ⓔ
5. Ⓐ Ⓑ Ⓒ Ⓓ Ⓔ
6. Ⓐ Ⓑ Ⓒ Ⓓ Ⓔ
7. Ⓐ Ⓑ Ⓒ Ⓓ Ⓔ
8. Ⓐ Ⓑ Ⓒ Ⓓ Ⓔ
9. Ⓐ Ⓑ Ⓒ Ⓓ Ⓔ
10. Ⓐ Ⓑ Ⓒ Ⓓ Ⓔ
11. Ⓐ Ⓑ Ⓒ Ⓓ Ⓔ
12. Ⓐ Ⓑ Ⓒ Ⓓ Ⓔ
13. Ⓐ Ⓑ Ⓒ Ⓓ Ⓔ
14. Ⓐ Ⓑ Ⓒ Ⓓ Ⓔ
15. Ⓐ Ⓑ Ⓒ Ⓓ Ⓔ
16. Ⓐ Ⓑ Ⓒ Ⓓ Ⓔ
17. Ⓐ Ⓑ Ⓒ Ⓓ Ⓔ
18. Ⓐ Ⓑ Ⓒ Ⓓ Ⓔ
19. Ⓐ Ⓑ Ⓒ Ⓓ Ⓔ
20. Ⓐ Ⓑ Ⓒ Ⓓ Ⓔ
21. Ⓐ Ⓑ Ⓒ Ⓓ Ⓔ
22. Ⓐ Ⓑ Ⓒ Ⓓ Ⓔ
23. Ⓐ Ⓑ Ⓒ Ⓓ Ⓔ
24. Ⓐ Ⓑ Ⓒ Ⓓ Ⓔ
25. Ⓐ Ⓑ Ⓒ Ⓓ Ⓔ
26. Ⓐ Ⓑ Ⓒ Ⓓ Ⓔ
27. Ⓐ Ⓑ Ⓒ Ⓓ Ⓔ
28. Ⓐ Ⓑ Ⓒ Ⓓ Ⓔ
29. Ⓐ Ⓑ Ⓒ Ⓓ Ⓔ
30. Ⓐ Ⓑ Ⓒ Ⓓ Ⓔ
31. Ⓐ Ⓑ Ⓒ Ⓓ Ⓔ
32. Ⓐ Ⓑ Ⓒ Ⓓ Ⓔ

33. Ⓐ Ⓑ Ⓒ Ⓓ Ⓔ
34. Ⓐ Ⓑ Ⓒ Ⓓ Ⓔ
35. Ⓐ Ⓑ Ⓒ Ⓓ Ⓔ
36. Ⓐ Ⓑ Ⓒ Ⓓ Ⓔ
37. Ⓐ Ⓑ Ⓒ Ⓓ Ⓔ
38. Ⓐ Ⓑ Ⓒ Ⓓ Ⓔ
39. Ⓐ Ⓑ Ⓒ Ⓓ Ⓔ
40. Ⓐ Ⓑ Ⓒ Ⓓ Ⓔ
41. Ⓐ Ⓑ Ⓒ Ⓓ Ⓔ
42. Ⓐ Ⓑ Ⓒ Ⓓ Ⓔ
43. Ⓐ Ⓑ Ⓒ Ⓓ Ⓔ
44. Ⓐ Ⓑ Ⓒ Ⓓ Ⓔ
45. Ⓐ Ⓑ Ⓒ Ⓓ Ⓔ
46. Ⓐ Ⓑ Ⓒ Ⓓ Ⓔ
47. Ⓐ Ⓑ Ⓒ Ⓓ Ⓔ
48. Ⓐ Ⓑ Ⓒ Ⓓ Ⓔ
49. Ⓐ Ⓑ Ⓒ Ⓓ Ⓔ
50. Ⓐ Ⓑ Ⓒ Ⓓ Ⓔ
51. Ⓐ Ⓑ Ⓒ Ⓓ Ⓔ
52. Ⓐ Ⓑ Ⓒ Ⓓ Ⓔ
53. Ⓐ Ⓑ Ⓒ Ⓓ Ⓔ
54. Ⓐ Ⓑ Ⓒ Ⓓ Ⓔ
55. Ⓐ Ⓑ Ⓒ Ⓓ Ⓔ
56. Ⓐ Ⓑ Ⓒ Ⓓ Ⓔ
57. Ⓐ Ⓑ Ⓒ Ⓓ Ⓔ
58. Ⓐ Ⓑ Ⓒ Ⓓ Ⓔ
59. Ⓐ Ⓑ Ⓒ Ⓓ Ⓔ
60. Ⓐ Ⓑ Ⓒ Ⓓ Ⓔ
61. Ⓐ Ⓑ Ⓒ Ⓓ Ⓔ
62. Ⓐ Ⓑ Ⓒ Ⓓ Ⓔ
63. Ⓐ Ⓑ Ⓒ Ⓓ Ⓔ
64. Ⓐ Ⓑ Ⓒ Ⓓ Ⓔ

65. Ⓐ Ⓑ Ⓒ Ⓓ Ⓔ
66. Ⓐ Ⓑ Ⓒ Ⓓ Ⓔ
67. Ⓐ Ⓑ Ⓒ Ⓓ Ⓔ
68. Ⓐ Ⓑ Ⓒ Ⓓ Ⓔ
69. Ⓐ Ⓑ Ⓒ Ⓓ Ⓔ
70. Ⓐ Ⓑ Ⓒ Ⓓ Ⓔ
71. Ⓐ Ⓑ Ⓒ Ⓓ Ⓔ
72. Ⓐ Ⓑ Ⓒ Ⓓ Ⓔ
73. Ⓐ Ⓑ Ⓒ Ⓓ Ⓔ
74. Ⓐ Ⓑ Ⓒ Ⓓ Ⓔ
75. Ⓐ Ⓑ Ⓒ Ⓓ Ⓔ
76. Ⓐ Ⓑ Ⓒ Ⓓ Ⓔ
77. Ⓐ Ⓑ Ⓒ Ⓓ Ⓔ
78. Ⓐ Ⓑ Ⓒ Ⓓ Ⓔ
79. Ⓐ Ⓑ Ⓒ Ⓓ Ⓔ
80. Ⓐ Ⓑ Ⓒ Ⓓ Ⓔ
81. Ⓐ Ⓑ Ⓒ Ⓓ Ⓔ
82. Ⓐ Ⓑ Ⓒ Ⓓ Ⓔ
83. Ⓐ Ⓑ Ⓒ Ⓓ Ⓔ
84. Ⓐ Ⓑ Ⓒ Ⓓ Ⓔ
85. Ⓐ Ⓑ Ⓒ Ⓓ Ⓔ
86. Ⓐ Ⓑ Ⓒ Ⓓ Ⓔ
87. Ⓐ Ⓑ Ⓒ Ⓓ Ⓔ
88. Ⓐ Ⓑ Ⓒ Ⓓ Ⓔ
89. Ⓐ Ⓑ Ⓒ Ⓓ Ⓔ
90. Ⓐ Ⓑ Ⓒ Ⓓ Ⓔ
91. Ⓐ Ⓑ Ⓒ Ⓓ Ⓔ
92. Ⓐ Ⓑ Ⓒ Ⓓ Ⓔ
93. Ⓐ Ⓑ Ⓒ Ⓓ Ⓔ
94. Ⓐ Ⓑ Ⓒ Ⓓ Ⓔ
95. Ⓐ Ⓑ Ⓒ Ⓓ Ⓔ

(This page may be removed to mark answers.)

[This page intentionally blank.]

ANSWERS TO ADDRESS CROSS COMPARISON/EXAM 4

1.	A	33.	D	65.	D
2.	D	34.	D	66.	D
3.	D	35.	A	67.	A
4.	A	36.	D	68.	D
5.	A	37.	A	69.	D
6.	D	38.	D	70.	D
7.	D	39.	D	71.	A
8.	A	40.	A	72.	A
9.	A	41.	A	73.	D
10.	D	42.	D	74.	A
11.	D	43.	D	75.	A
12.	A	44.	D	76.	D
13.	D	45.	D	77.	D
14.	A	46.	D	78.	A
15.	D	47.	A	79.	D
16.	A	48.	A	80.	A
17.	A	49.	D	81.	A
18.	D	50.	A	82.	A
19.	A	51.	D	83.	D
20.	D	52.	A	84.	A
21.	D	53.	A	85.	D
22.	D	54.	A	86.	D
23.	D	55.	A	87.	D
24.	A	56.	D	88.	A
25.	A	57.	A	89.	A
26.	D	58.	A	90.	A
27.	A	59.	D	91.	D
28.	D	60.	A	92.	D
29.	A	61.	D	93.	A
30.	A	62.	A	94.	A
31.	A	63.	A	95.	D
32.	D	64.	A		

ANSWERS TO MEMORIZATION/EXAM 4

1.	E	31.	D	61.	B
2.	D	32.	A	62.	A
3.	A	33.	D	63.	D
4.	D	34.	B	64.	B
5.	A	35.	B	65.	A
6.	A	36.	C	66.	C
7.	C	37.	E	67.	E
8.	A	38.	D	68.	C
9.	C	39.	E	69.	C
10.	D	40.	B	70.	C
11.	B	41.	C	71.	D
12.	B	42.	E	72.	E
13.	A	43.	A	73.	E
14.	E	44.	E	74.	E
15.	B	45.	A	75.	D
16.	C	46.	B	76.	B
17.	C	47.	C	77.	D
18.	D	48.	C	78.	E
19.	C	49.	C	79.	C
20.	E	50.	E	80.	A
21.	D	51.	D	81.	B
22.	E	52.	B	82.	D
23.	D	53.	B	83.	B
24.	E	54.	D	84.	C
25.	C	55.	A	85.	E
26.	B	56.	C	86.	A
27.	A	57.	D	87.	B
28.	D	58.	E	88.	B
29.	A	59.	E		
30.	A	60.	A		

ANSWERS TO NUMBERS SERIES/EXAM 4

1. A.
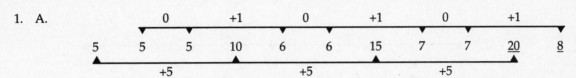

2. E.
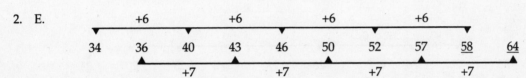

3. C.
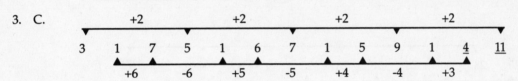

4. D.
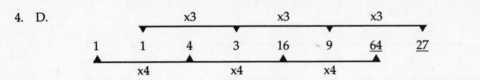

5. D.
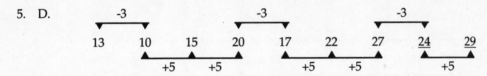

6. E.
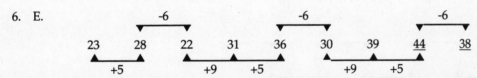

7. B.
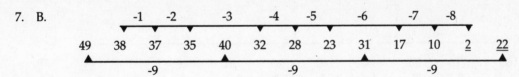

8. C.
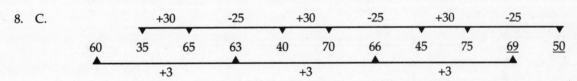

9. A.
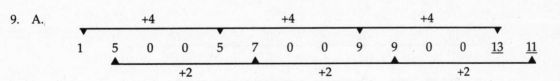

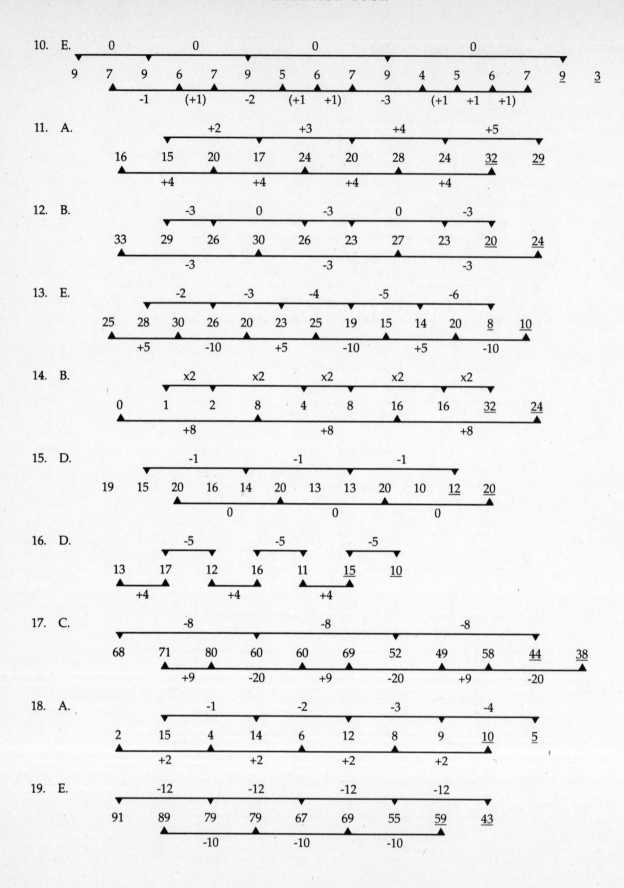

20. E.

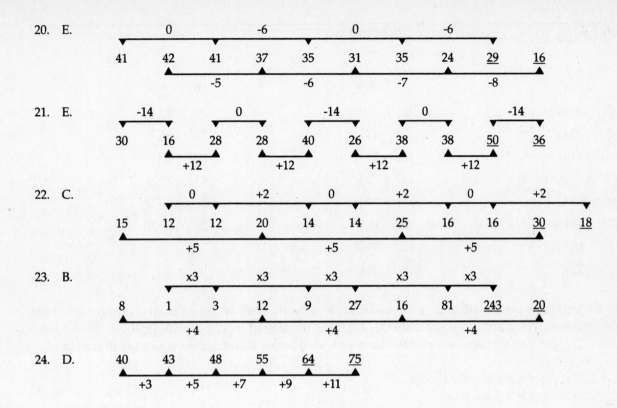

21. E.

22. C.

23. B.

24. D.

ANSWERS TO FOLLOWING DIRECTIONS/EXAM 4

1.	91 C	10.	49 E	19.	29 B
2.	90 A	11.	66 B	20.	82 C
3.	20 C	12.	4 C	21.	36 E
4.	13 B	13.	79 A	22.	67 E
5.	14 A	14.	72 E	23.	73 A
6.	39 C	15.	19 B	24.	60 D
7.	44 C	16.	10 D	25.	65 A
8.	55 D	17.	50 B		
9.	52 C	18.	28 C		

To determine your performance on this exam, add the number of correct answers from each of the four sections of the test. Subtract from this total the number of incorrect answers from the Address Cross Comparison section. Ratings have been provided below to determine your overall standing.

225-232 correct is an excellent score.
208-224 correct is a good score.
207 or fewer correct requires more practice.

Exam 5

**DO NOT OPEN THIS TEST BOOKLET UNTIL
YOU ARE TOLD TO START BY THE INDIVIDUAL
ASSISTING YOU IN THIS EXERCISE**

[This page intentionally blank.]

1.	1717 Wasbash Ave.	1717 Wabash Ave.
2.	2035 Kewanna Dr. SW	2035 Kawanna Dr. SW
3.	404 E. Attica St.	440 E. Attica St.
4.	New Carlisle, Ind. 48113	New Carlile, Ind. 48113
5.	31310 Hartford Ave.	31310 Heartford Ave.
6.	1112 Warsaw Lane NE	1112 Warsaw Lane NE
7.	41141 Maquoketa Blvd.	4114 Maquoketa Blvd.
8.	Hutchinson, Kan. 50897	Hutchinson, Kan. 50897
9.	304 Osborne Dr.	304 Osborn Dr.
10.	1299 Hiawatha Pl.	9912 Hiawatha Pl.
11.	155 NW Bancroft Ave.	155 NW Bancroft Ave.
12.	Cheyenne, Wyo. 79333	Cheyenne, Wyo. 79333
13.	6044 Ullysses Ct.	6044 Ulysses Ct.
14.	Route 4, Box 20053	Route 4, Box 20503
15.	5132 NE Kendall Circle	5132 NE Kendall Circle
16.	106 Murray Dr.	106 Murray Dr.
17.	Council Bluffs, Ia 53215	Council Bluffs, Ia. 53215
18.	9090 Pocahontas Place	9090 Pocohontas Place
19.	4152 Bondurant Blvd.	4152 Bondurant Blvd.
20.	1119 Versailles Point	1191 Versailles Point
21.	Brandywine, MD 04320	Brandywine, MD 04320
22.	73444 Randolph Trail	74344 Randolph Trail
23.	Battlecreek, Mich 67022	Battlecreek, Mich 67202

24.	4091 Somerset Place	4091 Somerset Place
25.	503 N. Watseka Cr.	503 N. Watsaka Cr.
26.	4017 Ladora Dr.	4017 Ladora Dr.
27.	1514-M Windsor Hts. Apts.	1514-M Windsor Hts. Apts.
28.	3093 NW Ellinwood Ave.	3093 SW Ellinwood Ave.
29.	404 31st St.	404 33rd St.
30.	Acomita, NM 79443	Acomita, NM 79443
31.	7474 Granite Hill Rd.	7474 Granate Hill Rd.
32.	202 W. Bismark Ave.	202 W. Bismark Ave.
33.	70009 Decator Dr.	70009 Decaitor Dr.
34.	113 Phillips Pt.	113 Phillips Pt.
35.	4531 Rosewood Lane	4531 Rosemary Lane
36.	Barneston, Neb. 67901	Barnesston, Neb. 67901
37.	3031 Springdale Dr.	3130 Springdale Dr.
38.	1418 White Pine Dr.	1418 White Pine Dr.
39.	6060 62nd Ave. SW	606 62nd Ave. SW
40.	322 Chadron Ct.	322 Chadron Ct.
41.	97388 Clinton St. N.	97388 Clinton St.
42.	7070 Ironside Dr.	70707 Ironside Dr.
43.	32-C Chinook Pl.	32-C S. Chinook Pl.
44.	8013 Dodson	8013 Dodson
45.	Contoocook, NH 09433	Contoocook, NH 09433
46.	13133 Hampstead Blvd.	13131 Hampstead Blvd.
47.	7274 Esmeralda Way	7274 Esmerelda Way
48.	702 Beatrice St.	702 Beatrice Street

49.	9093 Moccasin Trail	9093 Moccasin Trail
50.	300 Simms Ave.	300 Simms Ave.
51.	Bayonne, NJ 09444	Bayonne, NJ 09444
52.	4075 Daniels Dr.	4075 Daniels Dr. SW
53.	1091 Osage Beach	1091 Osage Beach
54.	31372 Henrietta Blvd.	31372 Henrietta Blvd.
55.	1696 Bucklin Hill Rd.	1669 Bucklin Hill Rd.
56.	73051 Dekalb Ave.	73051 Dekelb Ave.
57.	47910 Magnolia Dr.	47910 Magnolia Dr.
58.	Batesville, Miss 49330	Batsville, Miss 49330
59.	707 Maple Grove	7070 Maple Grove
60.	126 Lucerne Ln.	126 Lucerne Ln.
61.	Bellefontaine, MO 54355	Bellefontaine, MO 54355
62.	40002 Laddonia Dr.	40003 Laddonia Dr.
63.	1313 Wilkinson Blvd.	1313 Wilkenson Blvd.
64.	988 Raymond Way S.	988 S. Raymond Way
65.	5577 Beaumont St.	7755 Beaumont St.
66.	1111 Concordia Jct.	1111 Concordia Jct.
67.	Golconda, NEV 84328	Golkonda, NEV 84328
68.	48932 Marshall Terrace	48932 Marshall Terrace
69.	3197 Dolomite Ridge	3197 Dolomitic Ridge
70.	811 Robins	811 Robins
71.	80706 Jasper Jct. SW	80706 Jasper Jct. SW
72.	Mount Edgecumbe, AK	Mt. Edgecumbe, AK
73.	9810 Oak Knolls S.	9810 Oak Knolls S.

74.	7351 Hollister Ave.	7315 Hollister Ave.
75.	1507 Yellow Pine	1508 Green Pine Dr.
76.	Ehrenberg, Ariz. 85123	Ehrenburg, Ariz. 85123
77.	1413 3rd St. SW	1413 6th Ave. SW
78.	41378 Tallapoosa Circle	41378 Tallapoosa Circle
79.	105 NW Addison Dr.	105 NW Addison Dr.
80.	4899 Winston Hill	48999 Winston Hill
81.	2043 Fremont Way	2043 Fremont Way
82.	77-D Grandview Apts.	77-D Grandview Apts.
83.	1414 Frazier Park	1414 Frazier Park
84.	4149 Capistrano Beach	4149 Capistreno Beach
85.	83140 Holliwood Blvd.	83410 Holliwood Blvd.
86.	Attawaugan, Conn. 48590	Atawaugan, Conn. 48590
87.	5020 Bristol St.	5020 Bristol St.
88.	10956 Cromwell Dr.	10956 Cromwell Ct.
89.	198 Kent	198 Kent
90.	401 Willow Branch	401 Willow Branch
91.	Cheswold, DEL 03211	Cheswald, DEL 03211
92.	3400 Bowers	3400 Bowens
93.	2020 N. Laporte Ave.	2020 N. Laport Ave.
94.	120 Santa Cruz Circle	120 Santa Cruz Circle
95.	9011 Sedgwick Dr. SW	9011 Segwick Dr. SW

ANSWER SHEET TO ADDRESS CROSS COMPARISON/EXAM 5

1. (A) (D)
2. (A) (D)
3. (A) (D)
4. (A) (D)
5. (A) (D)
6. (A) (D)
7. (A) (D)
8. (A) (D)
9. (A) (D)
10. (A) (D)
11. (A) (D)
12. (A) (D)
13. (A) (D)
14. (A) (D)
15. (A) (D)
16. (A) (D)
17. (A) (D)
18. (A) (D)
19. (A) (D)
20. (A) (D)
21. (A) (D)
22. (A) (D)
23. (A) (D)
24. (A) (D)
25. (A) (D)
26. (A) (D)
27. (A) (D)
28. (A) (D)
29. (A) (D)
30. (A) (D)
31. (A) (D)
32. (A) (D)

33. (A) (D)
34. (A) (D)
35. (A) (D)
36. (A) (D)
37. (A) (D)
38. (A) (D)
39. (A) (D)
40. (A) (D)
41. (A) (D)
42. (A) (D)
43. (A) (D)
44. (A) (D)
45. (A) (D)
46. (A) (D)
47. (A) (D)
48. (A) (D)
49. (A) (D)
50. (A) (D)
51. (A) (D)
52. (A) (D)
53. (A) (D)
54. (A) (D)
55. (A) (D)
56. (A) (D)
57. (A) (D)
58. (A) (D)
59. (A) (D)
60. (A) (D)
61. (A) (D)
62. (A) (D)
63. (A) (D)
64. (A) (D)

65. (A) (D)
66. (A) (D)
67. (A) (D)
68. (A) (D)
69. (A) (D)
70. (A) (D)
71. (A) (D)
72. (A) (D)
73. (A) (D)
74. (A) (D)
75. (A) (D)
76. (A) (D)
77. (A) (D)
78. (A) (D)
79. (A) (D)
80. (A) (D)
81. (A) (D)
82. (A) (D)
83. (A) (D)
84. (A) (D)
85. (A) (D)
86. (A) (D)
87. (A) (D)
88. (A) (D)
89. (A) (D)
90. (A) (D)
91. (A) (D)
92. (A) (D)
93. (A) (D)
94. (A) (D)
95. (A) (D)

(This page may be removed to mark answers.)

[This page intentionally blank.]

MEMORIZATION/EXAM 5

A	B	C	D	E
1300-1399 Bowen	7900-7999 Bowen	8300-8399 Bowen	1500-1599 Bowen	5500-5599 Bowen
Border St.	Elkhart	Pine Cone Dr.	Elbe Blvd.	Borden Ave.
8300-8399 Lyle	7900-7999 Lyle	1500-1599 Lyle	5500-5599 Lyle	1300-1399 Lyle
Millstone Ln.	Constantine	Park Ave.	Illinois St.	Morgan Dr.
7900-7999 Kolbe	1500-1599 Kolbe	1300-1399 Kolbe	8300-8399 Kolbe	5500-5599 Kolbe

NOTE: Follow the same step by step format established for the memorization exercises studied earlier. (See page 41.)

PRACTICE MEMORIZATION/EXAM 5

STEP 2 TIME: 3 MINUTES
STEP 3 TIME: 3 MINUTES (cover key)

A	B	C	D	E
1300-1399 Bowen	7900-7999 Bowen	8300-8399 Bowen	1500-1599 Bowen	5500-5599 Bowen
Border St.	Elkhart	Pine Cone Dr.	Elbe Blvd.	Borden Ave.
8300-8399 Lyle	7900-7999 Lyle	1500-1599 Lyle	5500-5599 Lyle	1300-1399 Lyle
Millstone Ln.	Constantine	Park Ave.	Illinois St.	Morgan Dr.
7900-7999 Kolbe	1500-1599 Kolbe	1300-1399 Kolbe	8300-8399 Kolbe	5500-5599 Kolbe

1. 7900-7999 Kolbe
2. Constantine
3. Pine Cone Dr.
4. 1500-1599 Lyle
5. 5500-5599 Bowen
6. Morgan Dr.
7. Border St.
8. 8300-8399 Lyle
9. 8300-8399 Bowen
10. Park Ave.
11. 5500-5599 Kolbe
12. Illinois St.
13. 1300-1399 Kolbe
14. Elbe Blvd.
15. Millstone Ln.
16. Borden Ave.
17. 1300-1399 Lyle
18. 7900-7999 Lyle
19. 1300-1399 Bowen
20. 8300-8399 Kolbe
21. Pine Cone Dr.
22. 1500-1599 Kolbe
23. Morgan Dr.
24. 5500-5599 Bowen
25. 7900-7999 Bowen
26. Elbe Blvd.
27. 1300-1399 Bowen
28. 1500-1599 Kolbe
29. 8300-8399 Bowen
30. 5500-5599 Lyle

31. Border St.
32. Illinois St.
33. Morgan Dr.
34. Constantine
35. 8300-8399 Bowen
36. 5500-5599 Lyle
37. 7900-7999 Kolbe
38. 1300-1399 Bowen
39. 8300-8399 Lyle
40. 1500-1599 Lyle
41. Elkhart
42. 8300-8399 Kolbe
43. Morgan Dr.
44. 5500-5599 Kolbe
45. 1500-1599 Lyle
46. Pine Cone Dr.
47. Borden Ave.
48. 8300-8399 Bowen
49. 1500-1599 Kolbe
50. 1300-1399 Bowen
51. Illinois St.
52. Park Ave.
53. 7900-7999 Lyle
54. 5500-5599 Bowen
55. Millstone Ln.
56. 1500-1599 Kolbe
57. 5500-5599 Bowen
58. 7900-7999 Bowen
59. 1300-1399 Kolbe
60. 8300-8399 Kolbe

61. Elbe Blvd.
62. 5500-5599 Lyle
63. Park Ave.
64. Millstone Ln.
65. 8300-8399 Lyle
66. 8300-8399 Bowen
67. 8300-8399 Kolbe
68. Illinois St.
69. Border St.
70. 7900-7999 Lyle
71. 1500-1599 Lyle
72. 1300-1399 Lyle
73. 8300-8399 Bowen
74. 7900-7999 Kolbe
75. Constantine
76. 1500-1599 Bowen
77. 1500-1599 Kolbe
78. 7900-7999 Bowen
79. Pine Cone Dr.
80. Borden Ave.
81. 1500-1599 Kolbe
82. Border St.
83. 5500-5599 Lyle
84. 8300-8399 Bowen
85. 1500-1599 Kolbe
86. Millstone Ln.
87. 7900-7999 Bowen
88. Elbe Blvd.

PRACTICE ANSWER SHEET TO MEMORIZATION/EXAM 5

1. (A) (B) (C) (D) (E)
2. (A) (B) (C) (D) (E)
3. (A) (B) (C) (D) (E)
4. (A) (B) (C) (D) (E)
5. (A) (B) (C) (D) (E)
6. (A) (B) (C) (D) (E)
7. (A) (B) (C) (D) (E)
8. (A) (B) (C) (D) (E)
9. (A) (B) (C) (D) (E)
10. (A) (B) (C) (D) (E)
11. (A) (B) (C) (D) (E)
12. (A) (B) (C) (D) (E)
13. (A) (B) (C) (D) (E)
14. (A) (B) (C) (D) (E)
15. (A) (B) (C) (D) (E)
16. (A) (B) (C) (D) (E)
17. (A) (B) (C) (D) (E)
18. (A) (B) (C) (D) (E)
19. (A) (B) (C) (D) (E)
20. (A) (B) (C) (D) (E)
21. (A) (B) (C) (D) (E)
22. (A) (B) (C) (D) (E)
23. (A) (B) (C) (D) (E)
24. (A) (B) (C) (D) (E)
25. (A) (B) (C) (D) (E)
26. (A) (B) (C) (D) (E)
27. (A) (B) (C) (D) (E)
28. (A) (B) (C) (D) (E)
29. (A) (B) (C) (D) (E)
30. (A) (B) (C) (D) (E)

31. (A) (B) (C) (D) (E)
32. (A) (B) (C) (D) (E)
33. (A) (B) (C) (D) (E)
34. (A) (B) (C) (D) (E)
35. (A) (B) (C) (D) (E)
36. (A) (B) (C) (D) (E)
37. (A) (B) (C) (D) (E)
38. (A) (B) (C) (D) (E)
39. (A) (B) (C) (D) (E)
40. (A) (B) (C) (D) (E)
41. (A) (B) (C) (D) (E)
42. (A) (B) (C) (D) (E)
43. (A) (B) (C) (D) (E)
44. (A) (B) (C) (D) (E)
45. (A) (B) (C) (D) (E)
46. (A) (B) (C) (D) (E)
47. (A) (B) (C) (D) (E)
48. (A) (B) (C) (D) (E)
49. (A) (B) (C) (D) (E)
50. (A) (B) (C) (D) (E)
51. (A) (B) (C) (D) (E)
52. (A) (B) (C) (D) (E)
53. (A) (B) (C) (D) (E)
54. (A) (B) (C) (D) (E)
55. (A) (B) (C) (D) (E)
56. (A) (B) (C) (D) (E)
57. (A) (B) (C) (D) (E)
58. (A) (B) (C) (D) (E)
59. (A) (B) (C) (D) (E)
60. (A) (B) (C) (D) (E)

61. (A) (B) (C) (D) (E)
62. (A) (B) (C) (D) (E)
63. (A) (B) (C) (D) (E)
64. (A) (B) (C) (D) (E)
65. (A) (B) (C) (D) (E)
66. (A) (B) (C) (D) (E)
67. (A) (B) (C) (D) (E)
68. (A) (B) (C) (D) (E)
69. (A) (B) (C) (D) (E)
70. (A) (B) (C) (D) (E)
71. (A) (B) (C) (D) (E)
72. (A) (B) (C) (D) (E)
73. (A) (B) (C) (D) (E)
74. (A) (B) (C) (D) (E)
75. (A) (B) (C) (D) (E)
76. (A) (B) (C) (D) (E)
77. (A) (B) (C) (D) (E)
78. (A) (B) (C) (D) (E)
79. (A) (B) (C) (D) (E)
80. (A) (B) (C) (D) (E)
81. (A) (B) (C) (D) (E)
82. (A) (B) (C) (D) (E)
83. (A) (B) (C) (D) (E)
84. (A) (B) (C) (D) (E)
85. (A) (B) (C) (D) (E)
86. (A) (B) (C) (D) (E)
87. (A) (B) (C) (D) (E)
88. (A) (B) (C) (D) (E)

1. 1300-1399 Bowen	31. 1500-1599 Kolbe	61. Border St.
2. 1500-1599 Lyle	32. 5500-5599 Kolbe	62. 1500-1599 Kolbe
3. Pine Cone Dr.	33. Border St.	63. Elbe Blvd.
4. Illinois St.	34. Millstone Ln.	64. 1500-1599 Bowen
5. 5500-5599 Kolbe	35. 7900-7999 Lyle	65. Constantine
6. 5500-5599 Bowen	36. Morgan Dr.	66. 7900-7999 Lyle
7. Elbe Blvd.	37. Illinois St.	67. Park Ave.
8. 1500-1599 Kolbe	38. 5500-5599 Lyle	68. Illinois St.
9. Millstone Ln.	39. 1500-1599 Bowen	69. Morgan Dr.
10. 7900-7999 Kolbe	40. 1500-1599 Kolbe	70. 1300-1399 Kolbe
11. 1300-1399 Kolbe	41. Elkhart	71. 8300-8399 Bowen
12. Borden Ave.	42. Park Ave.	72. 7900-7999 Kolbe
13. Border St.	43. Elbe Blvd.	73. 8300-8399 Lyle
14. Elkhart	44. 8300-8399 Bowen	74. 5500-5599 Bowen
15. 5500-5599 Lyle	45. Constantine	75. 8300-8399 Kolbe
16. Morgan Dr.	46. 8300-8399 Kolbe	76. Pine Cone Dr.
17. 7900-7999 Lyle	47. 8300-8399 Lyle	77. 1500-1599 Bowen
18. Pine Cone Dr.	48. Elkhart	78. 5500-5599 Bowen
19. 8300-8399 Bowen	49. 1500-1599 Bowen	79. Elkhart
20. 1300-1399 Kolbe	50. 5500-5599 Bowen	80. 7900-7999 Bowen
21. 1500-1599 Kolbe	51. 5500-5599 Kolbe	81. Constantine
22. 1500-1599 Bowen	52. Pine Cone Dr.	82. Millstone Ln.
23. 5500-5599 Bowen	53. Border St.	83. 7900-7999 Bowen
24. Borden Ave.	54. 8300-8399 Bowen	84. 8300-8399 Bowen
25. Constantine	55. 5500-5599 Lyle	85. 5500-5599 Bowen
26. 8300-8399 Lyle	56. 7900-7999 Kolbe	86. 7900-7999 Kolbe
27. 1300-1399 Bowen	57. 1500-1599 Lyle	87. Park Ave.
28. Elbe Blvd.	58. Park Ave.	88. Border St.
29. Park Ave.	59. 7900-7999 Bowen	
30. 1300-1399 Kolbe	60. Millstone Ln.	

ANSWER SHEET TO MEMORIZATION/EXAM 5

1. A B C D E
2. A B C D E
3. A B C D E
4. A B C D E
5. A B C D E
6. A B C D E
7. A B C D E
8. A B C D E
9. A B C D E
10. A B C D E
11. A B C D E
12. A B C D E
13. A B C D E
14. A B C D E
15. A B C D E
16. A B C D E
17. A B C D E
18. A B C D E
19. A B C D E
20. A B C D E
21. A B C D E
22. A B C D E
23. A B C D E
24. A B C D E
25. A B C D E
26. A B C D E
27. A B C D E
28. A B C D E
29. A B C D E
30. A B C D E

31. A B C D E
32. A B C D E
33. A B C D E
34. A B C D E
35. A B C D E
36. A B C D E
37. A B C D E
38. A B C D E
39. A B C D E
40. A B C D E
41. A B C D E
42. A B C D E
43. A B C D E
44. A B C D E
45. A B C D E
46. A B C D E
47. A B C D E
48. A B C D E
49. A B C D E
50. A B C D E
51. A B C D E
52. A B C D E
53. A B C D E
54. A B C D E
55. A B C D E
56. A B C D E
57. A B C D E
58. A B C D E
59. A B C D E
60. A B C D E

61. A B C D E
62. A B C D E
63. A B C D E
64. A B C D E
65. A B C D E
66. A B C D E
67. A B C D E
68. A B C D E
69. A B C D E
70. A B C D E
71. A B C D E
72. A B C D E
73. A B C D E
74. A B C D E
75. A B C D E
76. A B C D E
77. A B C D E
78. A B C D E
79. A B C D E
80. A B C D E
81. A B C D E
82. A B C D E
83. A B C D E
84. A B C D E
85. A B C D E
86. A B C D E
87. A B C D E
88. A B C D E

[This page intentionally blank.]

1. 10   15   20   15   25   30   20   35   ___   ___
    - A. 40, 20
    - B. 40, 25
    - C. 25, 40
    - D. 40, 30
    - E. 35, 40

2. 39   30   32   37   40   42   35   50   ___   ___
    - A. 33, 45
    - B. 33, 52
    - C. 52, 33
    - D. 45, 33
    - E. 45, 45

3. 7   0   1   2   7   1   2   3   7   2   3   ___   ___
    - A. 7, 4
    - B. 5, 7
    - C. 6, 7
    - D. 4, 7
    - E. 6, 6

4. 0   1   1   7   2   49   3   ___   ___
    - A. 4, 343
    - B. 340, 9
    - C. 9, 340
    - D. 349, 4
    - E. 343, 4

5. 12   10   11   10   8   9   8   6   ___   ___
    - A. 8, 9
    - B. 6, 7
    - C. 10, 11
    - D. 8, 8
    - E. 7, 6

6. 75   63   71   67   67   71   63   ___   ___
    - A. 75, 59
    - B. 75, 63
    - C. 70, 59
    - D. 70, 73
    - E. 70, 63

7. 51   53   57   54   56   60   57   ___   ___
    - A. 59, 63
    - B. 57, 63
    - C. 59, 59
    - D. 59, 62
    - E. 62, 59

8. 8   9   8   8   9   8   7   8   9   8   6   7   8   __   __

    A.   8, 9
    B.   9, 8
    C.   10, 8
    D.   10, 9
    E.   10, 10

9. 43   47   44   40   44   41   37   41   __   __

    A.   37, 34
    B.   38, 34
    C.   39, 33
    D.   40, 35
    E.   38, 33

10. 25   30   30   28   22   25   27   21   19   16   __   __

    A.   23, 10
    B.   20, 8
    C.   24, 10
    D.   23, 8
    E.   20, 20

11. 3   18   6   17   9   15   12   12   __   __

    A.   8, 8
    B.   14, 7
    C.   15, 8
    D.   14, 9
    E.   15, 10

12. 69   75   83   93   __   __

    A.   103, 115
    B.   100, 112
    C.   103, 117
    D.   105, 119
    E.   98, 110

13. 70   55   66   51   62   __   __

    A.   47, 58
    B.   45, 56
    C.   45, 58
    D.   58, 47
    E.   48, 57

14. 52   33   52   38   45   44   45   51   __   __

    A.   35, 56
    B.   59, 38
    C.   36, 58
    D.   38, 59
    E.   59, 40

15.   6   1   2   12   4   8   18   16   ___ ___

    A. 30, 24
    B. 32, 20
    C. 30, 26
    D. 34, 24
    E. 32, 24

16.   87   69   75   61   63   53   51   ___ ___

    A. 46, 39
    B. 47, 39
    C. 45, 39
    D. 45, 38
    E. 44, 38

17.   20   23   23   23   25   25   26   27   27   ___ ___

    A. 27, 29
    B. 29, 29
    C. 30, 30
    D. 28, 28
    E. 28, 29

18.   77 87 88 88 81 89 88 88 85 91 88 88 ___ ___

    A. 89, 92
    B. 88, 89
    C. 90, 93
    D. 90, 94
    E. 89, 93

19.   1   4   3   2   9   4   9   2   3   4   ___ ___

    A. 3, 2
    B. 1, 2
    C. 2, 3
    D. 1, 4
    E. 1, 5

20.   54 38 37 35 45 32 28 23 36 17 10 ___ ___

    A. 2, 27
    B. 10, 27
    C. 27, 3
    D. 27, 2
    E. 4, 25

21.   1   5   5   9   9   13   ___ ___

    A. 9, 13
    B. 13, 16
    C. 13, 17
    D. 13, 18
    E. 13, 20

22.   8   10   10   12   11   11   16   12   __   __

        A.   12, 18
        B.   18, 12
        C.   20, 14
        D.   12, 20
        E.   14, 20

23.   29   34   27   32   25   __   __

        A.   30, 24
        B.   24, 17
        C.   28, 22
        D.   30, 23
        E.   30, 20

24.   30   28   32   38   40   42   46   52   60   60   64   68   74   82   __   __

        A.   90, 90
        B.   92, 90
        C.   90, 92
        D.   94, 86
        E.   86, 94

ANSWER SHEET TO NUMBER SERIES/EXAM 5

1. Ⓐ Ⓑ Ⓒ Ⓓ Ⓔ
2. Ⓐ Ⓑ Ⓒ Ⓓ Ⓔ
3. Ⓐ Ⓑ Ⓒ Ⓓ Ⓔ
4. Ⓐ Ⓑ Ⓒ Ⓓ Ⓔ
5. Ⓐ Ⓑ Ⓒ Ⓓ Ⓔ
6. Ⓐ Ⓑ Ⓒ Ⓓ Ⓔ
7. Ⓐ Ⓑ Ⓒ Ⓓ Ⓔ
8. Ⓐ Ⓑ Ⓒ Ⓓ Ⓔ

9. Ⓐ Ⓑ Ⓒ Ⓓ Ⓔ
10. Ⓐ Ⓑ Ⓒ Ⓓ Ⓔ
11. Ⓐ Ⓑ Ⓒ Ⓓ Ⓔ
12. Ⓐ Ⓑ Ⓒ Ⓓ Ⓔ
13. Ⓐ Ⓑ Ⓒ Ⓓ Ⓔ
14. Ⓐ Ⓑ Ⓒ Ⓓ Ⓔ
15. Ⓐ Ⓑ Ⓒ Ⓓ Ⓔ
16. Ⓐ Ⓑ Ⓒ Ⓓ Ⓔ

17. Ⓐ Ⓑ Ⓒ Ⓓ Ⓔ
18. Ⓐ Ⓑ Ⓒ Ⓓ Ⓔ
19. Ⓐ Ⓑ Ⓒ Ⓓ Ⓔ
20. Ⓐ Ⓑ Ⓒ Ⓓ Ⓔ
21. Ⓐ Ⓑ Ⓒ Ⓓ Ⓔ
22. Ⓐ Ⓑ Ⓒ Ⓓ Ⓔ
23. Ⓐ Ⓑ Ⓒ Ⓓ Ⓔ
24. Ⓐ Ⓑ Ⓒ Ⓓ Ⓔ

(This page may be removed to mark answers.)

[This page intentionally blank.]

FOLLOWING DIRECTIONS/EXAM 5

Note To Person Assisting In This Exam:

Remove from this test guide the pages of this exam that comprise the directions to be read out loud. The test applicant should be left with only the sample sheet and answer sheet. Read the following directions out loud at the suggested rate of 75-80 words per minute, pausing only where indicated in parentheses. Speak as clearly as possible: Once a statement has been read, it cannot be repeated.

Examine Sample 1. (Pause 2-3 seconds.) Write the letter B, as in "boy," beside the second highest number shown if it is less than 48. (Pause 2 seconds.) Otherwise, write the letter E, as in "elephant," beside the lowest number. (Pause 2 seconds.) Write the letter C, as in "cat," beside the highest number shown if it is greater than 49. (Pause 2 seconds.) Otherwise, write the letter A, as in "apple," beside the last number shown in the sample. (Pause 2 seconds.) Now, go to your answer sheet and darken both of the number-letter combinations just made. (Pause 10 seconds.)

Examine Sample 2. (Pause 2-3 seconds.) Write the number 10 beside the fourth letter in the alphabet. (Pause 2 seconds). Darken that number-letter combination on your answer sheet. (Pause 5 seconds.) Now, if the third letter in the sample is the first letter in the alphabet and the first letter in the sample is the second letter in the alphabet, go to number 5 on your answer sheet and darken the letter A, as in "apple." (Pause 5 seconds.) Otherwise, write the number 14 beside the second letter in the sample and darken that number-letter combination on your answer sheet. (Pause 5 seconds.)

Examine Sample 2 again. (Pause 2-3 seconds.) Write the numbers 15 and 17 beside the first and fourth letters in the sample, respectively. (Pause 5 seconds.) Now, darken the latter of the two number-letter combinations on your answer sheet. (Pause 5 seconds.)

Examine Sample 3. (Pause 2-3 seconds.) Write the letter C, as in "cat," in the box; then letter E, as in "elephant," in the circle; then letter D, as in "dog," in the triangle; and the letter B, as in "boy," beside the number not enclosed within a geometric shape. (Pause 10 seconds.) Now, darken the two highest number-letter combinations that are enclosed in geometric shapes on your answer sheet. (Pause 10 seconds.)

Examine Sample 4. (Pause 2-3 seconds.) If the third number in the sample is 10 less than the highest number shown, go to the smallest number in the sample shown on your answer sheet and darken the letter D, as in "dog." (Pause 5 seconds.) Otherwise, go to the next highest number shown in the sample and on that same number on your answer sheet darken the letter E, as in "elephant." (Pause 5 seconds.)

Examine Sample 4 again. (Pause 2-3 seconds.) If the fourth number from the right is greater than the third number shown, go to number 36 on your answer sheet and darken the letter A, as in "apple." (Pause 5 seconds.) If not, go to number 36 on your answer sheet anyway and darken the letter B, as in "boy," instead. (Pause 5 seconds.)

Examine Sample 5. (Pause 2-3 seconds.) Draw circles around only those numbers which are odd. (Pause 5 seconds.) Draw boxes around the remaining numbers. (Pause 5 seconds.) Now, select the smallest number enclosed in a box and go to that number on your answer sheet and darken the letter C, as in "cat." (Pause 5 seconds.) Select the second highest number you circled and go to that number on your answer sheet and darken the letter E, as in "elephant." (Pause 5 seconds.)

Examine Sample 5 again. (Pause 2-3 seconds.) If the fifth number from the right is 4 less than the fifth number in the sample, go to number 66 on your answer sheet and darken the letter A, as in "apple." (Pause 5 seconds.) If not, go to number 65 on your answer sheet and darken the letter B, as in "boy." (Pause 5 seconds.)

Examine Sample 6. (Pause 2-3 seconds.) Select the second highest odd number enclosed in a geometrical shape and go to that same number on your answer sheet and darken the letter B, as in "boy."

(Pause 5 seconds.) Select the highest even number not enclosed in a geometrical shape and go to that number on your answer sheet, and darken the letter C, as in "cat." (Pause 5 seconds.) Now, go to the number on your answer sheet that is shown in the square in the sample and darken the letter C, as in "cat." (Pause 5 seconds.)

Examine Sample 6 again. (Pause 2-3 seconds.) If the number in the circle is less than the highest number not enclosed in a geometrical shape and the number in the rectangle is higher than the number in the triangle, go to number 91 on your answer sheet and darken the letter D, as in "dog." (Pause 5 seconds.) If not, go to number 92 on your answer sheet and darken the letter B, as in "boy." (Pause 5 seconds.)

Examine Sample 7. (Pause 2-3 seconds.) Write the sum of 21 plus 21 on the line and darken the resulting number-letter combination on your answer sheet. (Pause 5 seconds.)

Examine Sample 8. (Pause 2-3 seconds.) Select the highest number associated with the letter B, as in "boy," and then go to that same number on your answer sheet and darken the letter D, as in "dog." (Pause 5 seconds.)

Examine Sample 8 again. (Pause 2-3 seconds.) Select the highest odd number associated with the letter E, as in "elephant," and then go to that same number on your answer sheet and darken the letter A, as in "apple." (Pause 5 seconds.)

Examine Sample 9. (Pause 2-3 seconds.) If 5 is less than either 4 or 6, write the number 13 beside the letter B, as in "boy." (Pause 2 seconds.) Otherwise, write the number 16 beside the letter C, as in "cat." (Pause 2 seconds.) If 15 is an odd number and is 6 less than 21, write the letter A, as in "apple," beside the only number shown in the sample. (Pause 2 seconds.) Otherwise, write the letter B, as in "boy," beside the number shown in the sample. (Pause 2 seconds.) If the letter C, as in "cat," is the third letter in the alphabet, and represents the only letter circled in the sample, write the number 83 beside the last letter shown. (Pause 2 seconds.) If not, write the number 84 instead of 83 as instructed in the previous statement. (Pause 2 seconds.) Now, go to your answer sheet and darken these three number-letter combinations. (Pause 15 seconds.)

Examine Sample 10. (Pause 2-3 seconds.) If the sum of the second number added to itself would be greater than the fourth number shown in the sample, go to number 75 on your answer sheet and darken the letter A, as in "apple." (Pause 5 seconds.) If not, go to that same number on your answer sheet, and darken the letter E, as in "elephant." (Pause 5 seconds.)

Examine Sample 10 again. (Pause 2-3 seconds.) If the sum of the first and second numbers equals the first number from the right, go to number 9 on your answer sheet and darken the letter C, as in "cat." (Pause 5 seconds.) If not, go to number 11 on your answer sheet and darken the letter D, as in "dog." (Pause 5 seconds.)

Examine Sample 11. (Pause 2-3 seconds.) Write the numbers 43, 48, 49, and 50 beside the letters A, B, D, and E, respectively. (Pause 7 seconds.) Now, select the third number-letter combination you just made and darken that same selection on your answer sheet. (Pause 5 seconds.)

-END OF TEST-

FOLLOWING DIRECTIONS/EXAM 5 SAMPLES

1.   46_____   48_____   50_____

2.   _____B   _____C   _____A   _____E   _____D

3.   [28_____]   29_____   (30_____)   △27_____

4.   80   85   105   75   110   115

5.   37   38   39   40   41

6.   2   △26   [29]   [61]   (79)   ⏢80   83

7.   _____E

8.   46 E   72 A   73 E   79 C   92 B   94 B

9.   _____B   15_____   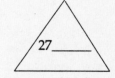

10.   15   14   30   29

11.   _____A   _____B   _____D   _____E

[This page intentionally blank.]

ANSWER SHEET TO FOLLOWING DIRECTIONS/EXAM 5

1. Ⓐ Ⓑ Ⓒ Ⓓ Ⓔ
2. Ⓐ Ⓑ Ⓒ Ⓓ Ⓔ
3. Ⓐ Ⓑ Ⓒ Ⓓ Ⓔ
4. Ⓐ Ⓑ Ⓒ Ⓓ Ⓔ
5. Ⓐ Ⓑ Ⓒ Ⓓ Ⓔ
6. Ⓐ Ⓑ Ⓒ Ⓓ Ⓔ
7. Ⓐ Ⓑ Ⓒ Ⓓ Ⓔ
8. Ⓐ Ⓑ Ⓒ Ⓓ Ⓔ
9. Ⓐ Ⓑ Ⓒ Ⓓ Ⓔ
10. Ⓐ Ⓑ Ⓒ Ⓓ Ⓔ
11. Ⓐ Ⓑ Ⓒ Ⓓ Ⓔ
12. Ⓐ Ⓑ Ⓒ Ⓓ Ⓔ
13. Ⓐ Ⓑ Ⓒ Ⓓ Ⓔ
14. Ⓐ Ⓑ Ⓒ Ⓓ Ⓔ
15. Ⓐ Ⓑ Ⓒ Ⓓ Ⓔ
16. Ⓐ Ⓑ Ⓒ Ⓓ Ⓔ
17. Ⓐ Ⓑ Ⓒ Ⓓ Ⓔ
18. Ⓐ Ⓑ Ⓒ Ⓓ Ⓔ
19. Ⓐ Ⓑ Ⓒ Ⓓ Ⓔ
20. Ⓐ Ⓑ Ⓒ Ⓓ Ⓔ
21. Ⓐ Ⓑ Ⓒ Ⓓ Ⓔ
22. Ⓐ Ⓑ Ⓒ Ⓓ Ⓔ
23. Ⓐ Ⓑ Ⓒ Ⓓ Ⓔ
24. Ⓐ Ⓑ Ⓒ Ⓓ Ⓔ
25. Ⓐ Ⓑ Ⓒ Ⓓ Ⓔ
26. Ⓐ Ⓑ Ⓒ Ⓓ Ⓔ
27. Ⓐ Ⓑ Ⓒ Ⓓ Ⓔ
28. Ⓐ Ⓑ Ⓒ Ⓓ Ⓔ
29. Ⓐ Ⓑ Ⓒ Ⓓ Ⓔ
30. Ⓐ Ⓑ Ⓒ Ⓓ Ⓔ
31. Ⓐ Ⓑ Ⓒ Ⓓ Ⓔ
32. Ⓐ Ⓑ Ⓒ Ⓓ Ⓔ

33. Ⓐ Ⓑ Ⓒ Ⓓ Ⓔ
34. Ⓐ Ⓑ Ⓒ Ⓓ Ⓔ
35. Ⓐ Ⓑ Ⓒ Ⓓ Ⓔ
36. Ⓐ Ⓑ Ⓒ Ⓓ Ⓔ
37. Ⓐ Ⓑ Ⓒ Ⓓ Ⓔ
38. Ⓐ Ⓑ Ⓒ Ⓓ Ⓔ
39. Ⓐ Ⓑ Ⓒ Ⓓ Ⓔ
40. Ⓐ Ⓑ Ⓒ Ⓓ Ⓔ
41. Ⓐ Ⓑ Ⓒ Ⓓ Ⓔ
42. Ⓐ Ⓑ Ⓒ Ⓓ Ⓔ
43. Ⓐ Ⓑ Ⓒ Ⓓ Ⓔ
44. Ⓐ Ⓑ Ⓒ Ⓓ Ⓔ
45. Ⓐ Ⓑ Ⓒ Ⓓ Ⓔ
46. Ⓐ Ⓑ Ⓒ Ⓓ Ⓔ
47. Ⓐ Ⓑ Ⓒ Ⓓ Ⓔ
48. Ⓐ Ⓑ Ⓒ Ⓓ Ⓔ
49. Ⓐ Ⓑ Ⓒ Ⓓ Ⓔ
50. Ⓐ Ⓑ Ⓒ Ⓓ Ⓔ
51. Ⓐ Ⓑ Ⓒ Ⓓ Ⓔ
52. Ⓐ Ⓑ Ⓒ Ⓓ Ⓔ
53. Ⓐ Ⓑ Ⓒ Ⓓ Ⓔ
54. Ⓐ Ⓑ Ⓒ Ⓓ Ⓔ
55. Ⓐ Ⓑ Ⓒ Ⓓ Ⓔ
56. Ⓐ Ⓑ Ⓒ Ⓓ Ⓔ
57. Ⓐ Ⓑ Ⓒ Ⓓ Ⓔ
58. Ⓐ Ⓑ Ⓒ Ⓓ Ⓔ
59. Ⓐ Ⓑ Ⓒ Ⓓ Ⓔ
60. Ⓐ Ⓑ Ⓒ Ⓓ Ⓔ
61. Ⓐ Ⓑ Ⓒ Ⓓ Ⓔ
62. Ⓐ Ⓑ Ⓒ Ⓓ Ⓔ
63. Ⓐ Ⓑ Ⓒ Ⓓ Ⓔ
64. Ⓐ Ⓑ Ⓒ Ⓓ Ⓔ

65. Ⓐ Ⓑ Ⓒ Ⓓ Ⓔ
66. Ⓐ Ⓑ Ⓒ Ⓓ Ⓔ
67. Ⓐ Ⓑ Ⓒ Ⓓ Ⓔ
68. Ⓐ Ⓑ Ⓒ Ⓓ Ⓔ
69. Ⓐ Ⓑ Ⓒ Ⓓ Ⓔ
70. Ⓐ Ⓑ Ⓒ Ⓓ Ⓔ
71. Ⓐ Ⓑ Ⓒ Ⓓ Ⓔ
72. Ⓐ Ⓑ Ⓒ Ⓓ Ⓔ
73. Ⓐ Ⓑ Ⓒ Ⓓ Ⓔ
74. Ⓐ Ⓑ Ⓒ Ⓓ Ⓔ
75. Ⓐ Ⓑ Ⓒ Ⓓ Ⓔ
76. Ⓐ Ⓑ Ⓒ Ⓓ Ⓔ
77. Ⓐ Ⓑ Ⓒ Ⓓ Ⓔ
78. Ⓐ Ⓑ Ⓒ Ⓓ Ⓔ
79. Ⓐ Ⓑ Ⓒ Ⓓ Ⓔ
80. Ⓐ Ⓑ Ⓒ Ⓓ Ⓔ
81. Ⓐ Ⓑ Ⓒ Ⓓ Ⓔ
82. Ⓐ Ⓑ Ⓒ Ⓓ Ⓔ
83. Ⓐ Ⓑ Ⓒ Ⓓ Ⓔ
84. Ⓐ Ⓑ Ⓒ Ⓓ Ⓔ
85. Ⓐ Ⓑ Ⓒ Ⓓ Ⓔ
86. Ⓐ Ⓑ Ⓒ Ⓓ Ⓔ
87. Ⓐ Ⓑ Ⓒ Ⓓ Ⓔ
88. Ⓐ Ⓑ Ⓒ Ⓓ Ⓔ
89. Ⓐ Ⓑ Ⓒ Ⓓ Ⓔ
90. Ⓐ Ⓑ Ⓒ Ⓓ Ⓔ
91. Ⓐ Ⓑ Ⓒ Ⓓ Ⓔ
92. Ⓐ Ⓑ Ⓒ Ⓓ Ⓔ
93. Ⓐ Ⓑ Ⓒ Ⓓ Ⓔ
94. Ⓐ Ⓑ Ⓒ Ⓓ Ⓔ
95. Ⓐ Ⓑ Ⓒ Ⓓ Ⓔ

(This page may be removed to mark answers.)

[This page intentionally blank.]

ANSWERS TO ADDRESS CROSS COMPARISON/EXAM 5

1.	D	33.	D	65.	D
2.	D	34.	A	66.	A
3.	D	35.	D	67.	D
4.	D	36.	D	68.	A
5.	D	37.	D	69.	D
6.	A	38.	A	70.	A
7.	D	39.	D	71.	A
8.	A	40.	A	72.	D
9.	D	41.	D	73.	A
10.	D	42.	D	74.	D
11.	A	43.	D	75.	D
12.	A	44.	A	76.	D
13.	D	45.	A	77.	D
14.	D	46.	D	78.	A
15.	A	47.	D	79.	A
16.	A	48.	D	80.	D
17.	A	49.	A	81.	A
18.	D	50.	A	82.	A
19.	A	51.	A	83.	A
20.	D	52.	D	84.	D
21.	A	53.	A	85.	D
22.	D	54.	A	86.	D
23.	D	55.	D	87.	A
24.	A	56.	D	88.	D
25.	D	57.	A	89.	A
26.	A	58.	D	90.	A
27.	A	59.	D	91.	D
28.	D	60.	A	92.	D
29.	D	61.	A	93.	D
30.	A	62.	D	94.	A
31.	D	63.	D	95.	D
32.	A	64.	D		

ANSWERS TO MEMORIZATION/EXAM 5

1.	A	31.	B	61.	A
2.	C	32.	E	62.	B
3.	C	33.	A	63.	D
4.	D	34.	A	64.	D
5.	E	35.	B	65.	B
6.	E	36.	E	66.	B
7.	D	37.	D	67.	C
8.	B	38.	D	68.	D
9.	A	39.	D	69.	E
10.	A	40.	B	70.	C
11.	C	41.	B	71.	C
12.	E	42.	C	72.	A
13.	A	43.	D	73.	A
14.	B	44.	C	74.	E
15.	D	45.	B	75.	D
16.	E	46.	D	76.	C
17.	B	47.	A	77.	D
18.	C	48.	B	78.	E
19.	C	49.	D	79.	B
20.	C	50.	E	80.	B
21.	B	51.	E	81.	B
22.	D	52.	C	82.	A
23.	E	53.	A	83.	B
24.	E	54.	C	84.	C
25.	B	55.	D	85.	E
26.	A	56.	A	86.	A
27.	A	57.	C	87.	C
28.	D	58.	C	88.	A
29.	C	59.	B		
30.	C	60.	A		

ANSWERS TO NUMBER SERIES/EXAM 5

1. B.
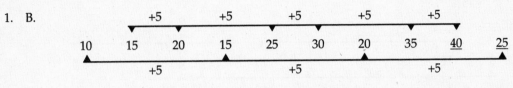

2. C.
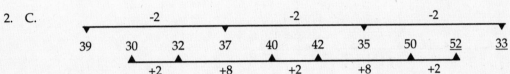

3. D.
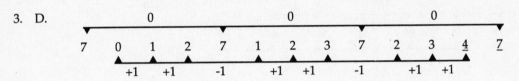

4. E.
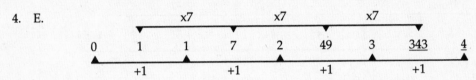

5. E.
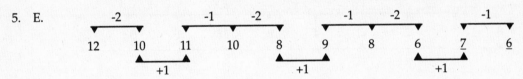

6. A.
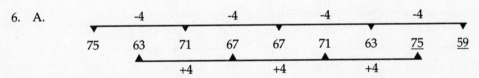

7. A.
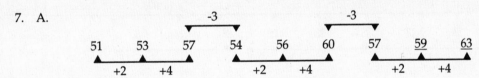

8. B.
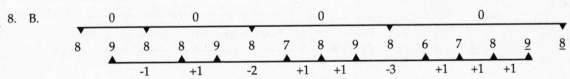

9. B.
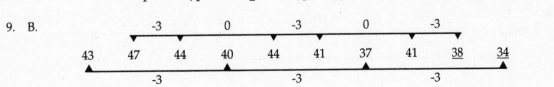

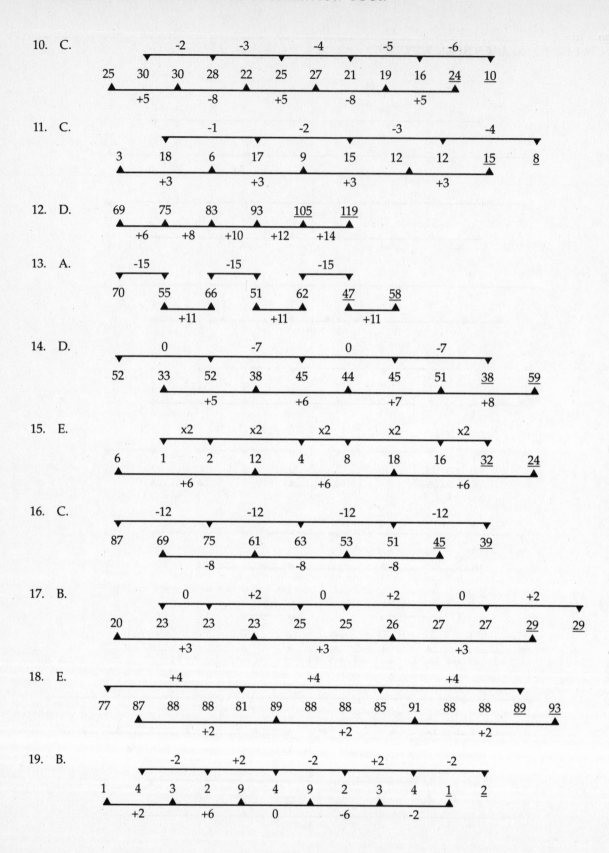

10. C.

	-2		-3		-4		-5		-6	
25	30	30	28	22	25	27	21	19	16	<u>24</u>	<u>10</u>
	+5		-8		+5		-8		+5	

11. C.

	-1		-2		-3		-4
3	18	6	17	9	15	12	12	<u>15</u>	<u>8</u>
	+3		+3		+3		+3

12. D.
69 75 83 93 <u>105</u> <u>119</u>
+6 +8 +10 +12 +14

13. A.
-15   -15   -15
70 55 66 51 62 <u>47</u> <u>58</u>
+11   +11   +11

14. D.
0   -7   0   -7
52 33 52 38 45 44 45 51 <u>38</u> <u>59</u>
+5   +6   +7   +8

15. E.
x2   x2   x2   x2   x2
6 1 2 12 4 8 18 16 <u>32</u> <u>24</u>
+6   +6   +6

16. C.
-12   -12   -12   -12
87 69 75 61 63 53 51 <u>45</u> <u>39</u>
-8   -8   -8

17. B.
0   +2   0   +2   0   +2
20 23 23 23 25 25 26 27 27 <u>29</u> <u>29</u>
+3   +3   +3

18. E.
+4   +4   +4
77 87 88 88 81 89 88 88 85 91 88 88 <u>89</u> <u>93</u>
+2   +2   +2

19. B.
-2   +2   -2   +2   -2
1 4 3 2 9 4 9 2 3 4 <u>1</u> <u>2</u>
+2   +6   0   -6   -2

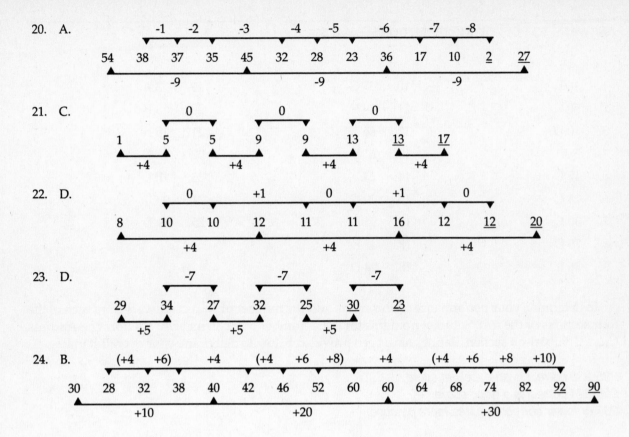

20. A.

	-1	-2		-3		-4	-5		-6		-7		-8		
54	38	37	35	45	32	28	23	36	17	10	2	27

-9   -9   -9

21. C.

0   0   0

1   5   5   9   9   13   13   17

+4   +4   +4   +4

22. D.

0   +1   0   +1   0

8   10   10   12   11   11   16   12   12   20

+4   +4   +4

23. D.

-7   -7   -7

29   34   27   32   25   30   23

+5   +5   +5

24. B.

(+4   +6)   +4   (+4   +6   +8)   +4   (+4   +6   +8   +10)

30   28   32   38   40   42   46   52   60   60   64   68   74   82   92   90

+10   +20   +30

ANSWERS TO FOLLOWING DIRECTIONS/EXAM 5

1.	46 E	10.	38 C	19.	73 A
2.	50 C	11.	39 E	20.	13 B
3.	10 D	12.	66 A	21.	15 A
4.	5 A	13.	61 B	22.	83 C
5.	17 E	14.	2 C	23.	75 E
6.	28 C	15.	29 C	24.	9 C
7.	30 E	16.	91 D	25.	49 D
8.	75 D	17.	42 E		
9.	36 B	18.	94 D		

To determine your performance on this exam, add the number of correct answers from each of the four sections of the test. Subtract from this total the number of incorrect answers from the Address Cross Comparison section. Ratings have been provided below to determine your overall standing.

225-232 correct is an excellent score.
208-224 correct is a good score.
207 or fewer correct requires more practice.

Exam 6

**DO NOT OPEN THIS TEST BOOKLET UNTIL
YOU ARE TOLD TO START BY THE INDIVIDUAL
ASSISTING YOU IN THIS EXERCISE**

[This page intentionally blank.]

1.	75011 Pearl Bay	75011 Pearl Bay
2.	Denver, Colo. 83007	Denver, Colo. 83007
3.	179-C Bauxite Gardens	179-C Bauxite Gardens
4.	8819 Lawrence Blvd.	8819 Lawrance Blvd.
5.	427 Imperial Way	427 Imperial Way
6.	Mineral Springs, Ark. 44041	Mineral Springs, Ark. 44041
7.	830 Ariton Dr. SW	803 Ariton Dr. SW
8.	7081 Grand Canyon Rd.	7081 Grand Canyon Rd.
9.	2453 St. Johns Rd.	2453 Saint Johns Rd.
10.	40744 Monteray Ln.	40474 Monteray Ln.
11.	4933 Cutler Ave.	4933 Cuttler Ave.
12.	3201 Ventura Blvd.	3021 Ventura Blvd.
13.	Kalaupapa, Hawaii 99831	Kalaupapa, Hawaii 99831
14.	4027 NW McNeil	4027 NE McNeil
15.	5151 Norwood Dr.	5151 Norwood Dr.
16.	6262 Bradley Ave.	6262 Bradly Ave.
17.	1520 Appleton Way	1520 Appleton Way
18.	2501 Sandy Ridge	2501 Sandy Ridge
19.	Guadalupe, Ariz. 84077	Guadalupe, Ariz. 84707
20.	91911 Alberta Dr.	91911 Alburta Dr.
21.	7921 22nd St. SW	7921 42nd St. SW
22.	8080 Maverick Ave.	8080 Maverick Ct.
23.	1293 Van Buran	1293 Van Burien

24.	601 Slyvan Way	601 Slyvan Way
25.	4358 Wauconda Dr.	4358 Wauconda Dr.
26.	1844 New Providence	1844 New Providence
27.	1308 Cherokee Lane	1380 Cherokee Lane
28.	991 Newton Blvd.	991 Newton Blvd.
29.	1345 Tripoli St. S.	1345 Tripoli St. N.
30.	494 Wheatcroft Dr.	494 Wheatcraft Dr.
31.	5535 Roxbury Ln.	5355 Roxbury Lane
32.	412 Plymoth Rock Pt.	412 Plymouth Rock Pt.
33.	67617 Knoxberry Ave.	67617 Knowberry Ave.
34.	741 Cottonwood St.	741 Cottonwood St.
35.	Bargersville, Ind. 49132	Bargersville, Ind. 41932
36.	Anacoco, LA 39542	Anacoca, LA 39542
37.	3052 Elkhorn Ln.	3052 Elkhorne Ln.
38.	Benton Harbour, Mich.	Benton Harbour, Mich.
39.	1588 Atchinson Place	1588 Atchinson Place
40.	70935 Biddeford Way	70935 Bideford Way
41.	311 Bellefonte	311 Bellefonte
42.	20716 Bloomfield Dr.	20761 Bloomfield Dr.
43.	1212 Panama Park	1212 Panama Place
44.	3838 Scott Ln.	3883 Scott Ln.
45.	91701 Woodridge Pl.	91701 Woodridge Pl.
46.	10013 Spencer Dr.	10013 Spencer Dr.
47.	181-E Oak Ridge Apts.	181-E Oak Ridge Apts.
48.	Bethleham, KY 54566	Bethlehem, KY 54566

49.	11190 Florence Dr.	11190 Florance Dr.
50.	4040 Hanover Blvd.	4040 Hanover Blvd.
51.	54990 Swanson Dr.	54990 Swanson Dr.
52.	165 W. Barthell St.	165 E. Barthell St.
53.	7833 Northbrook	7833 Northbrook
54.	1544 Greendale	1544 Greendale
55.	17178 Morgan View	17178 Morgan View Dr.
56.	505 Vermillian Blvd.	505 Vermillion Blvd.
57.	7039 Sheridan Rd.	7039 Sherman Rd.
58.	470 Shellfield Dr.	470 Shellfield Dr.
59.	Valantine, Neb. 67902	Valentine, Neb. 67902
60.	1419 Taft	1419 Taft
61.	540 Campbell Dr.	540 Campbell Dr.
62.	1111 Boston St.	1111 Boston St.
63.	Apt. F, Bayview Apts.	Apt. F, Bayview Apts.
64.	6060 Highland Ave.	60606 Highland Ave.
65.	711 Pleasant St.	711 Plesant
66.	4073 Hampson Way	4073 Hampson Way
67.	11 Bon Dileroy Rd.	11 Bon Dilleroy Rd.
68.	7018 Clifton Ave.	7018 Clifton Ave.
69.	90681 Paramount Blvd	90861 Paramount Blvd.
70.	1616 Madrona St.	1616 Madrona St.
71.	Gainsville, FLA 08911	Gainsville, FLA 09811
72.	1733 Copper Dr.	1733 Copper Dr.
73.	Memphis, Tenn 24101	Memphis, TN 24101

74.	4027 Sinclair Pl.	4027 Sinclair Place
75.	30391 Peppermint Ave.	30391 Peppermint Ave.
76.	108-B Briarcliff	108-B Briarcliff
77.	9041 Balkner Pl.	9041 Balkner Pl.
78.	8011 Sutherland Ct.	8011 Sutherland Pkwy
79.	Fredericksburg, Ind. 80541	Fredericksburg, Ind. 80541
80.	2793 Armstrong St.	2379 Armstrong St.
81.	Toledo, Ohio 89400	Toledo, Ohio 89400
82.	6869 Stronghurst Dr.	6869 Stronghurst Ave.
83.	2425 Huntington Pt.	2425 Huntington Pl.
84.	181 Pennington Dr.	181 Penington Dr.
85.	59540 Parker Blvd.	59540 Parker Blvd.
86.	4012 Sullivan Pl.	4012 Sulliven Pl.
87.	3384 Ballard Dr. SW	3384 Ballard Dr. NW
88.	301 N. Victor Lane	103 N. Victor Lane
89.	Brownville Jct., Maine	Brownsville Jct., Maine
90.	2340 Zackery Ct.	2340 Zackery Ct.
91.	Alexandria, LA 54911	Alexandria, LA 54191
92.	415 Jennings Ave.	415 Jennings Ave.
93.	2010 Livingston Ln.	2010 Livingston Ln.
94.	NW Evangeline Way	429 NW Evangeline Way
95.	121 Newcastle Dr.	211 New Castle, Drive.

ANSWER SHEET TO ADDRESS CROSS COMPARISON/EXAM 6

1. (A) (D)	33. (A) (D)	65. (A) (D)
2. (A) (D)	34. (A) (D)	66. (A) (D)
3. (A) (D)	35. (A) (D)	67. (A) (D)
4. (A) (D)	36. (A) (D)	68. (A) (D)
5. (A) (D)	37. (A) (D)	69. (A) (D)
6. (A) (D)	38. (A) (D)	70. (A) (D)
7. (A) (D)	39. (A) (D)	71. (A) (D)
8. (A) (D)	40. (A) (D)	72. (A) (D)
9. (A) (D)	41. (A) (D)	73. (A) (D)
10. (A) (D)	42. (A) (D)	74. (A) (D)
11. (A) (D)	43. (A) (D)	75. (A) (D)
12. (A) (D)	44. (A) (D)	76. (A) (D)
13. (A) (D)	45. (A) (D)	77. (A) (D)
14. (A) (D)	46. (A) (D)	78. (A) (D)
15. (A) (D)	47. (A) (D)	79. (A) (D)
16. (A) (D)	48. (A) (D)	80. (A) (D)
17. (A) (D)	49. (A) (D)	81. (A) (D)
18. (A) (D)	50. (A) (D)	82. (A) (D)
19. (A) (D)	51. (A) (D)	83. (A) (D)
20. (A) (D)	52. (A) (D)	84. (A) (D)
21. (A) (D)	53. (A) (D)	85. (A) (D)
22. (A) (D)	54. (A) (D)	86. (A) (D)
23. (A) (D)	55. (A) (D)	87. (A) (D)
24. (A) (D)	56. (A) (D)	88. (A) (D)
25. (A) (D)	57. (A) (D)	89. (A) (D)
26. (A) (D)	58. (A) (D)	90. (A) (D)
27. (A) (D)	59. (A) (D)	91. (A) (D)
28. (A) (D)	60. (A) (D)	92. (A) (D)
29. (A) (D)	61. (A) (D)	93. (A) (D)
30. (A) (D)	62. (A) (D)	94. (A) (D)
31. (A) (D)	63. (A) (D)	95. (A) (D)
32. (A) (D)	64. (A) (D)	

(This page may be removed to mark answers.)

[This page intentionally blank.]

MEMORIZATION/EXAM 6

A	B	C	D	E
2300-2399 Kenmore	1800-1899 Kenmore	7800-7899 Kenmore	9900-9999 Kenmore	1200-1299 Kenmore
Reese Ct.	Buckner St.	Evanston	Hatfield Dr.	Hargrove
7800-7899 Hoover	1200-1299 Hoover	9900-9999 Hoover	2300-2399 Hoover	1800-1899 Hoover
Kimberly Ln.	Honeydew Rd.	Clayton St.	Simpson Dr.	Drexel Ln.
1800-1899 Cranston	2300-2399 Cranston	1200-1299 Cranston	7800-7899 Cranston	9900-9999 Cranston

NOTE: Follow the same step by step format established for the memorization exercises studied earlier. (See page 41.)

PRACTICE MEMORIZATION/EXAM 6   **STEP 2 TIME: 3 MINUTES**
STEP 3 TIME: 3 MINUTES (cover key)

A	B	C	D	E
2300-2399 Kenmore	1800-1899 Kenmore	7800-7899 Kenmore	9900-9999 Kenmore	1200-1299 Kenmore
Reese Ct.	Buckner St.	Evanston	Hatfield Dr.	Hargrove
7800-7899 Hoover	1200-1299 Hoover	9900-9999 Hoover	2300-2399 Hoover	1800-1899 Hoover
Kimberly Ln.	Honeydew Rd.	Clayton St.	Simpson Dr.	Drexel Ln.
1800-1899 Cranston	2300-2399 Cranston	1200-1299 Cranston	7800-7899 Cranston	9900-9999 Cranston

1. 2300-2399 Cranston
2. Honeydew Rd.
3. Reese Ct.
4. 1800-1899 Kenmore
5. 7800-7899 Kenmore
6. Hatfield Dr.
7. Drexel Ln.
8. 9900-9999 Cranston
9. 1200-1299 Hoover
10. 9900-9999 Hoover
11. Simpson Dr.
12. Hargrove
13. Evanston
14. 1800-1899 Kenmore
15. Clayton St.
16. 1200-1299 Cranston
17. 9900-9999 Kenmore
18. Kimberly Ln.
19. Reese Ct.
20. 1800-1899 Cranston
21. Honeydew Rd.
22. 2300-2399 Hoover
23. 1200-1299 Kenmore
24. 2300-2399 Cranston
25. 7800-7899 Cranston
26. Buckner St.
27. Kimberly Ln.
28. 1800-1899 Cranston
29. 7800-7899 Kenmore
30. 9900-9999 Kenmore

31. Evanston
32. Reese Ct.
33. Simpson Dr.
34. 9900-9999 Cranston
35. 7800-7899 Kenmore
36. 1200-1299 Hoover
37. 7800-7899 Hoover
38. 2300-2399 Cranston
39. Buckner St.
40. 1800-1899 Kenmore
41. Kimberly Ln.
42. 1200-1299 Kenmore
43. Hargrove
44. 9900-9999 Kenmore
45. Honeydew Rd.
46. 1800-1899 Cranston
47. Simpson Dr.
48. Hatfield Dr.
49. 7800-7899 Cranston
50. Drexel Ln.
51. 9900-9999 Hoover
52. Buckner St.
53. Kimberly Ln.
54. 2300-2399 Cranston
55. 1200-1299 Kenmore
56. Hargrove
57. 9900-9999 Hoover
58. 7800-7899 Hoover
59. 1800-1899 Cranston
60. 9900-9999 Cranston

61. 1800-1899 Kenmore
62. Buckner St.
63. Clayton St.
64. 1200-1299 Cranston
65. Honeydew Rd.
66. 7800-7899 Cranston
67. Reese Ct.
68. Drexel Ln.
69. Evanston
70. 1200-1299 Hoover
71. 7800-7899 Cranston
72. 1800-1899 Hoover
73. 9900-9999 Kenmore
74. 1200-1299 Hoover
75. 7800-7899 Hoover
76. 2300-2399 Cranston
77. Evanston
78. Simpson Dr.
79. 2300-2399 Kenmore
80. 7800-7899 Cranston
81. 9900-9999 Cranston
82. 2300-2399 Cranston
83. Kimberly Ln.
84. Buckner St.
85. Drexel Ln.
86. 7800-7899 Cranston
87. Hatfield Dr.
88. 1200-1299 Kenmore

PRACTICE ANSWER SHEET TO MEMORIZATION/EXAM 6

1. A B C D E
2. A B C D E
3. A B C D E
4. A B C D E
5. A B C D E
6. A B C D E
7. A B C D E
8. A B C D E
9. A B C D E
10. A B C D E
11. A B C D E
12. A B C D E
13. A B C D E
14. A B C D E
15. A B C D E
16. A B C D E
17. A B C D E
18. A B C D E
19. A B C D E
20. A B C D E
21. A B C D E
22. A B C D E
23. A B C D E
24. A B C D E
25. A B C D E
26. A B C D E
27. A B C D E
28. A B C D E
29. A B C D E
30. A B C D E

31. A B C D E
32. A B C D E
33. A B C D E
34. A B C D E
35. A B C D E
36. A B C D E
37. A B C D E
38. A B C D E
39. A B C D E
40. A B C D E
41. A B C D E
42. A B C D E
43. A B C D E
44. A B C D E
45. A B C D E
46. A B C D E
47. A B C D E
48. A B C D E
49. A B C D E
50. A B C D E
51. A B C D E
52. A B C D E
53. A B C D E
54. A B C D E
55. A B C D E
56. A B C D E
57. A B C D E
58. A B C D E
59. A B C D E
60. A B C D E

61. A B C D E
62. A B C D E
63. A B C D E
64. A B C D E
65. A B C D E
66. A B C D E
67. A B C D E
68. A B C D E
69. A B C D E
70. A B C D E
71. A B C D E
72. A B C D E
73. A B C D E
74. A B C D E
75. A B C D E
76. A B C D E
77. A B C D E
78. A B C D E
79. A B C D E
80. A B C D E
81. A B C D E
82. A B C D E
83. A B C D E
84. A B C D E
85. A B C D E
86. A B C D E
87. A B C D E
88. A B C D E

1. 1800-1899 Kenmore	31. Evanston	61. Hargrove
2. Buckner St.	32. 2300-2399 Hoover	62. Drexel Ln.
3. Evanston	33. Drexel Ln.	63. 7800-7899 Kenmore
4. 2300-2399 Hoover	34. 7800-7899 Hoover	64. Simpson Dr.
5. 9900-9999 Cranston	35. Buckner St.	65. Kimberly Ln.
6. Drexel Ln.	36. 1200-1299 Cranston	66. 1800-1899 Cranston
7. 1200-1299 Hoover	37. Simpson Dr.	67. Reese Ct.
8. Kimberly Ln.	38. 1800-1899 Hoover	68. 2300-2399 Hoover
9. Honeydew Rd.	39. 1800-1899 Cranston	69. Clayton St.
10. 1200-1299 Cranston	40. 7800-7899 Cranston	70. 9900-9999 Kenmore
11. 1200-1299 Kenmore	41. Reese Ct.	71. 9900-9999 Cranston
12. Hatfield Dr.	42. 1200-1299 Cranston	72. 1800-1899 Kenmore
13. 2300-2399 Cranston	43. 9900-9999 Kenmore	73. Buckner St.
14. Hargrove	44. Hargrove	74. 1200-1299 Cranston
15. 1800-1899 Kenmore	45. Honeydew Rd.	75. 2300-2399 Hoover
16. 9900-9999 Kenmore	46. 1800-1899 Kenmore	76. 1200-1299 Hoover
17. 7800-7899 Cranston	47. Kimberly Ln.	77. 7800-7899 Hoover
18. Simpson Dr.	48. 2300-2399 Cranston	78. 2300-2399 Hoover
19. 1200-1299 Hoover	49. 1200-1299 Kenmore	79. 1800-1899 Hoover
20. Clayton St.	50. 9900-9999 Cranston	80. 9900-9999 Hoover
21. 1800-1899 Kenmore	51. 9900-9999 Hoover	81. Simpson Dr.
22. Reese Ct.	52. 9900-9999 Kenmore	82. Honeydew Rd.
23. 1800-1899 Cranston	53. 1200-1299 Hoover	83. Buckner St.
24. 2300-2399 Kenmore	54. Honeydew Rd.	84. Drexel Ln.
25. 1200-1299 Cranston	55. 1800-1899 Cranston	85. 1800-1899 Cranston
26. 7800-7899 Cranston	56. 1800-1899 Kenmore	86. 1200-1299 Cranston
27. Hargrove	57. 1800-1899 Hoover	87. Hatfield Dr.
28. 9900-9999 Hoover	58. Hatfield Dr.	88. Hargrove
29. Honeydew Rd.	59. 2300-2399 Cranston	
30. Kimberly Ln.	60. Simpson Dr.	

ANSWER SHEET TO MEMORIZATION/EXAM 6

1. Ⓐ Ⓑ Ⓒ Ⓓ Ⓔ	31. Ⓐ Ⓑ Ⓒ Ⓓ Ⓔ	61. Ⓐ Ⓑ Ⓒ Ⓓ Ⓔ
2. Ⓐ Ⓑ Ⓒ Ⓓ Ⓔ	32. Ⓐ Ⓑ Ⓒ Ⓓ Ⓔ	62. Ⓐ Ⓑ Ⓒ Ⓓ Ⓔ
3. Ⓐ Ⓑ Ⓒ Ⓓ Ⓔ	33. Ⓐ Ⓑ Ⓒ Ⓓ Ⓔ	63. Ⓐ Ⓑ Ⓒ Ⓓ Ⓔ
4. Ⓐ Ⓑ Ⓒ Ⓓ Ⓔ	34. Ⓐ Ⓑ Ⓒ Ⓓ Ⓔ	64. Ⓐ Ⓑ Ⓒ Ⓓ Ⓔ
5. Ⓐ Ⓑ Ⓒ Ⓓ Ⓔ	35. Ⓐ Ⓑ Ⓒ Ⓓ Ⓔ	65. Ⓐ Ⓑ Ⓒ Ⓓ Ⓔ
6. Ⓐ Ⓑ Ⓒ Ⓓ Ⓔ	36. Ⓐ Ⓑ Ⓒ Ⓓ Ⓔ	66. Ⓐ Ⓑ Ⓒ Ⓓ Ⓔ
7. Ⓐ Ⓑ Ⓒ Ⓓ Ⓔ	37. Ⓐ Ⓑ Ⓒ Ⓓ Ⓔ	67. Ⓐ Ⓑ Ⓒ Ⓓ Ⓔ
8. Ⓐ Ⓑ Ⓒ Ⓓ Ⓔ	38. Ⓐ Ⓑ Ⓒ Ⓓ Ⓔ	68. Ⓐ Ⓑ Ⓒ Ⓓ Ⓔ
9. Ⓐ Ⓑ Ⓒ Ⓓ Ⓔ	39. Ⓐ Ⓑ Ⓒ Ⓓ Ⓔ	69. Ⓐ Ⓑ Ⓒ Ⓓ Ⓔ
10. Ⓐ Ⓑ Ⓒ Ⓓ Ⓔ	40. Ⓐ Ⓑ Ⓒ Ⓓ Ⓔ	70. Ⓐ Ⓑ Ⓒ Ⓓ Ⓔ
11. Ⓐ Ⓑ Ⓒ Ⓓ Ⓔ	41. Ⓐ Ⓑ Ⓒ Ⓓ Ⓔ	71. Ⓐ Ⓑ Ⓒ Ⓓ Ⓔ
12. Ⓐ Ⓑ Ⓒ Ⓓ Ⓔ	42. Ⓐ Ⓑ Ⓒ Ⓓ Ⓔ	72. Ⓐ Ⓑ Ⓒ Ⓓ Ⓔ
13. Ⓐ Ⓑ Ⓒ Ⓓ Ⓔ	43. Ⓐ Ⓑ Ⓒ Ⓓ Ⓔ	73. Ⓐ Ⓑ Ⓒ Ⓓ Ⓔ
14. Ⓐ Ⓑ Ⓒ Ⓓ Ⓔ	44. Ⓐ Ⓑ Ⓒ Ⓓ Ⓔ	74. Ⓐ Ⓑ Ⓒ Ⓓ Ⓔ
15. Ⓐ Ⓑ Ⓒ Ⓓ Ⓔ	45. Ⓐ Ⓑ Ⓒ Ⓓ Ⓔ	75. Ⓐ Ⓑ Ⓒ Ⓓ Ⓔ
16. Ⓐ Ⓑ Ⓒ Ⓓ Ⓔ	46. Ⓐ Ⓑ Ⓒ Ⓓ Ⓔ	76. Ⓐ Ⓑ Ⓒ Ⓓ Ⓔ
17. Ⓐ Ⓑ Ⓒ Ⓓ Ⓔ	47. Ⓐ Ⓑ Ⓒ Ⓓ Ⓔ	77. Ⓐ Ⓑ Ⓒ Ⓓ Ⓔ
18. Ⓐ Ⓑ Ⓒ Ⓓ Ⓔ	48. Ⓐ Ⓑ Ⓒ Ⓓ Ⓔ	78. Ⓐ Ⓑ Ⓒ Ⓓ Ⓔ
19. Ⓐ Ⓑ Ⓒ Ⓓ Ⓔ	49. Ⓐ Ⓑ Ⓒ Ⓓ Ⓔ	79. Ⓐ Ⓑ Ⓒ Ⓓ Ⓔ
20. Ⓐ Ⓑ Ⓒ Ⓓ Ⓔ	50. Ⓐ Ⓑ Ⓒ Ⓓ Ⓔ	80. Ⓐ Ⓑ Ⓒ Ⓓ Ⓔ
21. Ⓐ Ⓑ Ⓒ Ⓓ Ⓔ	51. Ⓐ Ⓑ Ⓒ Ⓓ Ⓔ	81. Ⓐ Ⓑ Ⓒ Ⓓ Ⓔ
22. Ⓐ Ⓑ Ⓒ Ⓓ Ⓔ	52. Ⓐ Ⓑ Ⓒ Ⓓ Ⓔ	82. Ⓐ Ⓑ Ⓒ Ⓓ Ⓔ
23. Ⓐ Ⓑ Ⓒ Ⓓ Ⓔ	53. Ⓐ Ⓑ Ⓒ Ⓓ Ⓔ	83. Ⓐ Ⓑ Ⓒ Ⓓ Ⓔ
24. Ⓐ Ⓑ Ⓒ Ⓓ Ⓔ	54. Ⓐ Ⓑ Ⓒ Ⓓ Ⓔ	84. Ⓐ Ⓑ Ⓒ Ⓓ Ⓔ
25. Ⓐ Ⓑ Ⓒ Ⓓ Ⓔ	55. Ⓐ Ⓑ Ⓒ Ⓓ Ⓔ	85. Ⓐ Ⓑ Ⓒ Ⓓ Ⓔ
26. Ⓐ Ⓑ Ⓒ Ⓓ Ⓔ	56. Ⓐ Ⓑ Ⓒ Ⓓ Ⓔ	86. Ⓐ Ⓑ Ⓒ Ⓓ Ⓔ
27. Ⓐ Ⓑ Ⓒ Ⓓ Ⓔ	57. Ⓐ Ⓑ Ⓒ Ⓓ Ⓔ	87. Ⓐ Ⓑ Ⓒ Ⓓ Ⓔ
28. Ⓐ Ⓑ Ⓒ Ⓓ Ⓔ	58. Ⓐ Ⓑ Ⓒ Ⓓ Ⓔ	88. Ⓐ Ⓑ Ⓒ Ⓓ Ⓔ
29. Ⓐ Ⓑ Ⓒ Ⓓ Ⓔ	59. Ⓐ Ⓑ Ⓒ Ⓓ Ⓔ	
30. Ⓐ Ⓑ Ⓒ Ⓓ Ⓔ	60. Ⓐ Ⓑ Ⓒ Ⓓ Ⓔ	

[This page intentionally blank.]

1.   36   38   42   38   40   44   40   42   ___   ___
       A.   42, 46
       B.   46, 46
       C.   45, 42
       D.   46, 42
       E.   45, 45

2.   1   2   2   6   4   18   8   54   ___   ___
       A.   30, 152
       B.   16, 160
       C.   20, 160
       D.   66, 126
       E.   16, 162

3.   55   8   51   16   47   24   43   ___   ___
       A.   39, 32
       B.   33, 32
       C.   32, 39
       D.   37, 33
       E.   30, 37

4.   19   16   18   16   13   15   13   10   ___   ___
       A.   12, 9
       B.   9, 12
       C.   12, 10
       D.   10, 12
       E.   12, 12

5.   10   8   11   9   8   12   10   9   8   13   11   10   9   ___   ___
       A.   8, 14
       B.   9, 14
       C.   10, 13
       D.   10, 14
       E.   12, 14

6.   36   30   28   33   28   26   30   26   ___   ___
       A.   27, 23
       B.   27, 24
       C.   24, 26
       D.   24, 27
       E.   24, 28

7.   18   20   21   24   25   28   30   32   ___   ___
       A.   34, 34
       B.   36, 34
       C.   34, 36
       D.   35, 35
       E.   36, 36

8. 15   22   15   27   20   33   20   40   25   ___   ___

    A. 48, 25
    B. 48, 15
    C. 46, 30
    D. 44, 25
    E. 50, 25

9. 93   94   89   87   88   83   81   82   ___   ___

    A. 76, 75
    B. 77, 75
    C. 75, 75
    D. 75, 77
    E. 78, 79

10. 42   45   50   57   ___   ___

    A. 67, 77
    B. 66, 77
    C. 65, 75
    D. 66, 78
    E. 66, 66

11. 13   10   17   14   21   ___   ___

    A. 17, 25
    B. 18, 24
    C. 19, 25
    D. 18, 25
    E. 20, 25

12. 58   40   58   42   50   44   50   46   42   ___   ___

    A. 42, 48
    B. 40, 42
    C. 48, 42
    D. 58, 42
    E. 46, 42

13. 30   29   34   35   39   42   45   50   ___   ___

    A. 50, 59
    B. 59, 62
    C. 52, 59
    D. 62, 69
    E. 55, 59

14. 24   27   27   28   32   32   32   37   ___   ___

    A. 36, 37
    B. 37, 35
    C. 35, 36
    D. 35, 35
    E. 37, 36

15.   0   4   3   7   6   __   __

     A.   10, 9
     B.   9, 11
     C.   11, 10
     D.   12, 12
     E.   9, 9

16.   28   29   31   34   36   33   35   38   44   37   39   __   __

     A.   43, 51
     B.   42, 52
     C.   40, 52
     D.   52, 43
     E.   43, 43

17.   0   3   8   9   16   27   __   __

     A.   20, 80
     B.   24, 80
     C.   26, 81
     D.   24, 81
     E.   34, 80

18.   67   65   54   53   41   41   28   29   __   __

     A.   16, 18
     B.   17, 15
     C.   15, 17
     D.   18, 16
     E.   20, 17

19.   40   47   46   45   42   47   48   45   44   47   __   __

     A.   50, 54
     B.   48, 47
     C.   45, 50
     D.   48, 48
     E.   50, 45

20.   23   20   30   29   38   38   47   47   __   __

     A.   56, 55
     B.   55, 56
     C.   57, 55
     D.   57, 57
     E.   57, 56

21.   0   8   10   10   1   6   10   10   2   4   10   10   __   __

     A.   3, 2
     B.   3, 3
     C.   3, 5
     D.   2, 3
     E.   2, 2

22. 48   50   52   39   43   41   30   32   ___   ___

      A.   30, 19
      B.   28, 19
      C.   28, 21
      D.   30, 21
      E.   26, 21

23. 16   20   24   30   26   30   34   40   48   46   48   52   58   66   ___   ___

      A.   66, 77
      B.   66, 76
      C.   76, 76
      D.   65, 75
      E.   65, 65

24. 30   37   25   31   20   25   15   ___   ___

      A.   20, 10
      B.   10, 19
      C.   19, 10
      D.   10, 20
      E.   20, 20

ANSWER SHEET TO NUMBER SERIES/EXAM 6

1. Ⓐ Ⓑ Ⓒ Ⓓ Ⓔ
2. Ⓐ Ⓑ Ⓒ Ⓓ Ⓔ
3. Ⓐ Ⓑ Ⓒ Ⓓ Ⓔ
4. Ⓐ Ⓑ Ⓒ Ⓓ Ⓔ
5. Ⓐ Ⓑ Ⓒ Ⓓ Ⓔ
6. Ⓐ Ⓑ Ⓒ Ⓓ Ⓔ
7. Ⓐ Ⓑ Ⓒ Ⓓ Ⓔ
8. Ⓐ Ⓑ Ⓒ Ⓓ Ⓔ

9. Ⓐ Ⓑ Ⓒ Ⓓ Ⓔ
10. Ⓐ Ⓑ Ⓒ Ⓓ Ⓔ
11. Ⓐ Ⓑ Ⓒ Ⓓ Ⓔ
12. Ⓐ Ⓑ Ⓒ Ⓓ Ⓔ
13. Ⓐ Ⓑ Ⓒ Ⓓ Ⓔ
14. Ⓐ Ⓑ Ⓒ Ⓓ Ⓔ
15. Ⓐ Ⓑ Ⓒ Ⓓ Ⓔ
16. Ⓐ Ⓑ Ⓒ Ⓓ Ⓔ

17. Ⓐ Ⓑ Ⓒ Ⓓ Ⓔ
18. Ⓐ Ⓑ Ⓒ Ⓓ Ⓔ
19. Ⓐ Ⓑ Ⓒ Ⓓ Ⓔ
20. Ⓐ Ⓑ Ⓒ Ⓓ Ⓔ
21. Ⓐ Ⓑ Ⓒ Ⓓ Ⓔ
22. Ⓐ Ⓑ Ⓒ Ⓓ Ⓔ
23. Ⓐ Ⓑ Ⓒ Ⓓ Ⓔ
24. Ⓐ Ⓑ Ⓒ Ⓓ Ⓔ

(This page may be removed to mark answers.)

[This page intentionally blank.]

FOLLOWING DIRECTIONS/EXAM 6

Note To Person Assisting In This Exam:
Remove from this test guide the pages of this exam that comprise the directions to be read out loud. The test applicant should be left with only the sample sheet and answer sheet. Read the following directions out loud at the suggested rate of 75-80 words per minute, pausing only where indicated in parentheses. Speak as clearly as possible. Once a statement has been read, it cannot be repeated.

Examine Sample 1. (Pause 2-3 seconds.) Write the letter B, as in "boy," beside the middle number in the sample if it is greater than or equal to 31. (Pause 2 seconds.) Otherwise, write the letter D, as in "dog," beside the highest number in the sample. (Pause 2 seconds.) Now, write the letter E, as in "elephant," beside the only even number shown in the sample. (Pause 2 seconds.) Darken both of these number-letter combinations on your answer sheet. (Pause 10 seconds.)

Examine Sample 2. (Pause 2-3 seconds.) Draw a line under the third number from the right. (Pause 2 seconds.) Now, go to the same number on your answer sheet that you just underlined and write the letter C, as in "cat." (Pause 5 seconds.)

Examine Sample 2 again. (Pause 2-3 seconds.) Go to number 63 on your answer sheet, provided this number is the least of those seen in the sample, and darken the letter D, as in "dog." (Pause 5 seconds.) Otherwise, write the letter D, as in "dog," beside the second number in the sample and darken that number-letter combination on your answer sheet. (Pause 5 seconds.)

Examine Sample 3. (Pause 2-3 seconds.) Write the letter D, as in "dog," in the second circle from the right and the letter A, as in "apple," in the first circle. (Pause 5 seconds.) Now, go to your answer sheet and darken the resulting number-letter combinations. (Pause 10 seconds.)

Examine Sample 3 again. (Pause 2-3 seconds.) If the number in the third circle is one less than the number in the second circle from the right, but one greater than the number in the second circle from the right, go to the same number on your answer sheet that is shown in the third circle and darken the letter E, as in "elephant." (Pause 5 seconds.) If any part of the preceding question is false, go to number 18 on your answer sheet and darken the letter D, as in "dog." (Pause 5 seconds.)

Examine Sample 4. (Pause 2-3 seconds.) Pick out the number that represents the shape which is different from the others shown in the sample and go to that same number on your answer sheet and darken the letter B, as in "boy." (Pause 5 seconds.)

Examine Sample 4 again. (Pause 2-3 seconds.) If the first odd number in the sample is two less than the next highest odd number and only one less than the lowest even number, go to number 50 on your answer sheet and darken the letter B, as in "boy." (Pause 5 seconds.) Otherwise, go to number 49 on your answer sheet and darken the letter C, as in "cat." (Pause 5 seconds.)

Examine Sample 5. (Pause 2-3 seconds.) Write the numbers 3, 5, 7, and 9 beside the letters L, M, N, and O, respectively. (Pause 5 seconds.) Now, go to the same number beside the letter O on your answer sheet and darken the letter E, as in "elephant." (Pause 5 seconds.)

Examine Sample 6. (Pause 2-3 seconds.) The five times shown in this sample represent the actual times that mail was collected from a downtown outgoing mail drop. (Pause 2 seconds.) Underline the minutes portion of the earliest time shown. (Pause 2 seconds.) Also, underline the minutes portion of the second earliest time shown. (Pause 2 seconds.) Now, go to both of these numbers on your answer sheet and darken the letter D, as in "dog." (Pause 10 seconds.)

Examine Sample 6 again. (Pause 2-3 seconds.) If the fourth collection time from the right is later than the fifth collection time from the left, go to number 23 on your answer sheet and darken the letter A, as in "apple." (Pause 5 seconds.) If not, go to number 24 on your answer sheet and darken the letter E, as in "elephant." (Pause 5 seconds.)

Examine Sample 2. (Pause 2-3 seconds.) If the third number from the right is greater than the third number from the left, darken the letter D, as in "dog," for number 27 on your answer sheet. (Pause 5 seconds.) If this is not the case, go to number 28 on your answer sheet and darken the letter C, as in "cat." (Pause 5 seconds.)

Examine Sample 7. (Pause 2-3 seconds.) Write the number 54 beside the third letter in the alphabet if that letter happens to be enclosed by a circle. (Pause 2 seconds.) Write the number 55 beside the second letter of the alphabet if that letter happens to be enclosed in a circle. (Pause 2 seconds.) Write the number 56 beside the fifth letter in the alphabet if that letter happens to be enclosed in a box. (Pause 2 seconds.) Now, darken all of these number-letter combinations on your answer sheet. (Pause 10 seconds.)

Examine Sample 7 again. (Pause 2-3 seconds.) Write the number 67 beside the only letter not enclosed in either a circle or a square. (Pause 2 seconds.) Write the number 93 beside the letter enclosed in the larger circle shown. (Pause 2 seconds.) Now, go to your answer sheet and darken only the former of the two number-letter combination written. (Pause 5 seconds.)

Examine Sample 8. (Pause 2-3 seconds.) The numbers shown are Zip Plus Four Codes from two different locations. (Pause 2 seconds.) The last four digits of each code represent Post Office box numbers. (Pause 2 seconds.) Now, go to number 85 on your answer sheet and darken the letter that represents the highest Post Office box number for the 98320 Zip Code. (Pause 5 seconds.)

Examine Sample 8 again. (Pause 2-3 seconds.) Go to number 1 on your answer sheet and darken the letter that represents the lowest Post Office box number for the 98330 zip code. (Pause 5 seconds.)

Examine Sample 9. (Pause 2-3 seconds.) Write the letter C, as in "cat," beside the lowest odd number shown in the sample. (Pause 2 seconds.) Write the letter E, as in "elephant," beside the highest even number shown in the sample. (Pause 2 seconds.) Write the number 89 beside the letter A, as in "apple," only if it is less than the lowest number odd number in the sample. (Pause 2 seconds.) Otherwise, write that same number beside the other letter shown in the sample. (Pause 2 seconds.) Now, go to your answer sheet and darken all of the number-letter combinations you made from this sample. (Pause 15 seconds.)

Examine Sample 10. (Pause 2-3 seconds.) Underline the fifth digit from the right of this number. (Pause 2 seconds.) Now, go to that same number on your answer sheet and darken the letter B, as in "boy," only if that number is greater than or equal to 8. (Pause 5 seconds.) Otherwise, go to number 6 on your answer sheet and darken the letter B, as in "boy." (Pause 5 seconds.)

Examine Sample 11. (Pause 2-3 seconds.) Write the number 61 beside the last letter in the sample. (Pause 2 seconds.) Write the number 71 beside the middle letter in the sample. (Pause 2 seconds.) Write the number 11 beside the first letter in the sample. (Pause 2 seconds.) Now, go to the number on your answer sheet that you marked beside the letter S, and darken the letter A, as in "apple," only if the letter S precedes the letter T in the alphabet. (Pause 5 seconds.) Otherwise, go to number 72 on your answer sheet and darken the letter D, as in "dog." (Pause 5 seconds.)

Examine Sample 11 again. (Pause 2-3 seconds.) Go to the same number on your answer sheet that you have marked before the letter R, according to the previous question and darken the letter E, as in "elephant." (Pause 5 seconds.)

-END OF TEST-

FOLLOWING DIRECTIONS/EXAM 6 SAMPLES

1. 29_____   30_____   31_____

2. 63   72   75   76

3.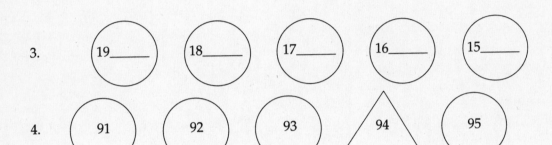

4.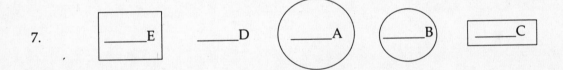

5. _____L   _____M   _____N   _____O

6.   9:36 AM   11:25 PM   10:05 AM   1:47 PM   3:30 PM

7.

8. A. 98330-0455   D. 98320-0466
    B. 98330-0465   E. 98320-0435
    C. 98320-0455

9. 2_____   91_____   _____E   81_____   _____A

10.   5399486721

11.   _____R   _____S   _____T

ANSWER SHEET FOR FOLLOWING DIRECTIONS/EXAM 6

1. Ⓐ Ⓑ Ⓒ Ⓓ Ⓔ
2. Ⓐ Ⓑ Ⓒ Ⓓ Ⓔ
3. Ⓐ Ⓑ Ⓒ Ⓓ Ⓔ
4. Ⓐ Ⓑ Ⓒ Ⓓ Ⓔ
5. Ⓐ Ⓑ Ⓒ Ⓓ Ⓔ
6. Ⓐ Ⓑ Ⓒ Ⓓ Ⓔ
7. Ⓐ Ⓑ Ⓒ Ⓓ Ⓔ
8. Ⓐ Ⓑ Ⓒ Ⓓ Ⓔ
9. Ⓐ Ⓑ Ⓒ Ⓓ Ⓔ
10. Ⓐ Ⓑ Ⓒ Ⓓ Ⓔ
11. Ⓐ Ⓑ Ⓒ Ⓓ Ⓔ
12. Ⓐ Ⓑ Ⓒ Ⓓ Ⓔ
13. Ⓐ Ⓑ Ⓒ Ⓓ Ⓔ
14. Ⓐ Ⓑ Ⓒ Ⓓ Ⓔ
15. Ⓐ Ⓑ Ⓒ Ⓓ Ⓔ
16. Ⓐ Ⓑ Ⓒ Ⓓ Ⓔ
17. Ⓐ Ⓑ Ⓒ Ⓓ Ⓔ
18. Ⓐ Ⓑ Ⓒ Ⓓ Ⓔ
19. Ⓐ Ⓑ Ⓒ Ⓓ Ⓔ
20. Ⓐ Ⓑ Ⓒ Ⓓ Ⓔ
21. Ⓐ Ⓑ Ⓒ Ⓓ Ⓔ
22. Ⓐ Ⓑ Ⓒ Ⓓ Ⓔ
23. Ⓐ Ⓑ Ⓒ Ⓓ Ⓔ
24. Ⓐ Ⓑ Ⓒ Ⓓ Ⓔ
25. Ⓐ Ⓑ Ⓒ Ⓓ Ⓔ
26. Ⓐ Ⓑ Ⓒ Ⓓ Ⓔ
27. Ⓐ Ⓑ Ⓒ Ⓓ Ⓔ
28. Ⓐ Ⓑ Ⓒ Ⓓ Ⓔ
29. Ⓐ Ⓑ Ⓒ Ⓓ Ⓔ
30. Ⓐ Ⓑ Ⓒ Ⓓ Ⓔ
31. Ⓐ Ⓑ Ⓒ Ⓓ Ⓔ
32. Ⓐ Ⓑ Ⓒ Ⓓ Ⓔ

33. Ⓐ Ⓑ Ⓒ Ⓓ Ⓔ
34. Ⓐ Ⓑ Ⓒ Ⓓ Ⓔ
35. Ⓐ Ⓑ Ⓒ Ⓓ Ⓔ
36. Ⓐ Ⓑ Ⓒ Ⓓ Ⓔ
37. Ⓐ Ⓑ Ⓒ Ⓓ Ⓔ
38. Ⓐ Ⓑ Ⓒ Ⓓ Ⓔ
39. Ⓐ Ⓑ Ⓒ Ⓓ Ⓔ
40. Ⓐ Ⓑ Ⓒ Ⓓ Ⓔ
41. Ⓐ Ⓑ Ⓒ Ⓓ Ⓔ
42. Ⓐ Ⓑ Ⓒ Ⓓ Ⓔ
43. Ⓐ Ⓑ Ⓒ Ⓓ Ⓔ
44. Ⓐ Ⓑ Ⓒ Ⓓ Ⓔ
45. Ⓐ Ⓑ Ⓒ Ⓓ Ⓔ
46. Ⓐ Ⓑ Ⓒ Ⓓ Ⓔ
47. Ⓐ Ⓑ Ⓒ Ⓓ Ⓔ
48. Ⓐ Ⓑ Ⓒ Ⓓ Ⓔ
49. Ⓐ Ⓑ Ⓒ Ⓓ Ⓔ
50. Ⓐ Ⓑ Ⓒ Ⓓ Ⓔ
51. Ⓐ Ⓑ Ⓒ Ⓓ Ⓔ
52. Ⓐ Ⓑ Ⓒ Ⓓ Ⓔ
53. Ⓐ Ⓑ Ⓒ Ⓓ Ⓔ
54. Ⓐ Ⓑ Ⓒ Ⓓ Ⓔ
55. Ⓐ Ⓑ Ⓒ Ⓓ Ⓔ
56. Ⓐ Ⓑ Ⓒ Ⓓ Ⓔ
57. Ⓐ Ⓑ Ⓒ Ⓓ Ⓔ
58. Ⓐ Ⓑ Ⓒ Ⓓ Ⓔ
59. Ⓐ Ⓑ Ⓒ Ⓓ Ⓔ
60. Ⓐ Ⓑ Ⓒ Ⓓ Ⓔ
61. Ⓐ Ⓑ Ⓒ Ⓓ Ⓔ
62. Ⓐ Ⓑ Ⓒ Ⓓ Ⓔ
63. Ⓐ Ⓑ Ⓒ Ⓓ Ⓔ
64. Ⓐ Ⓑ Ⓒ Ⓓ Ⓔ

65. Ⓐ Ⓑ Ⓒ Ⓓ Ⓔ
66. Ⓐ Ⓑ Ⓒ Ⓓ Ⓔ
67. Ⓐ Ⓑ Ⓒ Ⓓ Ⓔ
68. Ⓐ Ⓑ Ⓒ Ⓓ Ⓔ
69. Ⓐ Ⓑ Ⓒ Ⓓ Ⓔ
70. Ⓐ Ⓑ Ⓒ Ⓓ Ⓔ
71. Ⓐ Ⓑ Ⓒ Ⓓ Ⓔ
72. Ⓐ Ⓑ Ⓒ Ⓓ Ⓔ
73. Ⓐ Ⓑ Ⓒ Ⓓ Ⓔ
74. Ⓐ Ⓑ Ⓒ Ⓓ Ⓔ
75. Ⓐ Ⓑ Ⓒ Ⓓ Ⓔ
76. Ⓐ Ⓑ Ⓒ Ⓓ Ⓔ
77. Ⓐ Ⓑ Ⓒ Ⓓ Ⓔ
78. Ⓐ Ⓑ Ⓒ Ⓓ Ⓔ
79. Ⓐ Ⓑ Ⓒ Ⓓ Ⓔ
80. Ⓐ Ⓑ Ⓒ Ⓓ Ⓔ
81. Ⓐ Ⓑ Ⓒ Ⓓ Ⓔ
82. Ⓐ Ⓑ Ⓒ Ⓓ Ⓔ
83. Ⓐ Ⓑ Ⓒ Ⓓ Ⓔ
84. Ⓐ Ⓑ Ⓒ Ⓓ Ⓔ
85. Ⓐ Ⓑ Ⓒ Ⓓ Ⓔ
86. Ⓐ Ⓑ Ⓒ Ⓓ Ⓔ
87. Ⓐ Ⓑ Ⓒ Ⓓ Ⓔ
88. Ⓐ Ⓑ Ⓒ Ⓓ Ⓔ
89. Ⓐ Ⓑ Ⓒ Ⓓ Ⓔ
90. Ⓐ Ⓑ Ⓒ Ⓓ Ⓔ
91. Ⓐ Ⓑ Ⓒ Ⓓ Ⓔ
92. Ⓐ Ⓑ Ⓒ Ⓓ Ⓔ
93. Ⓐ Ⓑ Ⓒ Ⓓ Ⓔ
94. Ⓐ Ⓑ Ⓒ Ⓓ Ⓔ
95. Ⓐ Ⓑ Ⓒ Ⓓ Ⓔ

(This page may be removed to mark answers.)

[This page intentionally blank.]

ANSWERS TO ADDRESS CROSS COMPARISON/EXAM 6

1.	A	33.	D	65.	D
2.	A	34.	A	66.	A
3.	A	35.	D	67.	D
4.	D	36.	D	68.	A
5.	A	37.	D	69.	D
6.	A	38.	A	70.	A
7.	D	39.	A	71.	D
8.	A	40.	D	72.	A
9.	D	41.	A	73.	D
10.	D	42.	D	74.	D
11.	D	43.	D	75.	A
12.	D	44.	D	76.	A
13.	A	45.	A	77.	A
14.	D	46.	A	78.	D
15.	A	47.	A	79.	A
16.	D	48.	D	80.	D
17.	A	49.	D	81.	A
18.	A	50.	A	82.	D
19.	D	51.	A	83.	D
20.	D	52.	D	84.	D
21.	D	53.	A	85.	A
22.	D	54.	A	86.	D
23.	D	55.	D	87.	D
24.	A	56.	D	88.	D
25.	A	57.	D	89.	D
26.	A	58.	A	90.	A
27.	D	59.	D	91.	D
28.	A	60.	A	92.	A
29.	D	61.	A	93.	A
30.	D	62.	A	94.	D
31.	D	63.	A	95.	D
32.	D	64.	D		

ANSWERS TO MEMORIZATION/EXAM 6

1.	B	31.	C	61.	E
2.	B	32.	D	62.	E
3.	C	33.	E	63.	C
4.	D	34.	A	64.	D
5.	E	35.	B	65.	A
6.	E	36.	C	66.	A
7.	B	37.	D	67.	A
8.	A	38.	E	68.	D
9.	B	39.	A	69.	C
10.	C	40.	D	70.	D
11.	E	41.	A	71.	E
12.	D	42.	C	72.	B
13.	B	43.	D	73.	B
14.	E	44.	E	74.	C
15.	B	45.	B	75.	D
16.	D	46.	B	76.	B
17.	D	47.	A	77.	A
18.	D	48.	B	78.	D
19.	B	49.	E	79.	E
20.	C	50.	E	80.	C
21.	B	51.	C	81.	D
22.	A	52.	D	82.	B
23.	A	53.	B	83.	B
24.	A	54.	B	84.	E
25.	C	55.	A	85.	A
26.	D	56.	B	86.	C
27.	E	57.	E	87.	D
28.	C	58.	D	88.	E
29.	B	59.	B		
30.	A	60.	D		

ANSWERS TO NUMBER SERIES/EXAM 6

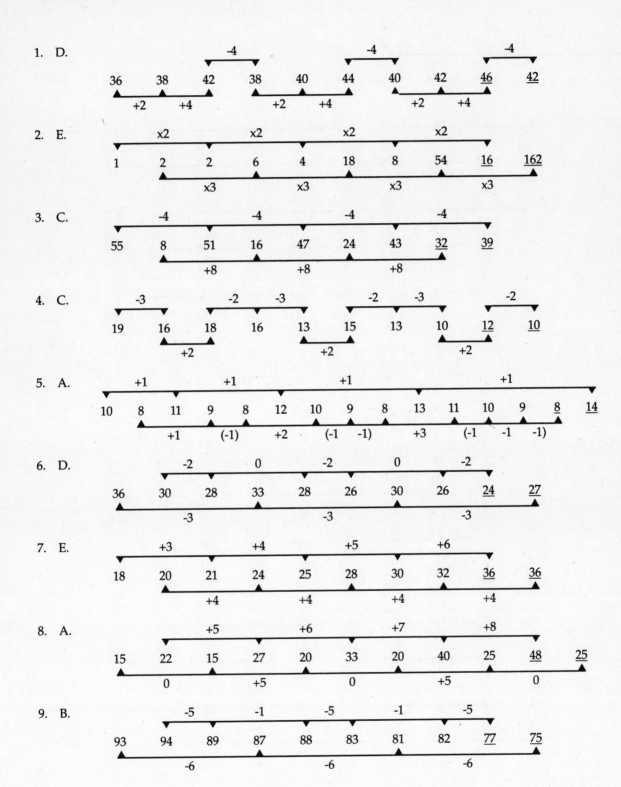

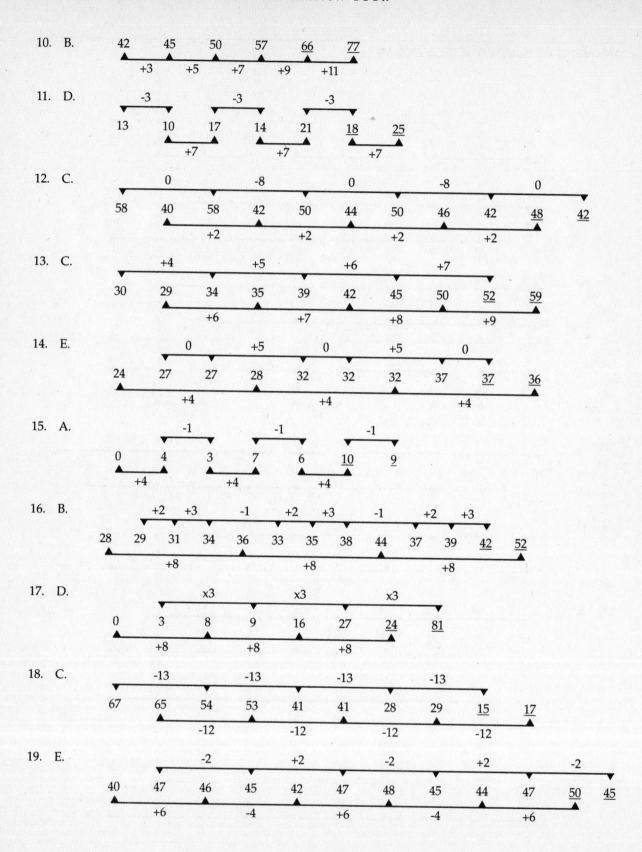

10. B.

42 45 50 57 66 77
+3 +5 +7 +9 +11

11. D.

-3   -3   -3
13 10 17 14 21 18 25
+7   +7   +7

12. C.

0   -8   0   -8   0
58 40 58 42 50 44 50 46 42 48 42
+2   +2   +2   +2

13. C.

+4   +5   +6   +7
30 29 34 35 39 42 45 50 52 59
+6   +7   +8   +9

14. E.

0   +5   0   +5   0
24 27 27 28 32 32 32 37 37 36
+4   +4   +4

15. A.

-1   -1   -1
0 4 3 7 6 10 9
+4   +4   +4

16. B.

+2 +3   -1   +2 +3   -1   +2 +3
28 29 31 34 36 33 35 38 44 37 39 42 52
+8   +8   +8

17. D.

x3   x3   x3
0 3 8 9 16 27 24 81
+8   +8   +8

18. C.

-13   -13   -13   -13
67 65 54 53 41 41 28 29 15 17
-12   -12   -12   -12

19. E.

-2   +2   -2   +2   -2
40 47 46 45 42 47 48 45 44 47 50 45
+6   -4   +6   -4   +6

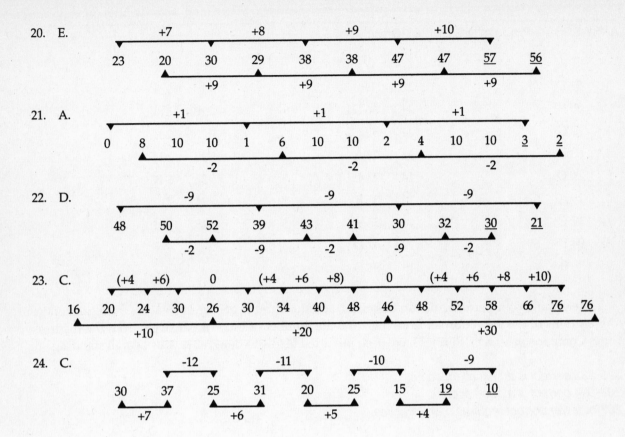

ANSWERS TO FOLLOWING DIRECTIONS/EXAM 6

1.	31 D	10.	9 E	19.	1 A
2.	30 E	11.	36 D	20.	81 C
3.	72 C	12.	5 D	21.	2 E
4.	63 D	13.	23 A	22.	89 E
5.	16 D	14.	28 C	23.	8 B
6.	19 A	15.	55 B	24.	71 A
7.	17 E	16.	56 E	25.	11 E
8.	94 B	17.	67 D		
9.	50 B	18.	85 D		

To determine your performance on this exam, add the number of correct answers from each of the four sections of the test. Subtract from this total the number of incorrect answers from the Address Cross Comparison section. Ratings have been provided below to determine your overall standing.

225-232 correct is an excellent score.
208-224 correct is a good score.
207 or fewer correct requires more practice.

What Follows After the Examination?

Once you have taken the exam, it will take two to eight weeks before your test results are mailed to you. If your score was 70 percent or better, your name will be placed on the Federal Register of the Post Office that offered the test. Your test score is not transferable to other Post Offices. Therefore, it is to your advantage to take as many of these exams as possible. The more Registers you are on, the better your chances for an interview.

It should be noted here that veteran preference is granted for employment in the United States Postal Service. Five-point preference is usually given to honorably discharged veterans who served in active duty in the U.S. Armed Forces under any of the following conditions:

- During World War II
- During a period extending from April 28, 1952, to July 1, 1955
- During February 1, 1955, through October 14, 1976, for which any part of more than 180 consecutive days was served
- In any campaign or expedition for which a campaign badge was authorized
- In Southeast Asia on or after August 2, 1990, if you were awarded the Southeast Asia Service Medal

NOTE: Active duty for training under the six-month Reserve or National Guard Program does not qualify.

Ten-point preference is given to honorably discharged veterans who served in active duty in the U.S. Armed Forces at any time and have a service-connected disability, for which they may or may not receive compensation. This preference may also be claimed by:

- Veterans who have been awarded the Purple Heart
- Spouses of certain veterans with a service-connected disability
- Mothers of certain disabled or deceased veterans
- Widows or widowers of an honorably discharged veteran, provided the deceased served in active duty during a war or died while in the Armed Forces

For those who are eligible, five-point veteran preference grants an applicant five additional points to his or her total test score, provided the score was a 70 percent or above. Those who qualify for ten-point veteran preference are given 10 additional points to their test score (provided the score was a minimum of 70 percent), and are also placed at the top of the hiring list (i.e., Federal Register), in descending order of their test scores. All other eligible candidates are listed below this group. For further information pertaining to veteran preference, contact the Department of Personnel at the Post Office where you intend to apply.

When you are among those to be considered for a Postal position, you will be notified by mail about the time and place of your interview. Pay particular attention to the date and become familiar, in advance, with the location of the interview. One sure way to disqualify yourself is to arrive late for the interview. You don't want to begin your interview with excuses.

Appearance is important, as well. Interviewers gain a distinct impression from the manner in which a candidate dresses. If you are not well-groomed (e.g., soiled clothes, uncombed hair), interviewers perceive you as being uncaring and somewhat sloppy, before asking you even one question. Even though you may be the most hardworking and concerned candidate available, you may undo all your hard work in the application process if you neglect your appearance. Proper dress for men includes a nice shirt (tie is optional), slacks, and a pair of dress shoes. For women, an attractive blouse, dress pants (or suit or skirt), and shoes are appropriate.

Also, avoid smoking or chewing gum prior to or during the interview. Habits like these can create a poor appearance. The whole idea is to put your best foot forward to indicate that you are the most enthusiastic and best qualified candidate for the job. Interview time is limited, so you'll want to make the most of it.

The beginning of the interview usually will focus on your application form. Your educational background, past employment history, and references will be examined. Before your interview, review everything you listed on your application form and have supportive reasoning for any career changes. If you can demonstrate that the direction you took has helped prepare you for work in the Postal Service, so much the better. However, do not deceive the interviewer regarding past choices. You may contradict yourself later in the interview. The best policy here is to answer all questions honestly, even if some past decisions were not necessarily the best ones. If you feel that you have made a questionable career move or have had a falling out with one or more past employers, explain why. If you can also show that something was learned or gained from a past mistake, point that out as well. Interviewers will appreciate your honesty and sincerity.

You will additionally be asked to sign an Authorization and Release Form (2181-A) for pre-employment screening. As permitted by law, this authorization is used to obtain information pertaining to your character and current or prior employment. This information is used to determine your suitability for employment in the Postal Service. If you deny the Postal Service consent to obtain this information, it may have an adverse effect on your employment eligibility.

Once the interview is over, thank the interviewer for his or her time and don't loiter to see how well you did. It takes a week or two to make a hiring decision. The United States Postal Service is an Equal Opportunity Employer. All qualified applicants receive consideration for employment without regard to race, religion, color, national origin, sex, political affiliation, age, marital status, physical handicap, or memberships in an employee organization.

Having worked as a letter carrier for the Postal Service for many years, I can attest to the fact that it is a fine employer. The job satisfactions are many and the service you provide to the public at large is considered invaluable.

— Norman S. Hall

REFUND POLICY

If you receive a score lower than 90 percent on the Postal exam after having used this study guide, Adams Media Corporation will refund the purchase price.

The following conditions must be met before any refund will be made. All exercises in this guide must be completed to demonstrate that the applicant did make a real attempt to practice and prepare for the exam. Any refund must be claimed within ninety days of the date of purchase shown on your sales receipt. Anything submitted beyond this ninety-day period will be subject to the publisher's discretion. Refunds are only available for copies of the book purchased through retail bookstores. The refund amount is limited to the purchase price and may not exceed the cover price of the book.

If you mail this study guide back for a refund, please include your sales receipt, validated test results, and a self-addressed, stamped envelope. Requests for refunds should be addressed to Adams Media Corporation, Postal Exams Division, 260 Center Street, Holbrook, MA 02343. Please allow approximately four weeks for processing.

Other titles by Norman Hall

Money-Back guarantee! No other exam books make this offer because no other exam books are as comprehensive and up-to-date!

Corrections Officer Exam Preparation Book

Test expert Norman Hall shows readers guaranteed methods for scoring 80% to 100% on the corrections officer test. Hall analyzes every aspect of the most current version of the test and shows readers what they need to qualify, from memory tests to basic mathematics. Norman Hall covers everything you'll need to know to be hired, including:

- Written exams
- Physical abilities test
- Oral boards
- Psychological examinations
- And more

Careers, trade paperback, 8½" x 11", $10.95, 1-55850-793-0

State Trooper & Highway Patrol Exam Preparation Book

Guaranteed methods for scoring 80% to 100% on the state trooper and highway patrol officer qualification tests. Hall analyzes every aspect of the most current versions of the tests—from reading comprehension to simple math to physical fitness—and shows readers what they need to qualify including:

- Memory
- Reading Comprehension
- Reasoning and Judgment
- Map Reading
- Report Writing
- Grammar, Vocabulary, and Spelling

Careers, trade paperback, 8½" X 11", 296 pages, $12.95, 1-58062-077-9

Available wherever books are sold.

HOW TO ORDER: If you cannot find these titles at your favorite retail outlet, you may order them directly from the publisher. BY PHONE: Call 1-800-872-5627. We accept Visa, Mastercard, and American Express. $4.95 will be added to your total order for shipping and handling. BY MAIL: Write out the full titles of the books you'd like to order and send payment, including $4.95 for shipping and handling, to: Adams Media Corporation, 260 Center Street, Holbrook, MA 02343. 30-day money-back guarantee.

Other titles by Norman Hall

Money-Back guarantee! No other exam books make this offer because no other exam books are as comprehensive and up-to-date!

The Complete Firefighter's Exam Preparation Book

The most complete and comprehensive Firefighter Exam Book today! If you are planning to take an exam leading to a position as a firefighter, you should know that the competition can be fierce. Fortunately, if you use *The Complete Firefighter's Exam Preparation Book,* you won't have to worry about whether you'll come up with a strong performance on exam day.

The Complete Firefighter's Exam Preparation Book includes:

- Six samples and four full-length tests, complete with answer keys and self-scoring tables
- Test-taking strategies for the written exam
- Pointers on the most common trouble spots
- Proven tips for boosting your memory, reading comprehension, and vocabulary
- Everything you need to know about an exciting career in firefighting: how to apply, how to respond to tough job interview questions, taking the physical, and much, much more!

Careers, trade paperback, 8 ½" x 11", 312 pages, $10.95, 1-55850-052-9

Police Exam Preparation Book

Taking the exam to become a law enforcement officer can be challenging. Fortunately, if you use *The Complete Police Exam Preparation Book,* you won't have to worry about whether you'll come up with a positive performance on exam day.

Everything you need to know about a Career in Law Enforcement is thoroughly covered in one book. Complete coverage of ALL test subject areas. Everything you need to know to come out on top.

Norman Hall's *Complete Police Exam Preparation Book* includes:

- 7 practice tests covering key subject areas
- 2 full-length Police Officer Exams
- Answer keys and self-scoring tables
- Pointers on avoiding common trouble spots
- Meeting the physical requirements
- Plus: the latest test-taking strategies

Careers, trade paperback, 8 ½" x 11", 256 pages, $10.95, 1-55850-296-3

Available wherever books are sold.

HOW TO ORDER: If you cannot find these titles at your favorite retail outlet, you may order them directly from the publisher. BY PHONE: Call 1-800-872-5627. We accept Visa, Mastercard, and American Express. $4.95 will be added to your total order for shipping and handling. BY MAIL: Write out the full titles of the books you'd like to order and send payment, including $4.95 for shipping and handling, to: Adams Media Corporation, 260 Center Street, Holbrook, MA 02343. 30-day money-back guarantee.